Intrafirm Trade and
Global Transfer Pricing Regulations

Intrafirm Trade and
Global Transfer Pricing Regulations

ROGER Y. W. TANG

QUORUM BOOKS
Westport, Connecticut • London

382.
T161

Library of Congress Cataloging-in-Publication Data

Tang, Roger Y. W.
  Intrafirm trade and global transfer pricing regulations / Roger
Y.W. Tang.
    p.   cm.
  Includes bibliographical references and index.
  ISBN 1–56720–039–7 (alk. paper)
    1. Intra-firm trade.   2. Transfer pricing.   3. Transfer pricing—
Law and legislation.   4. International business enterprises.
I. Title.
  HD62.42T36   1997
  382—DC21   96–40910

British Library Cataloguing in Publication Data is available.

Library of Congress Catalog Card Number: 96–40910
ISBN: 1–56720–039–7

First published in 1997

Quorum Books, 88 Post Road West, Westport, CT 06881
An imprint of Greenwood Publishing Group, Inc.

Printed in the United States of America

The paper used in this book complies with the
Permanent Paper Standard issued by the National
Information Standards Organization (Z39.48–1984).

10 9 8 7 6 5 4 3 2 1

Copyright Acknowledgments

The author and publisher are grateful for permission to reproduce the following
copyrighted material:

Tables 1.3, 1.4, 7.1, and 7.2 reprinted from *OECD Reviews of Foreign Direct
Investment.* © OECD, 1995. Reproduced by permission of the OECD.

Table 1.5 reprinted from Gustano Lombo, "The 100 Largest Foreign Investments in
the U.S., the Land of Cheap Currency," *Forbes* (July 17, 1995). Reprinted by
permission of *Forbes* Magazine © Forbes Inc., 1995.

Tables 1.6 and 1.7 reprinted from Garrick Holmes, "Big Price Tags Make for a
Banner Year," *Mergers & Acquisitions* (March/April 1996). Reprinted with permission
of IDD. Copyright 1996 by IDD Enterprises L.P., New York, N.Y.

Table 1.8 reprinted from Lawrence G. Tesler, "Networked Computing in the 1990s,"
Scientific American (special issue, The Computer in the 21st Century). Copyright ©
1995 by Scientific American, Inc. All rights reserved.

Figure 7.1 reprinted from Christopher Pass, "Transfer Pricing in Multinational
Companies," *Management Accounting (U.K.)* (September 1994). Reprinted with
permission of The Chartered Institute of Management Accountants.

Figure 9.1 reprinted from Roger Y. W. Tang, *Transfer Pricing in the 1990s: Tax and
Management Perspectives* (Westport, CT: Quorum Books, an imprint of Greenwood
Publishing Group, Inc.), © 1993.

To

Ann, Sherri, and Kevin

Contents

Figures and Tables

FIGURES

TABLES

Preface

Intrafirm trade involves the sale or transfer of tangible and intangible goods between related companies in two or more countries. Multinational transfer pricing is concerned with the pricing of intrafirm trade. Like two sides of the same coin, many issues in intrafirm trade and transfer pricing are closely related to each other. For decades, both areas have captured the attention of tax authorities, corporate executives, tax accountants, and academicians. The stakes are extremely high, because about 40 percent of U.S. foreign trade and 20 percent of world trade are intrafirm trade. In other words, more than $500 billion of U.S. foreign trade and close to $2 trillion of world trade in 1996 are intrafirm trade and subject to transfer pricing regulations in various countries.

Many problems and issues in intrafirm trade and transfer pricing are dynamic and complex. Changes in global business and technological environments not only affect the environments within which multinational companies (MNCs) operate but also impact the volume and directions of intrafirm trade. Transfer pricing regulations in the United States and many other countries have also changed significantly over the past ten years. In 1995, the Organization for Economic Cooperation and Development (OECD) released its new transfer pricing guidelines after years of deliberation. By August 1996, more then ten countries were offering advance-pricing agreement (APA) programs to their taxpayers. Together, these changes have created new opportunities and challenges for multinational taxpayers. The new transfer pricing regulations and guidelines should provide badly needed stability and certainty for corporate transfer pricing practices. Many taxpayers can now apply for unilateral, bilateral, or even multilateral APAs to cover intrafirm trade of tangible and intangible goods. If it is done properly, the APA process can become a flexible problem-solving tool for resolving many issues in transfer pricing and intrafirm trade.

On the other hand, taxpayers have to adjust their transfer pricing practices to adapt to the changing environments and apply the new transfer pricing regulations and guidelines to intrafirm trade. The penalties can be extremely high for negligence of, or noncompliance with, tax regulations. These are the reasons why many MNCs now consider transfer pricing the single most important issue in international taxation.

To help readers understand many of the issues and corporate practices of transfer pricing, I have published three books since 1979: *Transfer Pricing Practices in the United States and Japan* (1979); *Multinational Transfer Pricing: Canadian and British Perspectives* (1981); and *Transfer Pricing in the 1990s* (1993). The primary purposes of this new book, *Intrafirm Trade and Global Transfer Pricing Regulations*, are to provide the latest information on intrafirm trade of MNCs and to explain the new transfer pricing regulations issued by· the U.S. government and by its major trading partners including Canada, Mexico, the United Kingdom, Germany, France, the Netherlands, Japan, Australia, South Korea, and China. I have taken a global, but comparative, perspective from which to review many issues in intrafirm trade and transfer pricing regulations.

The summer of 1996 marked the 20th anniversary of my research in transfer pricing and intrafirm trade. In the summer of 1976, I began my study in transfer pricing with the objective of writing a Ph.D. dissertation and obtaining a terminal degree in accounting and business. Never in my wildest dreams did I expect to publish four books and more than ten articles on transfer pricing and intrafirm trade. Over the past 20 years, I have learned a great deal from corporate executives, certified public accountants, management consultants, government officials, and my colleagues and friends in many institutions. These institutions include the University of Nebraska, McGill University, the University of Calgary, Western Michigan University, the Upjohn Company (Pharmacia & Upjohn), Hong Kong Baptist University, the United Nations Centre on Transnational Corporations, and the United Nations Development Programme. Research funding and facilities provided by these organizations enabled me to carry out many projects on multinational transfer pricing. I also want to take this opportunity to thank the many individuals who assisted me in my transfer pricing research over the past 20 years. They include Bob Raymond, C. K. Walter, Kung Chen, Herb Jensen, and Hung Chan.

For this new book, I am grateful to Western Michigan University, for granting me a sabbatical leave in 1996, and Hong Kong Baptist University, for offering me a visiting scholarship to complete the manuscript. My appreciation also extends to many other individuals who provided valuable suggestions and assistance for the study. Beverly Eby offered professional editorial assistance, and skillful typing services were provided by Jeanne Wagenfeld, Barb Peacock, and Luann Bigelow.

I also want to express my gratitude to the staff at Greenwood Publishing

Group, especially Eric Valentine, Publisher of Quorum Books, for their assistance and encouragement. Last, but not least, this volume is dedicated to my wife, Ann, and our children, Sherri and Kevin. This book would not have been completed without their patience, understanding, and constant support.

Intrafirm Trade and
Global Transfer Pricing Regulations

1

The Changing Environment, Intrafirm Trade, and Transfer Pricing

Transfer pricing is concerned with the pricing of goods or services transferred between two or more units within an organization. The organization can be a business enterprise or a nonprofit agency. The units involved in transferring goods or services can be departments, divisions, or related companies of the same corporate group. Transfers (or transactions) between related firms in one or more countries are also called intrafirm trade. For example, transactions between Ford Motor Company and the Hertz Corporation are considered intrafirm transfers now that Hertz is a wholly owned subsidiary of Ford. For the same reason, transfers between Ford Motor headquarters, Ford Motor (Canada), and Jaguar Cars Limited in Britain are intrafirm trade, and thus subject to multinational transfer pricing rules, because the last two units are overseas subsidiaries of Ford Motor Company.

Both transfer pricing and intrafirm trade have captured the attention of many academicians, financial executives, and tax authorities for several decades. The volume of intrafirm trade is huge (about 40 percent of international trade) and is expanding rapidly as multinational companies (MNCs) globalize their investment and trade. Details of international intrafirm trade will be discussed in Chapter 2 of this book.

In the past, hundreds of papers and many books have been published that discuss various aspects of transfer pricing and intrafirm trade. Many issues in these two related areas are dynamic and multidimensional. For example, the environmental variables of transfer pricing (including tax regulations) have been changing constantly over the past ten years.

In a 1995 survey conducted by Ernst & Young LLP (1995), 82 percent of the 210 respondent MNCs considered transfer pricing as the most important international tax issue facing multinationals in 1995, and 71 percent of the firms expected it to remain so for the near future. These 210 companies were selected from eight industrial countries (Australia, Canada, France, Germany, Japan, the Netherlands, the United Kingdom, and the United States). A majority of the companies surveyed by Ernst & Young have experienced a transfer pricing inquiry in the past (61 percent at home and 69 percent in a subsidiary country). Companies in the United States, the United Kingdom, and Canada reported the highest level of transfer pricing inquiries, both at home and abroad.

The primary purposes of this book are to provide the latest information on intrafirm trade of MNCs and to explain the new transfer pricing regulations issued by the U.S. government and by its major trading partners including Canada, Mexico, Japan, selected European Union (EU) countries, Australia, China, and the OECD.

In the remainder of this chapter, we will discuss the following issues closely related to intrafirm trade and transfer pricing:

—changes in the business environment around the globe and their impact on intrafirm trade and transfer pricing;

—transfer pricing and its major stakeholders; and

—changing regulations for multinational transfer pricing.

An overview of the book will be provided toward the end of this chapter.

CHANGING ENVIRONMENTS AND THEIR IMPACT ON INTRAFIRM TRADE AND TRANSFER PRICING

The past decade has witnessed enormous changes in social, political, economic, and technological environments in the United States and around the world. These changes not only affect the environments within which MNCs operate but also impact the volume and directions of intrafirm trade. Figure 1.1 highlights the relationships between environmental changes and major issues of intrafirm trade and transfer pricing. Changes in the global business environment, such as globalization and trade expansion, will affect many international business and economic issues of intrafirm trade. New tax regulations and investigations of transfer pricing practices will make many tax issues of transfer pricing more complicated. Organizational changes such as mergers, acquisitions, and reengineering may require an overhaul of the corporate transfer pricing system. Advances in information technologies will speed up the decision-making process and facilitate the expansion of international trade, including intrafirm transactions. Several books have been published previously that discuss the changes in the global business environment. For example, Naisbitt's *Megatrends* (1982) explained ten "megatrends" that were shaping the 1980s, while Naisbitt and Aburdene, in *Megatrends 2000* (1990), cover another ten new trends that are influencing our lives in the 1990s. Five of the 20 megatrends presented by

Figure 1.1
Environmental Changes and Major Issues of Intrafirm Trade and Transfer Pricing

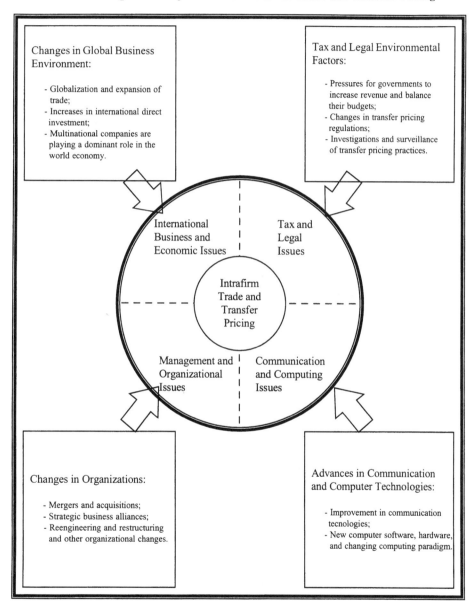

Naisbitt (1982) and Naisbitt and Aburdene (1990) may have significant implications for intrafirm trade and transfer pricing:

—the move from an industrial society to an information society;

—the transformation of the U.S. economy from a national economy to a world economy;

—the global economic boom of the 1990s;

—the emergence of free-market socialism; and

—the rise of the Pacific Rim.

(The implications of these five trends are discussed in Tang, 1993).

In his book *The New Realities*, Drucker (1989) attempted to define the concerns, issues, and controversies that will become realities during the 1990s and
the twenty-first century. One of his assertions is that the world economy has
changed from international to transnational. According to Drucker (1989), a
transnational economy has the following characteristics:

—In the transnational economy, the transnational production factors (land and labor)
  increasingly become secondary. Management has emerged as the decisive production
  factor and will shape the competitive position of a business enterprise.

—The goal of the transnational economy is not "profit maximization," but "market
  maximization." Trade increasingly follows investment.

—In the transnational economy, economic policy implies neither "free trade" nor "protectionism," but "reciprocity" between regions.

—Top management in an MNC should be transnational, as should the company's business plans, business strategies, and business decisions.

Many of the "new realities" predicted by Drucker are more true today than
in 1989. The increase in international direct investment has been followed by
an expansion of global trade. Business strategies and decisions are becoming
transnational. In this chapter, we will not attempt to review all the changes in
the new global business environment. However, we shall address several areas
that may have significant impact on the volume and directions of intrafirm
trade:

—the globalization and expansion of trade;

—international direct investment and the role of multinational companies;

—mergers, acquisitions, and the formation of strategic alliances among businesses;

—restructuring, reengineering, and other organizational changes; and

—advances in communication and information technologies.

Of course, many of these changes are closely tied to each other. Together, they facilitate the globalization process and expansion of world trade (including intrafirm trade).

Globalization and Expansion of Trade

The globalization of the world economy is an evolutionary and ongoing process that has existed since the birth of international commerce. However, the pace of globalization accelerated in the 1980s with the expansion of international trade and cross-border investment. A truly globalized company can produce its products anywhere, using resources and a subsidiary located anywhere. Moreover, it can meet quality standards found anywhere, allowing its product to be sold anywhere (Naisbitt, 1994). As explained by Goman (1994), globalization is also an attitude, a business strategy, and a management challenge:

Globalization is an attitude—a way of thinking of the world as a unified marketplace rather than a collection of national markets. . . . Globalization is a business strategy—a plan to develop and transfer innovations to subsidiaries around the world, to compete and collaborate internationally, and to manage independent multinational operations coordingated by a global mission. . . . Globalization is a management challenge—a process that includes building worldwide teams, customizing products and services to diverse national preferences, communicating to a multinational workforce, and developing career strategies with a global view. (p. 4)

In order to understand the magnitude of changes in international trade, we need to review some statistics related to world trade. Table 1.1 presents the statistics on world exports and imports for selected years between 1970 and 1994. Those statistics were obtained from various issues of *International Financial Statistics*, published by the International Monetary Fund. As shown in the table, in 1970, the world export total was $280.5 billion, whereas the world import total was $294.6 billion. In 1980, the world's exports totaled $1,845.6 billion, about six times higher than in 1970. A similar increase was recorded for world imports from 1970 to 1980.

Surprisingly, the volume of world trade did not change much between 1980 and 1985. However, significant increases were recorded throughout the second half of the 1980s. World trade continued to expand in the early 1990s, but at a slower rate than that recorded in the scond half of the 1980s. This phenomenon may be due to the recession experienced by some industrial countries from 1991 to 1993. Despite the slow growth rate in the early 1990s, the total amounts of world exports and imports ($4.4 trillion and $4.3 trillion, respectively) in 1994 were still quite significant.

We can also observe the trend of trade expansion by reviewing the statistics of major trading countries. Such statistics of ten major trading nations for 1970

Table 1.1
World Exports and Imports, Selected Years, 1970–1994 (Billions of U.S. Dollars)

Year	World Exports		World Imports	
	Total	% Change from previous year	Total	% Change from previous year
1970	280.5		294.6	
1975	795.1		817.8	
1980	1,845.6		1,899.2	
1985	1,784.6	+1.1	1,881.2	+1.9
1986	2,003.0	+12.2	2,066.2	+9.8
1987	2,355.3	+17.6	2,418.1	+17.0
1988	2,694.3	+14.4	2,767.6	+14.5
1989	2,906.6	+7.9	3,005.6	+8.6
1990	3,430.2	+18.0	3,431.8	+14.2
1991	3,537.1	+3.1	3,552.7	+3.5
1992	3,754.9	+6.2	3,777.1	+6.3
1993	3,824.6	+1.9	3,766.7	-0.3
1994	4,364.3	+14.1	4,285.7	+13.8

Sources: International Monetary Fund (IMF), *International Financial Statistics* (various issues); IMF, *Direction of Trade Statistics Quarterly* (various issues).

and 1994 are provided in Table 1.2. Data on exports and imports are shown separately. From the table we can draw the following conclusions:

1. Trade volume for each of the major trading nations increased substantially from 1970 to 1994.

2. International trade was dominated by industrial countries in both 1970 and 1994. The seven largest trading countries in both 1970 and 1994 were members of the so-called G-7 industrial nations. In 1994, international trade conducted by these G-7 nations accounted for about half of total world trade.

Table 1.2
Major Trading Nations in 1970 and 1994 (Billions of U.S. Dollars)

Country	1970 Exports (rank)	Country	1994 Exports (rank)
United States	43.2 (1)	United States	512.5 (1)
Germany	34.2 (2)	Germany	427.2 (2)
United Kingdom	19.4 (3)	Japan	397.0 (3)
Japan	19.3 (4)	France	235.9 (4)
France	18.1 (5)	United Kingdom	204.9 (5)
Canada	16.7 (6)	Italy	189.8 (6)
Italy	13.2 (7)	Canada	165.4 (7)
Netherlands	11.8 (8)	Netherlands	·155.6 (8)
Belgium-Luxemburg	11.6 (9)	Hong Kong	151.4 (9)
Sweden	6.8 (10)	Belgium-Luxemburg	128.9(10)

Country	1970 Imports (rank)	Country	1994 Imports (rank)
United States	42.4 (1)	United States	689.2 (1)
Germany	29.8 (2)	Germany	381.7 (2)
United Kingdom	21.7 (3)	Japan	275.2 (3)
France	19.1 (4)	France	230.2 (4)
Japan	18.9 (5)	United Kingdom	227.0 (5)
Italy	15.0 (6)	Italy	167.7 (6)
Canada	14.5 (7)	Canada	155.1 (7)
Netherlands	13.4 (8)	Hong Kong	161.8 (8)
Belgium-Luxemburg	11.4 (9)	Netherlands	139.8 (9)
Sweden	7.0 (10)	Belgium-Luxemburg	132.6 (10)

Sources: International Monetary Fund, *International Financial Statistics* (various issues).

3. In 1994, Hong Kong replaced Sweden as one of the ten largest trading countries (or jurisdictions) in the world. Hong Kong is benefiting from its role as the gateway to China. The trade statistics for China in 1994 were also quite impressive. China's exports and imports for 1994 were $120 billion and $114.6 billion, respectively. Other countries in the Asian Pacific region (including Korea, Singapore, and Taiwan) were also important players in international trade in 1994 and 1995.

4. The United States was the largest trading nation in both 1970 and 1994. It also had the largest trade deficit ($166.4 billion) among all maor trading countries in 1994.

5. In 1994, Germany ranked second and Japan ranked third among all major trading countries. Both countries enjoyed large trade surpluses in 1994, but Japan's trade surplus of $121.8 billion was the largest among all major trading countries. Close to half of Japan's trade surplus in 1994 was generated from trade with the United States. A large portion of its trade surplus with the United States was created by the existence of an intrafirm trade deficit between Japanese MNCs and their U.S. subsidiaries. (We will discuss this deficit further in Chapters 2 and 8.)

The global expansion of trade is not limited to merchandise trade. Service exports and imports have also increased significantly in recent years. For example, in 1994, U.S. service exports totaled $195.3 billion, an increase of 6 percent over the amount recorded in 1993. U.S. service imports increased from $128.0 billion in 1993 to $135.3 billion in 1994. In 1994, the United States had a trade surplus of $60 billion in services.

International Direct Investment and Multinational Companies

As the world economy globalized in the 1980s and the early 1990s, we also observed substantial increases in foreign direct investment (FDI) by MNCs from industrial countries. Table 1.3 shows the outward direct investment flows by OECD member countries, while Table 1.4 provides the statistics on inward direct investment flows by OECD members. Foreign direct investment was defined by the OECD (1992) as capital invested for the purpose of acquiring a lasting interest in an enterprise and exerting a degree of influence on its operations.

Table 1.3 shows that outward direct investment from OECD countries increased more than fourfold in the 1980s ($48.4 billion in 1981 versus $213.8 billion in 1990) and grew much more rapidly than did world trade (as shown in Table 1.1) OECD researchers (1992) provided the following explanation for this spectacular increase in FDI from OECD countries.

Domestic deregulation, international liberalization, and greater integration of the OECD economies in the 1980s facilitated foreign investment flows. Better macroeconomic policies, structural reforms, and the liberalization of exchange controls and foreign investment regimes also contributed substantially. Strong economic performance during most of the decade was the key to FDI growth. (p. 11)

Table 1.3
Direct Investment Abroad from Selected OECD Countries, 1971–1993 (Millions of U.S. Dollars)

Country	Cumulative flows		Flows of direct investment for selected years					
	1971–1980	1981–1990	1981	1986	1990	1991	1992	1993
Australia	2,510	22,610	734	3,419	260	3,105	41	900
Austria	578	4,132	206	296	1,663	1,288	1,871	1,404
Belgium-Luxembourg	3,213	21,454	30	1,627	6,600	6,062	10,953	11,409
Canada	11,335	41,847	5,756	4,066	4,732	5,856	3,688	7,176
Denmark	1,063	6,292	141	646	1,509	1,851	2,225	1,379
Finland	605	12,132	129	810	3,263	1,049	406	1,831
France	13,940	85,618	4,615	5,230	26,920	20,501	19,097	12,167
Germany	24,846	86,573	3,862	9,616	23,168	22,879	17,745	11,673
Italy	3,597	28,707	1,404	2,661	7,612	7,326	5,948	7,231
Japan	18,052	185,826	4,894	14,480	48,024	30,726	17,222	13,714
Netherlands	27,829	52,940	3,629	3,147	13,589	12,270	14,096	10,079
Norway	1,079	8,995	185	1,605	1,478	1,840	434	885
Portugal	21	374	20	0	165	474	687	148
Spain	1,274	8,196	272	377	2,845	3,574	1,273	2,599
Sweden	4,597	47,802	854	3,707	14,588	7,008	237	1,328
Switzerland	N.A.	31,858	N.A.	1,461	6,372	6,543	5,673	6,539
United Kingdom	55,112	185,674	12,065	17,647	18,729	15,597	19,444	25,697
United States	134,354	170,041	9,624	18,679	29,950	31,294	41,004	57,871
Total	302,306	1,005,323	48,420	89,474	213,825	180,752	162,595	172,750

Note: N.A. = Not available.
Based on balance of payments data. The statistics of some small OECD countries (e.g., New Zealand and Iceland) are not shown in this table. Columnar totals are for all OECD countries.
Source: Organization for Economic Cooperation and Development (1995a).

Another important factor is the expansion of MNCs. Many businesses have to look beyond their national borders for new products, customers, and other business opportunities. Advances in computer and communication technologies also facilitate the performance of mergers, acquisitions, and other sophisticated financial transactions. The flows of direct investment from OECD countries declined somewhat in the early 1990s due to economic recession in some member countries. In 1993, the total direct investment abroad from all OECD countries was $172.8 billion.

Table 1.3 also shows that in the 1970s, the United States was the largest outward direct investor, with a cumulative outflow of $134.4 billion in that decade. However, in the 1980s, Japan and the United Kingdom surpassed the United States and became the two largest investors of the 1980s. Together, Japan, the United Kingdom, and the United States accounted for about 54 percent of all outward direct investment flows from OECD countries in the 1980s. In 1991, the United States became the largest international direct investor again. In 1993, the flow of U.S. direct investment abroad was $57.9 billion. This amount was substantially larger than the outflows of direct investment from Japan or the United Kingdom.

Table 1.4 indicates that the United States was the largest recipient of inward direct investment in both the 1970s and 1980s. Cumulative flows of direct investment to the United States for the 1970s and 1980s were $56.3 billion and $359.7 billion, respectively. The direct investment flows into the United States in the 1980s were six times larger than those in the 1970s. No other country had such a large increase in inward direct investment.

During the 1980s, the United Kingdom received $130.5 billion in foreign direct investment. Other countries receiving large sums of foreign direct investment included Spain ($46 billion), France ($43.2 billion), and Australia ($40.4 billion). Japan, the largest source of direct investment capital in the 1980s, recived only $3.3 billion of foreign direct investment during the same decade. In 1993, the United States was the largest recipient of foreign direct investment among OECD countries.

The flows of direct investment from country to country in the 1980s and early 1990s were carried out largely by MNCs in industrial countries. As these MNCs globalized their operations, they also become more dependent on foreign revenue and foreign net profit for survival and growth. Table 1.5 presents the 50 largest U.S. MNCs and shares of their foreign revenue, net profit, and assets for 1994. (The data were published in the July 17, 1995, issue of *Forbes* magazine.) One can observe that many of the largest U.S. MNCs depend heavily on foreign markets as sources of revenue and profits. They also keep large portions of their assets overseas. For example, about 68 percent of Coca-Cola's worldwide sales and 67 percent of the corporate profit in 1994 were generated by overseas markets. Similarly, more than 70 percent of Exxon's revenue and profit came from overseas.

Together, the total revenue of these 50 U.S. MNCs in 1994 was $1,463.5 billion, equivalent to about 22 percent of the U.S. gross national product (GNP).

Table 1.4
Foreign Direct Investment in Selected OECD Countries, 1971–1993 (Millions of U.S. Dollars)

	Cumulative flows		Flows of direct investment for selected years					
	1971–1980	1981–1990	1981	1986	1990	1991	1992	1993
Australia	11,295	40,369	2,349	3,457	7,060	4,904	5,286	2,460
Austria	1,455	3,274	318	181	647	359	940	982
Belgium-Luxembourg	9,215	28,182	1,352	631	8,162	8,919	10,956	10,458
Canada	5,534	33,699	-3,670	2,781	7,852	2,913	4,576	5,930
Denmark	1,561	3,388	100	161	1,133	1,530	1,015	1,684
Finland	376	2,838	99	340	787	-247	396	593
France	16,908	43,194	2,426	2,749	9,040	11,073	15,928	12,142
Germany	13,969	18,029	340	1,190	2,529	4,263	2,422	-286
Greece	N.A.	6,145	520	471	1,005	1,135	1,144	977
Italy	5,698	24,888	1,146	-21	6,344	2,481	3,210	3,751
Japan	1,424	3,281	189	226	1,753	1,368	2,728	86
Netherlands	10,822	28,203	1,520	1,497	9,167	5,002	6,994	5,651
Norway	3,074	4,831	686	1,023	1,004	-291	720	2,058
Portugal	535	6,918	177	241	2,608	2,451	1,914	1,311
Spain	7,060	46,000	1,714	3,442	13,681	10,423	8,115	6,746
Sweden	897	8,612	182	1,079	1,965	6,322	-139	3,786
Switzerland	N.A.	12,432	N.A.	1,778	4,458	2,613	411	64
United Kingdom	40,503	130,469	5,891	8,557	32,889	15,826	16,448	14,536
United States	56,276	359,650	25,195	35,623	47,916	26,086	9,888	21,366
Total	188,249	836,329	40,879	68,286	165,109	114,529	99,397	102,676

Note: N.A. = Not available.
Based on balance of payments data. The statistics of some small OECD countries (e.g., New Zealand and Iceland) are not shown in this table. Columnar totals are for all OECD countries.
Source: Organization for Economic Cooperation and Development (1995a).

Table 1.5
The 50 Largest U.S. MNCs and Shares of Their Foreign Revenue, Net Profit, and Assets, 1994

1994 Forbes Rank	Company	Total Revenue (In bil. of US $)	Foreign Revenue as % of Total Revenue	Foreign Net Profit as % of Total Revenue	Foreign Assets as % of Total Assets
1	Exxon	99.7	77.4	72.6	57.9
2	General Motors	155.0	28.4	63.6	25.6
3	Mobil	59.6	67.6	85.4	58.8
4	IBM	64.1	62.3	69.5	57.0
5	Ford Motor	128.4	29.6	21.6	27.6
6	Texaco	44.3	55.9	47.6	43.4
7	Citicorp	31.7	62.3	48.4	54.4
8	Chevron	38.5	42.9	42.9	42.0
9	Philip Morris Cos	53.8	30.4	28.8	34.2
10	Procter & Gamble	30.3	51.7	34.1	41.9
11	E.I. du Pont de Nemours	34.0	42.1	30.9	38.2
12	Hewlett-Packard	25.0	54.1	66.7	46.2
13	General Electric	60.1	19.8	12.1	17.4
14	American Intl. Group	22.4	51.8	57.4	37.2
15	Coca-Cola	16.2	68.3	66.8	49.9
16	Dow Chemical	22.4	50.3	47.7	44.2
17	Motorola	16.2	43.9	66.7	33.9
18	Xerox	20.0	47.8	51.4	31.3
19	United Technologies	21.2	39.2	69.4	30.4
20	Digital Equipment	13.5	61.5	D-D	57.1
21	PepsiCo	28.5	28.9	40.9	30.6
22	Johnson & Johnson	15.7	50.3	50.8	42.0
23	ITT	23.6	33.0	26.1	9.6
24	3M	15.1	50.2	29.6	40.6
25	AT&T	75.1	9.8	8.3	11.8

#	Firm				
26	Eastman Kodak	13.6	52.5	17.0	39.3
27	Chrysler	52.2	12.6	12.3	13.7
28	Amoco	27.0	21.7	21.1	29.1
29	Sara Lee	15.5	37.2	38.0	49.3
30	Intel	11.5	49.4	42.9	21.3
31	J.P. Morgan & Co	11.9	45.6	43.0	49.5
32	Compaq Computer	10.9	49.6	56.6	46.5
33	Colgate-Palmolive	7.6	68.4	76.2	49.9
34	Goodyear Tire & Rubber	12.3	42.0	49.2	38.7
35	Aflac	6.1	84.3	92.5	90.3
36	Bristol-Myers Squibb	12.0	41.8	48.0	33.0
37	UAL	14.0	35.3	NA	NA
38	Merrill Lynch	18.2	26.9	36.0	36.6
39	CPC International	7.4	64.4	57.5	68.0
40	RJR Nabisco	15.4	30.9	42.2	15.6
41	Chase Manhattan	11.2	39.9	45.3	34.7
42	Merck	15.0	29.4	29.0	16.6
43	Texas Instruments	10.3	42.4	NA	36.5
44	Alcoa	9.9	43.7	76.6	45.0
45	AMR	16.1	26.8	NA	NA
46	Apple Computer	9.2	45.8	125.8	33.3
47	American Express	15.2	27.6	42.6	20.8
48	McDonald's	8.3	50.1	46.9	50.8
49	Gillette	6.1	68.0	61.6	67.3
50	Pfizer	8.3	46.7	40.1	39.2
	Total Revenue for the 50 firms	1,463.5			
	Average percentage		44.9	48.7	39.3

Note: D-D = Deficit to deficit; NA = not available.
Source: Forbes (July 17, 1995), pp. 274–275.

On average, they obtained about 45 percent of their revenue and 49 percent of their profit from overseas markets in 1994. About 39 percent of their assets were in foreign countries.

The performances of foreign investors in the United States in the 1980s and early 1990s were also quite impressive. In particular, foreign interests invested a total of $354.7 billion in the United States in the 1980s to purchase U.S. businesses or to establish their own subsidiaries. Many large companies in the United States were invested in by MNCs from Japan, Switzerland, Germany, the Netherlands, and Canada. Examples include Shell Oil, invested by Royal Dutch/Shell Group; Burger King and Pillsbury, invested by Grand Metropolitan from the United Kingdom; and so forth.

Statistics show that the total sales revenue of U.S. subsidiaries invested by the 50 largest foreign MNCs was $361.6 billion in 1994 (Lombo, 1995). This amount is equivalent to about 5.5 percent of the GNP of the United States.

International investment remained strong in the first half of the 1990s. There are several reasons why the expansion of international trade and investment is also likely to continue in the second half of the 1990s and well into the twenty-first century. First, the movement toward regional economic integration will continue. In 1992, the 12 countries of the European Community (EC) removed most of the barriers to the free movement of goods, services, money, and people. By November 1993, all the EC member nations had also approved the Maastricht Treaty (the treaty on European Union), which commits its members to establish a monetary union by January 1999. The monetary union may include a single currency and a European Central Bank. Also in 1993, the EC was transformed into the European Union (EU). In 1995, the EU was expanded to include Austria, Finland, and Sweden. Further enlargement of EU membership is expected to continue in the future. In North America, the North American Free Trade Agreement (NAFTA) became effective on January 1, 1994. NAFTA will eliminate tariffs and other trade barriers among the United States, Canada, and Mexico over a 15-year period. Many restrictions imposed on cross-border investment will also be removed. In addition, other regional organizations, including the Association of Southeast Asian Nations (ASEAN) and the Asian Pacific Economic Council (APEC), are talking about forming their own free trade areas.

Second, the Uruguay Round of multilateral trade negotiations mediated by the General Agreement on Tariffs and Trade (GATT) was concluded with the signing of its Final Act in April 1994. At the end of October 1995, the 110 member countries of GATT formally became members of the World Trade Organization (WTO) (Levy and Srinivasan, 1996). The WTO will oversee the implementation of the new global trade rules negotiated in the Uruguay Round. Customs duties will be substantially reduced for many products and raw materials. Many other trade barriers will also be removed after the new rules are fully implemented.

Finally, the booming economies in the Far East, including China, Indonesia,

Table 1.6

Completion Record of Mergers and Acquisitions in the United States, 1986–1995

Year	No. of deals	% Change	Value (U.S. $ bil.)	% Change
1986	2,523	---	$220.8	---
1987	2,515	-0.3%	196.5	-11.0%
1988	3,013	19.8	271.8	38.3
1989	3,818	26.7	311.2	14.5
1990	4,307	12.8	199.7	-35.8
1991	3,573	-17.0	139.1	-30.3
1992	3,742	4.7	125.1	-10.1
1993	4,132	10.4	174.2	39.2
1994	4,923	19.4	280.4	61.0
1995	5,887	19.6	388.2	38.4

Source: SDC Mergers and Corporate Transactions Database; reprinted in Holmes (1996), p. 37.

Malaysia, Thailand, Taiwan, and Vietnam, attracted large-scale direct investment from Japan, Europe, and North America in the first half of the 1990s. The situation is expected to continue as these Far Eastern countries liberalize their industries and modernize their infrastructure for further industrial development. Together, these factors will promote further expansion of direct investment and trade. As a result, intrafirm trade will also be expanded further in the future.

Mergers, Acquisitions, and Business Alliances

Mergers, acquisitions, and business alliances were widely used as investment alternatives in the 1980s and the early 1990s. Table 1.6 shows the mergers and acquisitions completion record in the United States from 1986 to 1995. In 1986, there were 2,523 deals with a total merger and acquisition (M&A) value of $220.8 billion. In 1990, the number of deals reached 4,307, with a total M&A value of $199.7 billion. According to the OECD (1992), the growth of acquisitions was a key feature of inward investment in the United States during the 1980s. Statistics show that acquisitions exceeded new establishments of enterprises (in value terms) throughout the 1980s and the proportion of acquisition to total U.S. inward investment grew from 67 percent in the first half of the 1980s to about 80 percent in the second half.

By merging with or acquiring other companies, a firm may achieve one or more of the following objectives:

—enter a new market rapidly;

—gain access to new technologies and new products; and

—facilitate the establishment of supply and sitribution networks and improve the economy of scale.

In summary, the merger and acquisition option may improve the competitive advantages of an MNC in the global marketplace. As shown in Table 1.6, both the number of deals and M&A value reached their all-time record in 1995 (5,887 deals with a total value of $388.2 billion).

Merger and acquisition activities in major overseas markets in 1995 are summarized in Table 1.7. The table shows that the United Kingdom had 1,002 deals worth $87.2 billion; France had 407 deals with a total value of $15.8 billion; and Germany had 528 deals valued at $17.1 billion. However, these numbers are small when compared with the number of deals and the total value of M&A activities in the United States.

Strategic business alliances (or collaborative ventures) are other ways to bring together the specific skills and resources of two or more organizations to achieve such objectives as penetrating new markets, improving research and development capabilities, or establishing distribution or service networks to better serve customers. Some successful firms are the results of international strategic alliances. For example, NEC was set up in 1899 as Japan's first joint venture with Western Electric in the United States (Cowhey and Aronson, 1993). In 1925, ITT acquired Western Electric's interest, and NEC later freed itself from this affiliation and began to grow as an independent company in 1965. ITT was NEC's largest shareholder until the early 1970s. In 1995, NEC was a very successful MNC, with 37 production plants in 17 countries and 43 marketing and service firms in 22 countries. The company's total worldwide sales for 1994 were $37.9 billion.

The formation of business alliances became an appealing alternative in the 1980s for the following reasons (OECD, 1992):

—The convergence of consumer needs and preferences meant that buyers worldwide demanded the best products at the cheapest price, regardless of national origin. Many companies found that on their own, they could not meet customer needs globally.

—The rapid dispersion of technology meant that companies could not maintain a technological advantage for long, and they had to rely on others (including competitors) to help them develop new technologies.

—Companies could reduce costs and minimize risk by forming alliances, which at times is a fast and profitable way to go global without the complications and expenses associated with a merger.

Table 1.7
Mergers and Acquisitions Activity in Major Overseas Markets, 1995

Country	No. of Deals	Value (U.S. $bil)	Country	No. of Deals	Value (U.S. $bil)
Argentina	55	$2.3	Japan	42	2.2
Australia	286	26.6	Malaysia	155	3.6
Austria	50	1.3	Mexico	57	1.2
Belgium	90	1.2	Netherlands	193	4.3
Brazil	70	3.7	New Zealand	91	2.3
Canada	426	18.1	Norway	77	1.1
Chile	25	1.2	Peru	31	3.1
China	63	0.6	Poland	75	1.4
Czech Republic	43	9.5	Portugal	31	3.6
Denmark	92	1.3	Russia	39	1.2
Finland	110	2.5	Singapore	54	2.3
France	407	15.8	South Africa	102	0.7
Germany	528	17.1	Spain	112	2.3
Hong Kong	62	2.9	Sweden	162	11.3
Hungary	72	2.0	Switzerland	106	6.9
India	65	0.7	Thailand	24	0.4
Indonesia	24	2.3	United Kingdom	1,002	87.2
Ireland	44	0.3			
Italy	233	13.3	**Total**	**5,098**	**$257.8**

Source: SDC Mergers and Corporate Transactions Database; reprinted in Holmes (1996), p. 37.

Companies in many industries, including automobiles, aircraft, computers, and telecommunication, established strategic alliances in the 1980s and early 1990s. Many cases of international strategic alliances implemented in the 1980s were documented in Mowery (1988), Nevaer (1990), Dunning (1993), and Cowhey and Aronson (1993). One example was the agreement between Boeing and the Japan Commercial Aircraft Corporation (JCAC) to produce the Boeing 767 aircraft. JCAC is a consortium of Mitsubishi Heavy Industries, Kawasaki Heavy Industries, and Fuji Heavy Industries. Other examples include the agreement between AT&T and NEC to develop technologies for the next generation of semiconductors. Glaxo, a U.K. pharmaceutical firm, has several Japanese partners to establish sales and service networks in Japan. By September 1992, IBM alone had joined in over 400 strategic alliances with many companies in the United States and abroad (Sherman, 1992). Recent cases include the distribution and marketing agreement announced in June 1995 between the Miller Brewing Unit of Philip Morris and Asaki Breweries of Tokyo. On June 23, 1995, the two large credit-card rivals, Visa International and MasterCard International, announced that they had agreed to join forces to work on securing credit-card payments made over the Internet.

Mergers, acquisitions, and business alliances have significant implications for intrafirm trade and transfer pricing. Mergers and acquisitions between two companies creates new intrafirm transactions because the acquiring company and the target company become members of a new corporate family. Partners to a strategic alliance may have to share costs and revenue. Cross-border alliances may also create many related party transactions, which are subject to transfer pricing regulations of two or more countries.

Restructuring, Reengineering, and Other Organizational Changes

The concept of corporate restructuring is not new. American companies have been doing it for decades. The idea of reengineering drew wide attention after Hammer and Champy's *Reengineering the Corporation* was published in 1993. The book was based on joint research that began in the mid-1980s. Since then, the book has sold more than 500,000 copies in the United States and abroad. In 1995, Champy published another book, *Reengineering Management*, and Hammer and Stanton coauthored *The Reengineering Revolution*. Both books extend the ideas and principles of reengineering discussed in Hammer and Champy (1993). According to their first book, reengineering is "the fundamental rethinking and radical redesign of business processes to achieve dramatic improvement in critical, contemporary measures of performance, such as cost, quality, service, and speed" (Hammer and Champy, 1993, p. 32).

Reengineering is not the same as restructuring or downsizing; however, corporate reengineering often leads to these outcomes. The trend toward reengineering and restructuring will continue. The following gives some evidence:

—According to a survey of employment practices done by the American Management Association, almost half of the 870 companies surveyed had reduced their work forces from mid-1992 to mid-1993. For two-thirds of these companies, it was their second consecutive year of downsizing (Smith, 1994). For example, IBM laid off about 60,000 employees in 1993, and Sears Roebuck laid off 50,000 workers during the same year. Other companies with large layoffs in 1993 included Boeing (21,000 employees), Procter & Gamble (13,000 workers), and United Technologies (10,500 employees).

—Two of the "Big Six" accounting firms in the United States conducted separate studies in 1994 and found almost identical results: between 75 percent and 80 percent of the largest U.S. companies had already begun reengineering and would be increasing their commitment to it over the next few years (Hammer and Stanton, 1995).

Many large and well-known U.S. companies have achieved dramatic results through reengineering. The list of companies includes Chrysler, Ford, IBM, Pepsico, GTE, Hewlett-Packard, Hallmark, Amoco Oil, EDS, Johnson & Johnson, and many others. Some small companies have also adopted the concept and reengineered their business processes (Barrier, 1994). Because of these reengineering and restructuring efforts, the United States has replaced Japan as the world's most competitive economy for the first time since 1985, according to the 1994 World Competitiveness Report (cited in Roth, 1994).

Reengineering, restructuring, and other organizational changes that follow have a great impact on intrafirm transactions because the process may redefine (or reorganize) the sellers and buyers of those transactions. After the changes in business processes are implemented, they will impact the production costs of goods and services transferred between business units. For example, several years ago, after IBM Credit Corporation reengineered its credit approval process, the corporation slashed its seven-day turnaround time to just four hours (Hammer and Champy, 1993). Similarly, Kodak reduced the time it takes to develop the 35mm, single-use camera from 70 weeks to 38 weeks. In cases such as these, transfer prices for goods and services have to be recalculated or renegotiated.

Advances in Information Technologies

Over the past four decades, drastic improvements in communication and computer technologies have changed the way we work and how we communicate with each other. According to Behling and Records (1994–1995), the key enabling technologies in the communications and electronic computing industry include improved transmission capacity and speed through digital signal generation; speech processing; switching and data storage; fiber optics and light wave transmission; image, video, and audio compression; artificial intelligence applications such as image recognition; and wireless transmission. Changes in communication and computer technologies have also altered business practices in many MNCs. Business practices have to change from time to time because we need to catch up with new computing paradigms. According to Tesler (1995), "Computing paradigms are made possible by steady improvements in a variety of technologies, together with a maturation of the market. They seem to happen at intervals of about a decade" (p. 11). As shown in Table 1.8, we have gone through four different computing paradigms since the early 1960s. In the 1960s, the computer was treated as data processing equipment by many corporations. Data were processed in sequential batches using such languages as COBOL and FORTRAN. In the 1970s, large mainframe computers were essentially time-sharing computing systems shared among many subscribers. The paradigm shifted again in the early 1980s as personal computers entered many homes and offices. This transformed the computer into a desktop business and productivity tool for individuals. In the early 1990s, as we began to use more client-server

Table 1.8
The Four Paradigms of Computing

	Batch	Time-Sharing	Desktop	Network
Decade	1960s	1970s	1980s	1990s
Technology	Medium-Scale Integration	Large-Scale Integration	Very Large Scale	UltraLarge Scale
Location	Computer Room	Terminal Room	Desktop	Mobile
Users	Experts	Specialists	Individuals	Groups
User Status	Subservience	Dependence	Independence	Freedom
Data	Alpha-numeric	Text, Vector	Fonts, Graphs	Script, Voice
Objective	Calculate	Access	Present	Communication
User Activity	Punch & Try (Submit)	Remember & Type (Interact)	See & Point (Drive)	Ask & Tell (Delegate)
Operation	Process	Edit	Layout	Orchestration
Interconnect	Peripherals	Terminals	Desktops	Palmtops
Applications	Custom	Standard	Generic	Components
Languages	COBOL, FORTRAN	PL/I, BASIC	PASCAL, C	Object Oriented

Source: Tesler (1995).

technology and built more local-area networks (LANs) and wide-area networks (WANs), we moved into the so-called network computing paradigm. Many companies had also adopted groupware such as Lotus Notes to connect a widely dispersed work force. A fully networked corporation can now do business anywhere, anytime, and can share information and ideas with other colleagues through corporate networks. A good example is Sweden's L. M. Erickson, which has 17,000 engineers in 40 research centers located in 20 countries around the world, all of which are linked to one network. Similarly, development teams in Australia and England can now work together on the same design and then send off the final blueprint to a factory in China (Arnst, 1995).

Besides setting up its own computer network, a company can also use the Internet to obtain a variety of services and tools. The Internet is a global network of computers connecting millions of academic, business, and other users. Some of the major types of services and tools available on the Internet are shown below (Deloitte & Touche, 1995):

—E-mail—A store-and-forward mail service allowing communication throughout the network.

—bulletin boards—Central clearinghouses for information and correspondence about a large number of subjects and topics.

—file transfer—A package delivery service through which a company can request or send a wide variety of bulk data.

—Index and Retrieval Services—These may be used to find and communicate with information sources of interest or individuals with whom a company wants to establish contact.

In summary, the networking computing paradigm is still evolving. Many software companies are developing more sophisticated technologies that will make conducting business on the worldwide networks easier in the future (see Dertouzos, 1995; Cortese, 1995).

So far, the advances in communication and technologies have had the following positive effects that promote world trade and investment:

—Corporate executives and business people are better informed about international business developments, and they can absorb needed information in a more timely fashion.

—Through E-mail, voice mail, cellular phones, and fax machines, business executives can be more accessible and can personalize their communication with colleagues, customers, and others.

—Using sophisticated equipment and tools, currency, and bond traders, corporate executives can move large sums of capital and funds around the globe within seconds to take advantage of global business opportunities. Many international accounting and financial software programs are available to help companies deal with multilanguage, multicurrency, and other multicultural problems in international trade (O'Brien, 1995; Lebow and Adhikari, 1995).

Impact on Intrafirm Trade and Transfer Pricing

When we explained each environmental change earlier, we mentioned briefly that each of those changes may lead to expansion in intrafirm trade and create more issues and problems for corporate transfer pricing systems. Now we can look at all the changes together and assess their overall impact on intrafirm trade and transfer pricing. Figure 1.2 shows the cause-and-effect relationships between the environmental changes and their impact on intrafirm trade and transfer pricing.

Globalization and expansion in international trade usually lead to an enlargement of overseas operations by MNCs. This enlargement of operations may be reflected in increased international direct investment or greater numbers of cross-border mergers, acquisitions, and strategic alliances. These activities will lead to a further expansion of trade, including intrafirm trade. Many mergers and acquisitions lead to restructuring and other changes in corporate operations, which in turn may necessitate an overhaul of the corporate transfer pricing systems.

Improvements in communication and computer technologies have the poten-

Figure 1.2
Environmental Changes and Their Impact on Intrafirm Trade and Transfer Pricing

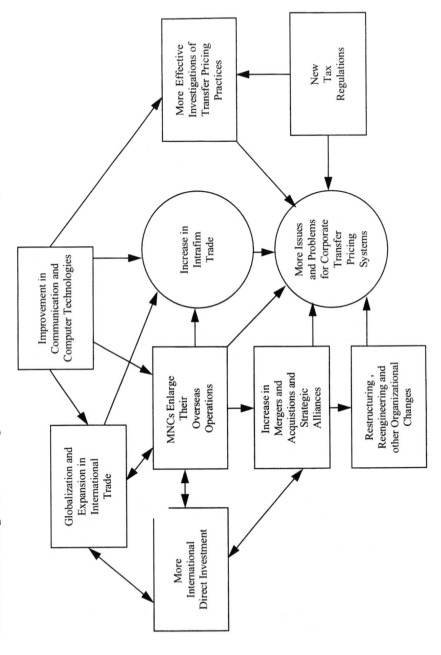

tial to facilitate the globalization process of MNCs and the expansion of all forms of trade and investment. These changes may create new problems and opportunities for corporate transfer pricing systems. Improvements in information technology have enabled the U.S. Internal Revenue Service (IRS) to implement the "Compliance 2000" program and systems modernization, which should lead to more effective investigations of corporate transfer pricing practices. The main purpose of "Compliance 2000" is to enhance voluntary compliance. It combines traditional enforcement efforts with other initiatives such as taxpayer outreach and education programs, advance pricing agreements, audit technique guides and the nonfiler program. New transfer pricing regulations, as announced periodically by the IRS and tax authorities of foreign governments, may also create new challenges for corporate transfer pricing administrators.

TRANSFER PRICING AND ITS MAJOR STAKEHOLDERS

Intrafirm trade and transfer pricing involve many different parties with conflicting interests. As shown in Figure 1.3, these stakeholders can be divided into five groups:

1. Stakeholders within the corporate family: they include the buying division(s), selling division(s), corporate financial management, top management, and other units involved. Normally, a buying division prefers low transfer prices for an intrafirm transaction to reduce the purchasing cost, whereas a selling division would like to receive a higher transfer price so that it can increase its revenue. The corporate finance department (division) usually wants a fair price for the transaction that is in compliance with tax regulations. Top management normally wants transfer prices to achieve such objectives as maximizing profit or minimizing global tax liability.

2. Domestic government agencies, which include the tax authority (the IRS), U.S. Customs Service, Congress, the General Accounting Office (GAO), and others. Obviously, the IRS would like to collect the maximum tax allowed by tax laws. The Customs Service wants to collect as many customs duties as possible. Congress wants to pass effective legislation that serves as a basis for the Treasury Department and the IRS to issue detailed regulations. From time to time, Congress may ask the GAO to investigate the extent of tax compliance by foreign-controlled and U.S. MNCs. The results of such investigations (e.g., GAO, 1995) will be reported in other chapters.

3. Foreign government agencies, which include their tax authorities, customs services, investment promotional agency, and others. Normally, the investment promotional agency would like to have the most liberal transfer pricing legislation, to attract foreign investors.

4. International organizations including the OECD, the United Nations (UN), the European Union (EU), and so forth. One important objective of these organizations is to promote the use of arm's-length prices for international intrafirm trade. In the past, the OECD took a leadership role in issuing guidelines for transfer pricing (e.g., OECD, 1979, 1984, 1995b). The United Nations Conference on Trade and Development (UNCTAD) has published several reports on transfer pricing (e.g., UNCTAD, 1978).

Figure 1.3
Stakeholders of Intrafirm Transactions and Transfer Pricing

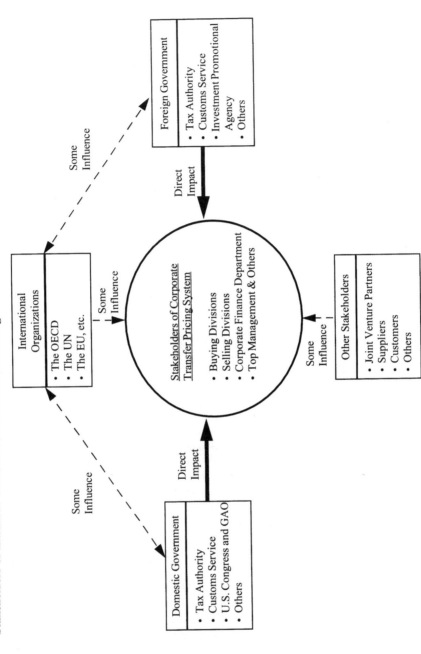

The United Nations Center on Transnational Corporations sponsored many transfer pricing workshops in developing countries. The EU issued a number of tax directives related to international taxation.

5. Other stakeholders include joint venture partners, suppliers, and final customers. This group of stakeholders will try to look after their own interests in intrafirm trade.

Because of the conflicting interests of these stakeholders, many issues in intrafirm trade and transfer pricing are bound to be controversial. To avoid unnecessary conflicts and disputes among corporate internal stakeholders and to comply with government regulations, corporate management must have a policy statement governing all aspects of intrafirm transactions and transfer pricing. We will discuss some issues related to the management of corporate transfer pricing systems in Chapter 9.

CHANGING REGULATIONS FOR MULTINATIONAL TRANSFER PRICING

As intrafirm trade between MNCs expands, tax authorities in many countries are changing their transfer pricing regulations and intensifying their investigations of corporate transfer pricing practices. A summary of new and proposed transfer pricing regulations in selected countries is shown in Table 1.9. In the United States, section 482 of the Internal Revenue Code authorizes the Internal Revenue Service (IRS) to allocate income or deductions among controlled taxpayers to prevent tax evasion and clearly reflect the income of controlled taxpayers. The final regulations for section 482 of the Internal Revenue Code were issued on July 1, 1994. The regulations contain 262 pages of rules and examples. New U.S. regulations under section 6662(e) may impose penalties of 20 to 40 percent in the case of underpayment of taxes attributable to large transfer pricing adjustments. Tax authorities in many other countries and the Organization for Economic Cooperation and Development (OECD) have also issued new transfer pricing regulations and guidelines in recent years. Together, the expansion of intrafirm trade and the proliferation of new transfer pricing regulations have the potential of creating a global tax war related to transfer pricing (see Reed, Holyoke, and Harbrecht, 1994; Steiner, 1994). The following cases are only some examples:

—Several years ago, the IRS claimed that Nissan's U.S. subsidiary inflated the prices it paid to its parent for finished cars imported from Japan and demanded $600 million payment of back taxes. The IRS later reached a settlement of $160 million with Nissan. In 1994, Pepsico Inc. was battling the IRS over an $880 million bill for 1985–1989, which was levied after an extensive tax audit of Pepsico's subsidiaries, including Pizza Hut, Taco Bell, and Kentucky Fried Chicken.

—In 1994, the Japanese National Tax Administration Agency claimed that Coca-Cola Co.'s Japanese subsidiary had paid excessive royalties to its U.S. parent in 1990–1992

Table 1.9

New and Proposed Transfer Pricing Regulations in Selected Countries

Country	New Regulations or Legislation	Date Issued
U.S.	Revenue Procedure 91-22 for advance pricing agreements	3/1/91
	Announcement 95-49 on proposed update of advance pricing agreement revenue procedure	5/19/95
	Final regulations under section 482	7/1/94
	Final cost sharing regulations under section 482	12/20/95
	Final regulations for section 6662—imposition of the accuracy-rated penalty	2/9/96
	Revenue Procedure 91-23 on requesting Competent Authority Assistance	3/19/91
	Announcement 95-9 on proposed competent authority revenue procedure	5/24/95
Canada	Revenue Canada Information Circular 94-4: International Transfer Pricing: Advance Pricing Agreement (APA)	12/30/94
Mexico	New transfer pricing rules with respect to Maquiladora companies	3/31/95
Australia	Draft Taxation Ruling TR95/D22: The use of arm's length transfer pricing methodologies in international dealings between associate enterprises;	9/29/95
	Draft Taxation Ruling TR95/D23: Documentation and other practical issues associated with transfer pricing; and	9/29/95
	Draft Taxation Ruling TR95/D24: Guidelines on the application of penalty tax for international transfer pricing adjustments.	9/29/95
China	Circular of state Taxation Administration on tax management between associated enterprises	10/29/92
Japan	Revised procedure for the pre-confirmation system	1993
South Korea	The International Tax Coordination Law and Enforcement Decree	Effective 1/1/96
The OECD	Transfer pricing guidelines for multinational enterprises and tax administrations	7/13/95

Source: Compiled by the author.

and demanded $145 million in back taxes. In addition, Japan has ordered 60 other companies to pay back taxes on profits totaling 120 billion yen (or about U.S. $1.2 billion).

—Also in 1994, the Spanish tax authority conducted a tax audit of Gillette Española, S.A., a Spanish subsidiary of the U.S.-based Gillette Corporation, and concluded that Gillette Española owed about $84.6 million in back taxes.

These and many other similar examples show that the focus of transfer pricing has shifted gradually from domestic to international and tax issues. Details of such legislation and regulations will be discussed in Chapters 3 through 8 of this book. Legislative changes implemented in recent years may have enormous ramifications for tax planning and the management of a multinational transfer pricing system in the future.

AN OVERVIEW OF THE BOOK

This book contains nine chapters. The first chapter is the introduction to the book. Changes in business environment and their implications for intrafirm trade and transfer pricing have been discussed. We also identified the major stakeholders in intrafirm trade and transfer pricing.

Chapter 2 reviews recent literature on intrafirm trade and current trends of international intrafirm trade from a U.S. perspective. Other topics to be discussed include U.S. direct investment abroad and profiles of foreign affiliates of U.S. MNCs. U.S. merchandise trade associated with U.S. MNCs and intrafirm trade among those corporations will be examined in detail.

Transfer pricing regulations in the United States will be reviewed in Chapter 3, which explains some historical developments of section 482, including the 1968 regulations, the 1992 proposed regulations, and the 1993 temporary regulations. The 1994 final regulations for section 482 will be discussed in detail. Also covered in Chapter 3 are final cost-sharing regulations and section 6662 regulations on the imposition of the accuracy-related penalty.

Chapter 4 presents the details of the advance-pricing agreement (APA) and other U.S. programs related to transfer pricing. We will review the APA process and explain its potential benefit and risks. Other programs, including the competent authority procedure and transfer pricing arbitration, will also be reviewed.

The OECD reports and guidelines for transfer pricing are discussed in Chapter 5. These reports include the 1979 OECD report, *Transfer Pricing and Multinational Enterprises*, and the 1984 report, *Transfer Pricing and Multinational Enterprises: Three Taxation Issues*. The OECD's *Transfer Pricing Guidelines for Multinational Enterprises and Tax Administrations* (1995b) will be discussed in detail.

Chapter 6 examines major issues on intrafirm trade and transfer pricing in Canada and Mexico, the two NAFTA partners of the United States. Bilateral investment and intrafirm trade between Canada, Mexico, and the United States will be reviewed. Transfer pricing regulations of Canada and Mexico will be examined, and the Canadian advance pricing agreement program will also be described.

Chapter 7 reviews the transfer pricing regulations of selected countries in the Europe Union. These countries include France, Germany, Italy, the Netherlands, and the United Kingdom. International investment activities of these five countries and their intrafirm trade with the United States will be discussed.

Chapter 8 examines major issues on intrafirm trade and transfer pricing of four selected countries in the Asian Pacific region: Australia, China, Japan and

South Korea. New transfer pricing regulations imposed by these countries and their implications will be explained.

Chapter 9 summarizes major research findings in the following areas related to intrafirm trade and transfer pricing: changes in the international environment, literature and realities of international intrafirm trade; changes in transfer pricing regulations in major trading nations; tax investigations of corporate transfer pricing practices, and advance pricing agreement programs. A new paradigm for resolving many problems and issues in transfer pricing will be provided, along with some general conclusions drawn from the research.

REFERENCES

Arnst, Catherine. 1995. Networked Corporation. *Business Week* (June 26): 86–89.

Barrier, Michael. 1994. Re-engineering Your Company. *Nation's Business* (February): 16–22.

Behling, Robert, and Hal Records. 1994–1995. Technology and International Competition in the Information Age. *Journal of Computer Information Systems* (Winter): 50–55.

Byrne, John A. 1994. The Pain of Downsizing. *Business Week* (May 9): 60–63.

Champy, James. 1995. *Reengineering Management.* New York: HarperCollins.

Cook, William J. 1994. Serving Up a New Era in Computing. *U.S. News & World Report* (October 17): 62–72.

Cortese, Amy. 1995. Group Therapy: Why IBM Paid All That Loot for Lotus. *Business Week* (June 26): 93–96.

Cortese, Amy, John Verity, Russell Mitchell, and Richard Brandt. 1995. Cyberspace. *Business Week* (February 27): 78–86.

Cowhey, Peter F., and Jonathan D. Aronson. 1993. *Managing the World Economy: The Consequences of Corporate Alliances.* New York: Council on Foreign Relations Press.

Cox, James. 1995. Move to Punish U.S. Firms May Hurt China More. *USA Today* (July 20): A1–A2.

Deloitte & Touche. 1994. Using Strategic Alliances to Manage Change. *Deloitte & Touche Review* (October 31): 1–2.

———. 1995. Business on the Internet—Potential Benefits and Dangers. *Deloitte & Touche Review* (June 26): 1–2.

Dertouzos, Michael L. 1995. Communications, Computers and Networks. *Scientific American* (special issue, The Computer in the 21st Century): 22–29.

Drucker, Peter F. 1989. *The New Realities.* New York: Harper & Row.

Dunning, John H. 1993. *The Globalization of Business.* London: Routledge.

Elmer-Dewitt, Philip. 1994. Battle for the Soul of the Internet. *Time* (July 25): 50–56.

Ernst & Young LLP. 1995. Transfer Pricing: Risk Reduction and Advance Pricing Agreements. *Tax Notes International* (July 31): 293–310.

Frigo, Mark L., and Howard Singer. 1994. Reengineering: A Controller's Perspective. *Small Business Controller* (Spring): 33–36.

Goman, Carol K. 1994. *Managing in a Global Organization.* Menlo Park, Calif.: Crisp Publications.

Hammer, Michael, and James Champy. 1993. *Reengineering the Corporation.* New York: HarperCollins.

Hammer, Michael, and Steven A. Stanton. 1995. *The Reengineering Revolution.* New York: HarperCollins.

Hielkirk, John. 1993. Challenging Status Quo Now in Vogue. *USA Today* (November 9): B1–B2.

Holland, Kelley, and Amy Cortese. 1995. The Future of Money. *Business Week* (June 12): 66–78.

Holmes, Garrick. 1996. Big Price Tags Make for a Banner Year. *Mergers & Acquisitions* (March/April): 13–17.

Lebow, Marc I., and Ajay Adhikari. 1995. Software That Speaks Your Language. *Journal of Accountancy* (July): 65–72.

Levy, Philip I., and T. N. Srinivasan. 1996. Regionalism and the (Dis)advantage of Dispute-Settlement Access. *American Economic Review* (Vol. 86, No. 2): 93–98.

Little, Jane Sneddon. 1986. Intra-Firm Trade and U.S. Protectionism: Thoughts Based on a Small Survey. *New England Economic Review* (January/February): 42–51.

———. 1987. Intra-Firm Trade: An Update. *New England Economic Review* (May/June): 46–51.

Lombo, Gustano. 1995. The 100 Largest Foreign Investments in the U.S., the Land of Cheap Currency. *Forbes* (July 17): 280–288.

Mowery, David C. 1988. *International Collaborative Ventures in U.S. Manufacturing.* Cambridge, Mass.: Ballinger.

Naisbitt, John. 1982. *Megatrends.* New York: Warner Books.

———. 1994. *Global Paradox.* New York: William Morrow and Co.

———. 1995. *Megatrends Asia.* London: Nicholas Brealey.

Naisbitt, John, and Patricia Aburdene. 1990. *Megatrends 2000.* New York: Avon Books.

Nevaer, Louis E. V. 1990. *Strategic Corporate Alliances.* Westport, Conn.: Quorum.

O'Brien, Michael. 1995. Going Global: What to Look for in Financial Software. *Management Accounting* (April): 59–60.

Organization for Economic Cooperation and Development (OECD). 1979. *Transfer Pricing and Multinational Enterprises.* Paris: OECD.

———. 1984. *Transfer Pricing and Multinational Enterprises: Three Taxation Issues.* Paris: OECD.

———. 1992. *International Direct Investment Policies and Trends in the 1980s.* Paris: OECD.

———. 1995a. *OECD Reviews of Foreign Direct Investment: United States.* Paris: OECD.

———. 1995b. *Transfer Pricing Guidelines for Multinational Enterprises and Tax Administrations.* Paris: OECD.

Reed, Stanley, Larry Holyoke, and Douglas Harbrecht. 1994. Here Comes the Great Global Tax War. *Business Week* (May 30): 55–56.

Roth, Terence. 1994. Global Report Finds U.S. Has Replaced Japan as Most Competitive Economy. *Wall Street Journal* (September 7).

Securities Data Co. 1996. 1995 M & A Profile. *Mergers & Acquisitions* (March/April): 37.

Sherman, Stratford. 1992. Are Strategic Alliances Working? *Fortune* (September 21): 77–78.

Smith, Lee. 1994. Burned-Out Bosses. *Fortune* (July 25): 44–52.

Steiner, Robert. 1994. Japan Orders 60 Firms to Pay Back-Taxes. *Wall Street Journal* (October 12): A13.

Tang, Roger Y. W. 1979. *Transfer Pricing Practices in the United States and Japan.* New York: Praeger.

———. 1981. *Multinational Transfer Pricing: Canadian and British Perspectives.* Toronto: Butterworths.

———. 1993. *Transfer Pricing in the 1990s: Tax and Management Perspectives.* Westport, Conn.: Quorum.

Tesler, Lawrence G. 1995. Networked Computing in the 1990s. *Scientific American* (special issue, The Computer in the 21st Century): 10–21.

UN Conference on Trade and Development (UNCTAD). 1978. *Dominant Positions of Market Power of Transnational Corporations: Use of the Transfer Pricing Mechanism.* New York: United Nations.

U.S. General Accounting Office (GAO). 1995. *International Taxation, Transfer Pricing and Information on Non-payment of Tax.* Washington, D.C.: GAO.

Zajac, Brian. 1995. The 100 Largest U.S. Multinationals: Weak Dollar, Strong Results. *Forbes* (July 17): 274–276.

2

Intrafirm Trade of U.S. Multinational Companies

Intrafirm trade has always been an important part of U.S. foreign trade. Recent estimates show that between one-third and one-half of all trade is intrafirm trade (Whitman, 1995). This chapter examines major issues and trends related to intrafirm trade of U.S. multinational companies (MNCs). More specifically, we will cover the following topics:

—a review of recent literature on U.S. intrafirm trade;

—recent trends in international intrafirm trade from a U.S. perspective;

—international investment activities relating to the United States;

—profile of foreign affiliates of U.S. MNCs; and

—an analysis of intrafirm trade between U.S. MNCs and their foreign affiliates.

An understanding of these topics is essential to the study of transfer pricing practices in the United States.

LITERATURE ON INTRAFIRM TRADE OF U.S. MULTINATIONAL COMPANIES (MNCs)

In the past, many researchers have studied various aspects of international intrafirm trade related to U.S. MNCs. Bisat (1967) conducted one of the earliest studies in this area, using statistics on direct foreign investment and foreign trade of the United States and the noncommunist world. He analyzed the data from 1946 to 1965 and discovered that a substantial, and rising, share of international trade was represented by intrafirm transactions. He estimated that intrafirm trade accounted for close to one-third of the noncommunist world's foreign trade in merchandise. Since then, many other researchers and organizations (e.g., Lall, 1978a; Helleiner and Lavergne, 1979; Little, 1986, 1987; Cho, 1988, 1990; Hipple, 1990, 1995; OECD, 1993) have conducted empirical studies on intrafirm trade. This author has also reviewed intrafirm trade statistics of U.S. and non-U.S. MNCs in two earlier works (Tang, 1981, 1993). In the following, we will review the key findings from these empirical studies.

Lall

Lall (1978a) attempted to explain interindustry differences in the pattern of intrafirm exports by U.S. manufacturing MNCS to their affiliates abroad in 1970. That study is related to others conducted by Lall (1973, 1978b) on transfer pricing. From the data published by the U.S. Tariff Commission (1973), Lall observed significant interindustry differences in the propensity to use intrafirm rather than unrelated-party trade.

Lall (1978a) selected two dependent variables (IFX and IFP) to express the extent of intrafirm exports by U.S. MNCs. IFX is the percentage of intrafirm exports to total exports by MNCs in a particular industry. IFP represents intrafirm exports as a percentage of production by majority-owned foreign affiliates (MOFAs) receiving those exports. The independent variables used by Lall to run ordinary regression analyses include the following:

RD   research and development expenditures as a percentage of industry sales in
         the United States;

VAL   value added per employee for each industry;

SALES   a dummy variable to denote the marketing requirements of each industry. A
         value of 1 was assigned when after-sales service requirements were high, and
         0 was assigned when service requirements were low;

AD   advertising as a percentage of sales;

TAR   a dummy variable, which was assigned a value of 1 when the industry used
         Tariff Schedules 807.00 and 806.30, and 0 when it did not;

FA   foreign assets as a percentage of domestic assets of each industry.

Data supplied by the U.S. Tariff Commission (1973) were collated to give 32 observations for IFX and 30 for IFP. Lall (1978a) used an ordinary least-squares linear regression analysis to analyze the data. He discovered that the independent variables were able to explain close to half of the variations in IFP and about 30 percent of the variations for IFX. The explanatory variables that performed best are RD, FA, TAR, and SALES. Therefore, Lall concluded that the following factors affect the pattern of intrafirm exports: technological intensity, the extent of foreign investment, the divisibility of production processes, and the need for after-sales services.

Lall's findings may provide some explanations for the interindustry differences among the amounts of intrafirm exports by U.S. MNCs. However, his findings can be treated only as tentative because multicollinearity problems existed among some of the independent variables. For example, RD was highly correlated with SALES, and both SALES and RD were significantly correlated with FA. It is also questionable whether an ordinary least-squares linear regression is appropriate for this type of statistical analysis.

Helleiner and Lavergne

Whereas Lall (1978a) was trying to explain the interindustry differences of intrafirm exports by U.S. MNCs, Helleiner and Lavergne (1979) attempted to interpret the interindustry differences in U.S. related-party imports using multiple regression analysis. In their investigations, Helleiner and Lavergne (1979) discovered that about 48.4 percent of U.S. imports in 1977 came from firms that were related by ownership to the importing firms. However, there were significant interindustry differences. While only 23.5 percent of nonpetroleum primary product imports were from related firms, 37.6 percent of semimanufactured and 53.6 percent of manufactured products were imported from related companies.

Findings from multiple regression analysis showed that the magnitude of related-party imports as a percentage of total imports was found to be significantly positively correlated with the average levels wage, research, and development expenditures as a percentage of sales and firm size. There were some differences between related-party imports from OECD countries and those from developing countries. For imports from the OECD only, the results were similar to those for total U.S. imports. In the case of imports from developing countries, however, neither firm size nor the average wage was significantly correlated with the level of related-party imports. Helleiner and Lavergne (1979) also discovered that ''some newly industrializing countries exporting manufacturing products to the U.S. do so through intrafirm channels to a much greater degree than others, whatever the product'' (p. 307). Countries that had high intrafirm trade ratios with the United States in 1975 through 1977 included Malaysia (87.9 percent), Singapore (83.3 percent), Mexico (71.0 percent), and Ireland (59.0 percent).

While Helleiner and Lavergne (1979) provided additional information on interindustry differences among U.S. intrafirm imports, their regression model explained less than half of the variations in intrafirm imports by U.S. MNCs. It is obvious that many important explanatory variables were not considered in the model.

Little

Little's findings are published in two separate issues of the *New England Economic Review* (in 1986 and 1987). In her first article, Little (1986) noted that increased foreign direct investment led to additional intrafirm trade. A good example is Mexico. By 1985, U.S. MNCs in industries such as electronics, textiles, drugs, automotive parts, and toys had established 772 plants employing 202,000 workers in Mexico under the maquiladora program. These plants used the materials and components imported from U.S. parents and then shipped the finished goods back to the United States free of Mexican customs duties.

Little (1986) conducted a survey of 475 New England firms to examine the impact of exchange rate fluctuations on affiliated versus unaffiliated trade. These firms were either active in international trade or were foreign-owned firms with a known mailing address. A total of 104 companies responded. Among the firms responding, the typical MNC conducted over half of its trade within its own firm in 1983. Little (1986) also discovered that "for the U.S. respondents the mean share of intrafirm exports in total exports was 50 percent while the mean share of intrafirm imports in total was 58 percent. For the typical U.S. affiliate of a foreign firm, 44 percent of exports were intrafirm while 70 percent of imports represented affiliate trade" (p. 46). The data provided by respondents suggested that intrafirm trade reacted to macro-developments differently than did unaffiliated trade between 1979 and 1983. Intrafirm exports and imports both grew faster than total U.S. trade (weighted according to the industries represented in the survey group). Between 1979 and 1983, U.S. intrafirm imports were more sensitive to the appreciation of the U.S. dollar than were unaffiliated imports, mainly because U.S. MNCs were establishing low-cost production sites abroad to protect domestic markets from foreign competition.

In her second article, Little (1987) provided updated statistics on the growth of intrafirm trade using data published by the U.S. Bureau of Economic Analysis. She noted that intrafirm transactions accounted for about 60 percent of U.S. parent manufacturers' imports and almost half of their exports. U.S. affiliates of foreign MNCs also relied on intrafirm imports to an equally great extent. However, their intrafirm exports were much less significant, because the affiliates' primary objective is to serve the huge U.S. market.

Cho

In his first study, Cho (1988) identified four groups of major determinants of intrafirm trade: product-specific factors; region-specific factors; government-specific factors; and firm-specific factors. Specific examples of these four groups of factors (determinants) are shown in Table 2.1.

Product-specific factors are those related to the nature of a product that permit international production and internal market exchange and make it more profitable than international external market exchange. Region-specific factors are the geographical and socioeconomic characteristics of home and host countries linked by trade. Government-specific factors are the political and fiscal environments of home and host countries that permit international production and internal market exchange and make it more profitable than international external market exchange. Firm-specific factors include the ability and incentives of a

Table 2.1
Major Determinants of Intrafirm Trade Patterns

1. Product-specific factors	3. Government-specific factors
Specificity of product: usage, technology quality, economies of scale, production, and marketing requirements, etc.	Fiscal and monetary policies
	Trade policies
Uncertainty: quality, price, supply, and demand	Foreign investment policies
	Foreign exchange policies
Nature of product market competition	Commercial and industrial policies
Divisibility of production processes	Tax and tariff regulations
	Foreign policies
	Political stability
	Legal environments, especially patent protection, contract enforcement, and dispute resolution
2. Region-specific factors	4. Firm-specific factors
Availability of cheap, quality inputs: raw materials, intermediate parts, technology, human resources, etc.	Possession of proprietary resources: information, technology, management skills, trademarks, human resources, access to factor and product markets, etc.
Transportation and communication	Excess capacity and resources
Availability of adequate infrastructure	
	Economies of joint operations in such areas as production, purchasing, marketing, and finance
Production costs	
Psychic distance, such as differences in language, culture, business, and customs	Special strategic and competitive needs
	Risk bearability
	International business experience

Source: Cho (1988).

firm to organize international production and internal market for the international exchange of goods and services. After examining these factors, Cho (1988) developed some testable hypotheses, as follows:

—Countries with relatively favorable positions regarding the region-specific and govern-ment-specific factors are more likely to be major intrafirm trading partners of U.S. MNCs.

—Industries/products with characteristics conducive to foreign direct investment are more likely to be amenable to intrafirm trade than others.

—The size and relative significance of intrafirm exports and imports in a particular product seem to reflect the dominant nature of U.S. foreign direct investment of the product.

—Countries with larger U.S. foreign direct investment presence tend to have larger intrafirm trade between U.S. parents and their foreign affiliates there, with the notable exception of Japan and Brazil.

In another article, Cho (1990) examined the role of major product-specific factors in the intrafirm trade of U.S. MNCs. Using pooled time-series (1982–1986), cross-sectional (19 products) regression analysis, Cho (1990) discovered that the technology intensity of a product has a strong positive effect on its demand via intrafirm trade. In other words, the more intensive a product's technological content, the more likely the product is to be intrafirm-traded by U.S. MNCs. (This finding is similar to that discovered in Lall, 1978a.) Cho (1990) also found that the level of economies of scale appears to have a constraining effect on the volume of intrafirm trade. The vertical integration intensity and international production intensity were found to have no significant bearings on the volume of trade.

The OECD

The OECD (1993) study was conducted by Marcos Bonturi and Kiichiro Fukasaku using data obtained from the U.S. Department of Commerce and Japan's Ministry of International Trade (MITI). The data indicate that over one-third of U.S. merchandise trade was intrafirm trade. U.S. intrafirm trade was concentrated in industries with relatively high research and development (R&D) and human capital intensity such as the machinery, electric/electronic equipment, and transportation equipment industries.

The overall share of intrafirm trade in U.S. trade did not show a significant increase between 1977 and 1989. However, one component that showed a significant increase during the same period is the level of the U.S.-based affiliates' imports from their foreign parents. As the authors explained, "This increase is mostly due to increased activity by firms from Japan and South Korea and is concentrated in the wholesale trade of motor vehicles and equipment" (p. 8). On the export side, Canada and Europe accounted for about 70 percent of total intrafirm trade of U.S. MNCs in 1989. On the import side, intrafirm trade by U.S. MNCs posted large increases with Mexico and Europe. Intrafirm imports from Canada increased only slightly between 1982 and 1989.

The authors also reported the regression analysis results of major determinants of intrafirm trade by U.S. parent companies in manufacturing using the 1989 data. The results indicate that the greater the R&D and skill intensities and the higher the international orientation, the more the U.S. parent firms are engaged in intrafirm exports. For intrafirm exports, there is a positive effect of R&D intensity, physical capacity intensity, and selling expense intensity, and a negative effect of pollution intensity. The human capital intensity of U.S. affiliates was found to be statistically insignificant. The finding related to pollution intensity was contrary to that reported by Siddharthan and Kumar (1990).

Hipple

Hipple's studies focused on the role of MNCs in U.S. international trade. In a 1990 article, Hipple, discussed the impact of intrafirm shipments on U.S. foreign trade between 1977 and 1982. He observed that intrafirm shipments comprised a significant share of U.S. international trade and contributed to the deficit pressures on the U.S. trade balance. Hipple (1990) also discovered that the nature of intrafirm shipments of manufactures by U.S. compared to foreign MNCs was quite different. U.S. MNCs played a large role in both manufactures exports and imports, with the more significant share on the export side. In contract, foreign-based MNCs were involved almost exclusively in imports of manufactures.

Hipple (1990) also noted two divergent trends in intrafirm shipments between 1977 and 1982. U.S. MNCs had a surplus change of $5.1 billion, but foreign-based MNCs had a deficit change of $13.7 billion. These changes contributed to the deficit pressures on the U.S. merchandise trade balance.

A 1995 book by Hipple presented extensive information on the trade role of MNCs in U.S. foreign trade, providing information on the geographic patterns of MNC-related trade and also on product patterns of trade related to multinational companies. On the geographic patterns of MNC-related trade, Hipple examined trade with Canada, Europe, Japan, and other areas for 1975, 1982, and 1989. (Those were the years when benchmark surveys of foreign direct investment were conducted by the U.S. Department of Commerce.) On product patterns of MNC-related trade, Hipple presented numerous tables on trade related to the categories of ''Road Vehicles and Parts,'' ''Petroleum and Products,'' ''Chemicals,'' other manufacturing industries, and nonmanufacturing trade. Hipple noted that the U.S. merchandise trade deficit increased to $152.1 billion in 1989. In affiliate-related trade, MNCs had a 51.2 percent share and a deficit of $89.5 billion. In intrafirm trade, MNCs as a group had a 38.2 percent share and a deficit of $61.8 billion. Hipple concluded that MNCs, as a group of trade transactors, remained linked to an excessive share of U.S. trade deficit.

Evaluation of Current Literature

All the studies reviewed in this section have provided great insight into different aspects of intrafirm transactions related to U.S. foreign trade. The study by Lall (1978a) represents one of the earlier attempts to explain interindustry differences in U.S. intrafirm exports, while Helleiner and Lavergne (1979) tried to interpret interindustry differences in U.S. intrafirm imports. Helleiner and Lavergne (1979) also noted that some developing countries (Malaysia, Singapore, and Mexico) had high intrafirm trade ratios with the United States during the period of 1975 to 1977. Both Lall (1978a) and Helleiner and Lavergne (1979) identified some variables that explained part of the variation in intrafirm trade of U.S. MNCs.

Little (1986, 1987) noted the relationship between increased direct investment and expanding intrafirm trade. Little (1986) also discovered that between 1979 and 1983, U.S. intrafirm imports were more sensitive to the appreciation of the U.S. dollar than were unaffiliated. imports In her second article, Little (1987) found that intrafirm trade accounted for about 60 percent of U.S. parent manufacturers' imports and almost half of their exports.

Cho (1988) provided a useful framework of major determinants of intrafirm trade: product-specific factors; region-specific factors; government-specific factors; and firm-specific factors. This conceptual framework has theoretical merits because it enhances our understanding of the elements that explain the variation in intrafirm trade. Cho (1988) also provided several hypotheses related to the four sets of major determinants. In his second article, Cho (1990) discovered that the more intensive a product's technological content, the more likely it will be intrafirm-traded by U.S. MNCs. It will be interesting to find out whether this finding remains valid for intrafirm trade in the 1990s.

The OECD (OECD, 1993) study, conducted by Marcos Bontuir and Kirchino Fukaskure, reconfirmed the importance of intrafirm trade in both U.S. and Japanese international trade. The study also found that the greater the R&D and skill intensities and the higher the international orientation, the more likely are U.S. parent firms to be engaged in intrafirm export.

Hipple (1990, 1995) provided a large volume of U.S. intrafirm trade information, organized by geographic patterns and product categories. Hipple (1990) noted that U.S. intrafirm trade comprised a significant share of foreign trade and contributed to the deficit pressures on the trade balance.

All these studies have broadened our understanding of intrafirm trade of MNCs from a U.S. perspective. Much remains to be learned, however, about intrafirm trade and multinational transfer pricing. Over the past five years, tax and legal environments for intrafirm transfer pricing have changed significantly in the United States and in other major trading nations of Europe and the Asian Pacific region. We need to study these changes and explore their impact on intrafirm trade and corporate transfer pricing practices. We should also examine the roles of some innovative programs (e.g., advance-pricing agreements, the competent authority procedure, and transfer pricing arbitration) in promoting international investment and intrafirm trade.

RECENT TRENDS IN INTERNATIONAL INTRAFIRM TRADE

In spite of the importance of international intrafirm trade, only a few industrial countries gather information regularly on international intrafirm trade; among these are Japan and the United States. Intrafirm trade data of U.S. MNCs and foreign companies operating in the United States are included in annual surveys conducted by the Bureau of Economic Analysis (BEA) of the U.S. Department of Commerce and published in various issues of its publications, *U.S. Direct Investment Abroad, Foreign Direct Investment in the United States*, and *Survey of Current Business*. Because the databases maintained by the BEA are very complete and comprehensive, we will use the information to analyze the overall trends of international intrafirm trade.

Table 2.2 reports the statistics of U.S. merchandise trade between U.S. parent companies and their majority-owned foreign affiliates (MOFAs) from 1982 to 1993. According to the U.S. Department of Commerce, a ''foreign affiliate'' is a foreign business enterprise in which a U.S. person owns or controls 10 percent of the voting securities or the equivalent. A ''majority-owned foreign affiliate'' is defined as a foreign affiliate in which the combined direct and indirect ownership interest of all U.S. parents exceeds 50 percent. The data for the years 1982 to 1993 are also shown in graphic format (in Figure 2.1). Both Table 2.2 and Figure 2.1 show that international intrafirm trade between U.S. parent companies and their MOFAs increased steadily from 1982 to 1993. In 1993 U.S. exports shipped to foreign affiliates by U.S. parents amounted to $105.0 billion, while U.S. imports shipped by those affiliates to U.S. parents amounted to $95.9 billion. The combined intrafirm trade volume for U.S. MNCs and their foreign affiliates was $200.9 billion. This represents a 142 percent increase over the $82.9 billion recorded in 1982.

The last column of Table 2.2 also shows the intrafirm trade as a percentage of U.S. merchandise trade for the 11-year period. On average, the international intrafirm trade between U.S. parent companies and their foreign affiliates accounted for about 19 percent of U.S. merchandise trade. Since the intrafirm trade percentage varied little from 1982 to 1993, we can assume that intrafirm trade of U.S. MNCs increased at about the same rate as that for U.S. merchandise trade.

Figure 2.1 shows that between 1982 and 1993, the United States enjoyed trade surpluses on intrafirm trade between U.S. parents and their MOFAs. In 1993, the intrafirm trade surplus of U.S. MNCs was about $9.1 billion. (We will discuss more details concerning the intrafirm trade of U.S. MNCs later in this chapter.)

Table 2.3 shows the intrafirm trade between U.S. affiliates and their foreign parent groups from 1982 to 1992. A U.S. affiliate is defined by the U.S. Department of Commerce as a U.S. business enterprise in which a single foreign

Table 2.2
U.S. Merchandise Trade between U.S. Parents and Their Majority-Owned
Foreign Affiliates, 1982–1993 (Millions of U.S. Dollars)

Year	U.S. exports shipped to affiliates by U.S. parents (1)	U.S. imports shipped by affiliates to U.S. parents (2)	Trade total between U.S. parents and their foreign affiliate	
			Amount (3) = (1) + (2)	As a % of U.S. merchandise trade (4)
1982	44,320	38,533	82,853	18.2%
1983	45,107	41,551	86,658	22.3%
1984	52,726	49,316	102,042	18.8%
1985	57,567	51,751	109,318	19.6%
1986	58,916	49,961	108,877	19.5%
1987	65,248	55,867	121,115	18.4%
1988	78,204	65,464	143,668	18.7%
1989	85,648	72,374	158,022	18.9%
1990	88,375	75,251	163,626	18.4%
1991	95,779	77,578	173,357	19.1%
1992	100,737	84,890	185,627	19.1%
1993	104,987	95,906	200,893	19.2%

Sources: U.S. Department of Commerce, *U.S. Direct Investment Abroad* (various years).

person owns or controls, directly or indirectly, 10 percent or more of the voting securities or equivalent. A ''foreign parent group'' is defined to include:

1. the foreign parent;
2. any foreign person, proceeding up the foreign parent's ownership chain, that owns more than 50 percent of the party below it, up to, and including, the ''ultimate beneficial owner'' (UBO); and
3. any foreign person, proceeding down the ownership chain(s) of each of these members, that is owned more than 50 percent by the party above.

The intrafirm trade data of non-U.S. MNCs for 1982 through 1993 are also shown in graphic format in Figure 2.2. Table 2.3 indicates that both the U.S.

Figure 2.1
Intrafirm Trade of U.S. Multinational Companies, 1982–1993

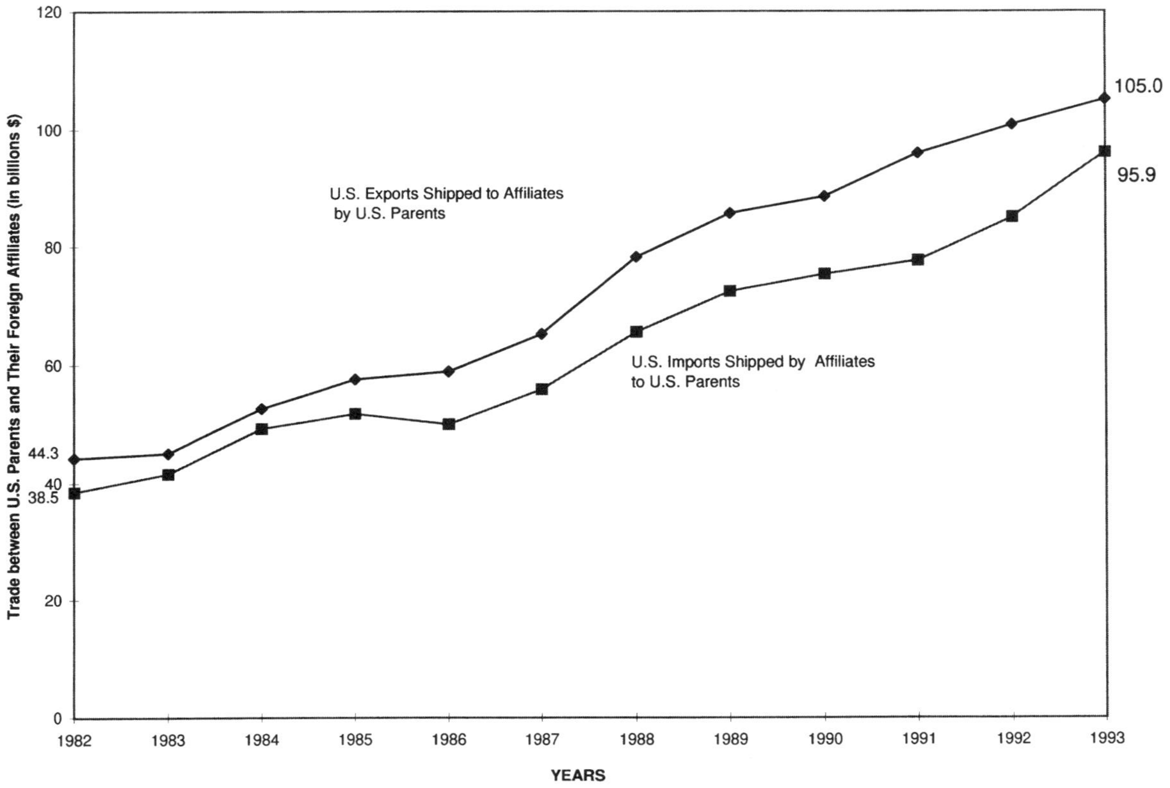

Sources: U.S. Department of Commerce, *U.S. Direct Investment Abroad* (various years).

Table 2.3
Intrafirm Trade between U.S. Affiliates and Their Foreign Parent Groups,
1982–1993 (Millions of U.S. Dollars)

Year	U.S. exports shipped by U.S. affiliates to foreign parent groups (1)	U.S. imports shipped to U.S. affiliates by foreign parent groups (2)	Trade total between U.S. parents and their foreign affiliates	
			Amount (3) = (1) + (2)	As a % of U.S. merchandise trade (4)
1982	25,024	51,915	76,939	16.9%
1983	22,577	54,802	77,379	16.9%
1984	27,100	70,500	97,600	18.0%
1985	25,900	81,740	107,640	19.3%
1986	21,873	93,418	115,291	19.6%
1987	19,109	108,201	127,310	19.3%
1988	32,348	121,522	153,870	20.0%
1989	40,717	132,270	172,987	20.7%
1990	45,322	141,847	187,169	21.1%
1991	50,356	137,043	187,399	20.6%
1992	57,198	140,993	198,191	20.3%
1993	47,166	148,540	195,706	18.7%

Sources: U.S. Department of Commerce, *Foreign Direct Investment in the United States* (various years).

exports shipped to U.S. affiliates to foreign parent groups (column 1) and U.S. imports shipped to U.S. affiliates by foreign parent groups (column 2) increased gradually between 1982 and 1993. However, the rate of increase in imports shipped to U.S. affiliates by foreign parent groups was much greater than for exports shipped by U.S. affiliates to foreign parent groups.

In 1982, the total amount of intrafirm trade between U.S. affiliates and their foreign parent groups (column 3) was $76.9 billion. By 1993, however, the total volume of intrafirm trade had increased to $195.7 billion, representing an increase of 154 percent over the 11-year period. In 1993, U.S. exports shipped by U.S. affiliates to foreign parent groups (column 1) amounted to $47.2 billion, while U.S. imports shipped to U.S. affiliates by foreign parent groups totaled $148.5 billion. During the same year, the United States experienced a significant

Figure 2.2
Intrafirm Trade of Non-American Multinational Companies in the United States, 1982–1993 (Billions of U.S. Dollars)

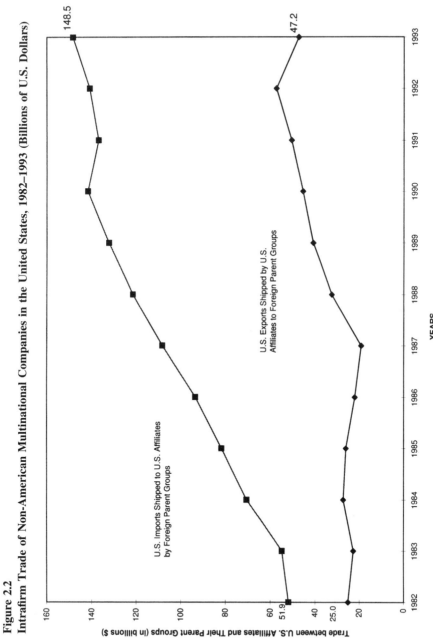

Sources: U.S. Department of Commerce, *Foreign Direct Investment in the United States* (various years).

trade deficit of $101.3 billion in intrafirm trade between non-U.S. MNCs and their affiliates in the United States.

Table 2.4 provides the details by country for exports shipped by U.S. affiliates to their foreign parent groups and U.S. imports shipped to U.S. affiliates by their foreign parent groups in 1993. Also provided are total exports shipped by U.S. affiliates and total imports shipped to U.S. affiliates for 1993. We can observe that total exports shipped by U.S. affiliates (column 1) in 1993 were $105.1 billion, of which about 44.9 percent (or $47.2 billion) were shipped to the foreign parent groups. Total imports shipped to U.S. affiliates (column 4) in 1993 were $198.5 billion, of which 74.8 percent ($148.5 billion) were shipped by the foreign parent groups. Therefore, the total amount and percentage of intrafirm imports ($148.5 billion; 74.8 percent) were substantially larger than the amount and percentage of intrafirm exports ($47.2 billion; 44.9 percent) of non-U.S. MNCs. This phenomenon created an immense deficit pressure on the U.S. trade balance. Thus, the observation made by Hipple (1990) based on 1982 data was still valid in 1993.

The statistics by country and region in Table 2.4 indicate that both intrafirm exports and imports related to U.S. affiliates of non-U.S. MNCs were dominated by affiliates of Japan and the European Union (EU) countries. Japanese affiliates imported $78.4 billion of goods from their foreign parent groups and exported $28.1 billion to those parent groups in 1993. In other words, the total intrafirm trade between Japanese MNCs and their U.S. affiliates amounted to $106.5 billion, or 51 percent of all intrafirm trade between non-U.S. MNCs and their U.S. affiliates. During the same year, U.S. affiliates of MNCs in the European Union imported $35.1 billion of merchandise from their EU parent groups and exported $11.4 billion to those groups. Total intrafirm trade between EU MNCs and their U.S. affiliates in 1993 was $46.5 billion and accounted for 23.8 percent of all intrafirm trade between U.S. affiliates and their foreign parent groups.

Within the EU, countries with large volumes of intrafirm trade involving U.S. affiliates in 1993 were Germany ($18.5 billion), France ($9.1 billion), the United Kingdom ($8.8 billion), and the Netherlands ($5.7 billion).

Columns (3) and (6) of Table 2.4 also show that the percentages of intrafirm exports and imports for Japanese MNCs were much higher than those of EU MNCs. In 1993, 65.2 percent of exports shipped by U.S. affiliates of Japanese MNCs and 83.9 percent of imports shipped to those affiliates involved intrafirm trade. In contrast 31.9 percent of exports shipped by EU affiliates and 62.9 percent of imports shipped to EU affiliates in the United States involved intrafirm trade.

Table 2.5 summarizes all intrafirm trade statistics of the United States from 1982 to 1993. (These statistics were transferred from Tables 2.2 and 2.3.) Column (1) of Table 2.5 shows the total intrafirm trade between U.S. parents and their foreign affiliates, and column (2) provides the total intrafirm trade figures between U.S. affiliates and their foreign parent groups. Column (3) shows the sum of columns (1) and (2) and represents the U.S. intrafirm trade total for each

Table 2.4
Exports Shipped by U.S. Affiliates of Non-U.S. MNCs and Imports Shipped to Those Affiliates, 1993 (Millions of U.S. Dollars)

Country	Exports Shipped by U.S. Affiliates			Imports Shipped to U.S. Affiliates		
	Total (1)	To the foreign parent groups (2)	Exports Shipped to the foreign parent groups as a % of total (3)	Total (4)	By the foreign parent groups (5)	Imports Shipped by the foreign parent groups as a % of total (6)
All countries	105,088	47,166	44.9%	198,469	148,540	74.8%
Canada	7,030	1,574	22.4%	7,597		60.1%
Europe	44,858	13,807	30.8%	68,764	45,072	65.6%
France	12,254	4,608	37.6%	9,067	4,525	49.9%
Germany	8,253	2,485	30.1%	20,149	16,055	79.7%
Italy	1,839	791	43.0%	2,785	1,807	64.9%
Netherlands	3,741	1,382	36.9%	8,678	4,274	49.3%
Sweden	2,413	513	21.3%	4,508	3,815	84.6%
Switzerland	5,543	1,582	28.5%	5,912	4,312	72.9%
United Kingdom	8,406	1,930	23.0%	12,322	6,859	55.7%
Other	2,409	516	21.4%	5,343	3,425	64.1%
Latin America & Other Western Hemisphere	3,316	1,163	35.1%	8,029	5,435	67.7%
Brazil	343	280	81.6%	1,003	791	78.9%
Mexico	418	232	55.5%	1,068	575	53.8%
Panama	619	129	20.8%	153	8	5.2%
Venezuela	226	1	0.4%	3,644	2,831	77.7%
Bermuda	97	48	49.5%	564	543	96.3%
Other	1,613	521	32.3%	2,161	687	31.8%
Asia and Pacific	48,365	30,335	62.7%	104,527	86,715	83.0%
Australia	715	105	14.7%	1,408	430	30.5%
China	735	426	58.0%	(D)	(D)	(D)
Hong Kong	157	37	23.6%	1,118	541	48.4%
Japan	43,045	28,062	65.2%	93,437	78,426	83.9%
South Korea	2,901	1,408	48.5%	6,048	5,370	88.8%
Singapore	111	21	18.9%	155	58	37.4%
Taiwan	546	174	31.9%	866	744	85.9%
Other	155	102	65.8%	N.A	N.A	N.A
Addenda:						
European Union	35,728	11,402	31.9%	55,813	35,102	62.9%
OPEC	551	250	45.4%	6,858	5,885	85.8%

Note: (D) = Data suppressed to avoid disclosure of data of individual companies.
Source: U.S. Department of Commerce, (1995a).

Table 2.5
International Intrafirm Trade of the United States, 1982–1993 (Millions of U.S. Dollars)

Year	Intrafirm trade between U.S. parents and their foreign affiliates (1)	Intrafirm trade between U.S. affiliates and their foreign parent groups (2)	U.S. international intrafirm trade total (3) = (1) + (2)	U.S. intrafirm trade as a % of U.S. merchandise trade (4)
1982	82,853	76,939	159,792	35.1%
1983	86,658	77,379	164,037	39.2%
1984	102,042	97,600	199,642	36.8%
1985	109,318	107,640	216,958	38.9%
1986	108,877	115,291	224,168	39.1%
1987	121,115	127,310	248,425	37.7%
1988	143,668	153,870	297,538	38.7%
1989	158,022	174,987	333,009	39.8%
1990	163,626	187,169	350,795	39.5%
1991	173,357	187,399	360,756	39.7%
1992	185,627	198,191	383,818	39.4%
1993	200,893	195,706	396,599	37.9%

Sources: Tables 2.2 and 2.3.

year. We can observe from column (3) that U.S. international intrafirm trade increased steadily from 1982 to 1993. In 1993, the total was $396.6 billion. Over the 11-year period, the total U.S. intrafirm trade increased by about 148.2 percent.

From 1982 to 1993, U.S. intrafirm trade as a percentage of U.S. merchandise trade varied between 35.1 percent and 39.8 percent. In 1993, the percentage was 37.9. One can notice the importance of intrafirm trade in U.S. foreign trade by looking at the totals in column (3) and the percentages in column (4). A small change in the transfer prices of intrafirm trade may have a significant impact on the U.S. balance of payments and tax revenue collected by the Internal Revenue Service (IRS). It is understandable why corporate transfer pricing practices are closely monitored by the U.S. Congress and the IRS.

INTERNATIONAL INVESTMENT AND INTRAFIRM TRADE OF U.S. MNCs

As suggested by Little (1986) and Cho (1988), the degree of intrafirm trade of U.S. MNCs may be related to the international direct investment made by those companies. Before discussing the details of intrafirm trade of U.S. MNCs, we will review international direct investment activities carried out by U.S. companies in recent years. For comparative purposes, we will present relevant information of foreign direct investment (FDI) in the United States. A profile of foreign affiliates of U.S. MNCs will also be provided so that we can better understand the nature and effect of U.S. direct investment abroad.

International Direct Investment Activities Related to the United States

In Chapter 1, we noted that outward direct investment from the OECD countries increased about fourfold in the 1980s. The United States is a major contributor, as well as the largest recipient, of outward direct investment from the OECD countries. Table 2.6 shows the statistics of U.S. direct investment position (DIP) abroad and foreign direct investment position (FDIP) in the United States from 1980 to 1994. (The numbers shown for U.S. DIP and FDIP are on a historical-cost basis.) Also shown are the annual increase (or decrease) percentages for U.S. DIP and FDIP and the ratio of DIP to FDI for each year.

As shown in Table 2.6, at the end of 1980, U.S. DIP abroad was $215.4 billion compared with $68.4 billion of FDIP in the United States. The ratio of U.S. DIP to FDIP in 1980 was 3.15:1 (column 5). Between 1981 and 1989, the rates of annual increases in FDIP were significantly higher than those for U.S. DIP, and by the end of 1989, the ratio of U.S. DIP to FDIP had declined to only 1.02:1. In other words, at the end of 1989, U.S. DIP ($381.8 billion) was only 2 percent larger than the FDIP ($373.8 billion). From 1990 to 1993, U.S. DIP abroad increased faster than that for FDIP. At the end of 1994, the total amount of U.S. DIP abroad was $612.1 billion, compared with $504.4 billion of FDIP in the United States. The ratio of U.S. DIP to FDIP was 1.21:1.

If we compare the statistics of U.S. DIP abroad and FDIP in the United States in 1994 with those for 1980, we can observe substantial expansion in international investment activities relating to the United States over the 14-year period. During that period, U.S. DIP abroad increased by 184 percent, while FDIP in the United States expanded by about 637 percent.

Table 2.7 shows the distribution of U.S. DIP abroad by countries for selected years from 1980 to 1994. One can notice that most U.S. DIP rankings abroad are invested in developed countries such as Canada, member countries of the EU, Japan, and Australia. In 1994, these countries were hosts to about 70 percent of U.S. DIP abroad. In the early 1980s, Canada was the largest host country of U.S. direct investment. However, since the late 1980s, the United Kingdom has replaced Canada as the most important host country of U.S. direct investment. U.S. DIP in Canada changed very little between 1990 and 1994, despite the fact that both countries are NAFTA partners and Canada is the largest trading partner of the United States. In contrast, U.S. direct investment expanded rapidly in Europe, Latin America, and the Asian Pacific region from 1990 to 1994. In 1994, Germany, Japan, and Switzerland became important host countries of U.S.

Table 2.6
U.S. Direct Investment Abroad and Foreign Direct Investment in the United States, 1980–1994 (Billions of U.S. Dollars)

Year	U.S. direct invesment position (DIP) abroad (1)	% Change in DIP from previous year (2)	Foreign direct investment (FDI) in the U.S. (3)	% Change in FDI from previous year (4)	Ratio of U.S. DIP/FDI (5)
1980	215.4		68.4		3.15
1981	228.3	+ 5.6	89.8	+31.3	2.54
1982	221.5	- 3.0	124.7	+38.9	1.78
1983	226.1	+ 2.1	137.1	+ 9.9	1.65
1984	211.5	- 6.5	164.6	+20.1	1.28
1985	230.3	+ 8.9	184.6	+12.2	1.25
1986	259.8	+12.8	209.3	+13.4	1.24
1987	308.0	+18.6	263.4	+25.9	1.17
1988	326.9	+ 6.1	314.8	+19.5	1.04
1989	381.8	+16.8	373.8	+18.7	1.02
1990	430.5	+12.8	403.7	+ 8.0	1.07
1991	467.8	+ 8.7	418.8	+ 3.7	1.12
1992	499.0	+ 6.7	425.6	+ 1.6	1.17
1993	548.6	+ 9.9	445.3	+ 4.6	1.23
1994	612.1	+11.6	504.4	+13.3	1.21

Note: Calculated on a historical-cost basis.
Source: U.S. Department of Commerce, Bureau of Economic Affairs, *Survey of Current Business* (various years).

direct investment. Even tiny Bermuda had attracted $29.2 billion of U.S. direct investment by the end of 1994. This may have something to do with the tax haven status of that island.

For comparative purposes, Table 2.8 shows the sources of foreign direct investment (FDI) in the United States for selected years from 1980 to 1994. We can observe that in 1980, only a few developed countries invested heavily in the United States, including the Netherlands, the United Kingdom, and Canada.

Table 2.7

U.S. Direct Investment Position Abroad on a Historical-Cost Basis, Selected Years, 1980–1994 (Billions of U.S. Dollars)

Countries	1980	1985	1990	1991	1992	1993	1994
All Countries	215.4	230.3	430.5	467.8	499.0	548.6	612.1
Canada	45.1	46.9	69.5	70.7	68.8	70.4	72.8
Europe	96.3	105.2	214.7	235.2	246.2	269.2	300.2
Belgium	6.3	5.0	9.5	10.6	11.1	11.6	14.0
France	9.3	7.6	19.2	21.6	24.7	23.6	27.9
Germany	15.4	16.8	27.6	32.4	33.6	37.5	40.0
Italy	5.4	5.9	14.1	15.1	13.9	13.9	15.0
Netherlands	8.0	7.1	19.1	20.3	20.1	19.9	24.2
Switzerland	11.3	15.8	25.1	25.7	29.2	32.9	34.5
United Kingdom	28.5	33.0	72.7	79.8	82.6	96.4	102.2
Other	12.1	14.0	27.4	29.7	31.0	33.4	42.4
Latin America and Other Western Hemisphere	38.8	28.3	71.4	77.7	90.6	101.9	115.0
Brazil	7.7	8.9	14.4	15.0	16.3	16.9	19.0
Mexico	6.0	5.1	10.3	12.5	13.7	15.4	16.4
Panama	3.2	4.0	9.3	10.5	11.3	12.6	13.8
Bermuda	11.0	13.1	20.2	22.3	25.7	28.2	29.2
Other	10.9	-2.8	17.2	17.4	23.6	28.8	36.6
Asia and Pacific	23.0	34.0	64.7	72.2	80.0	92.3	108.4
Australia	7.7	8.8	15.1	16.1	16.9	18.4	20.5
Hong Kong	2.1	3.3	6.1	6.7	8.7	10.5	12.0
Japan	6.2	9.2	22.6	25.4	26.6	31.4	37.0
Singapore	1.2	1.9	4.0	5.4	6.7	8.9	11.0
Other	5.8	10.8	16.9	18.6	21.1	23.1	27.9
Other Countries	12.2	15.9	10.2	12.0	13.4	14.8	15.7

Sources: U.S. Department of Commerce, Bureau of Economic Affairs, *Survey of Current Business* (various issues).

Table 2.8
Foreign Direct Investment in the United States on a Historical-Cost Basis, Selected Years, 1980–1994 (Billions of U.S. Dollars)

Country	1980	1985	1990	1991	1992	1993	1994
All countries	68.4	184.6	403.7	418.8	425.6	445.3	504.4
Canada	10.1	17.1	27.7	36.3	37.8	39.4	43.2
Europe	45.7	121.4	256.5	252.7	251.2	270.8	312.9
Belgium	1.9	2.3	4.2	3.2	4.3	4.6	3.6
France	3.0	6.7	19.6	25.4	25.5	28.5	33.5
Germany	5.4	14.8	27.8	28.6	29.6	34.7	39.6
Italy	0.4	1.2	1.6	2.7	.3	1.2	2.4
Netherlands	16.9	37.1	64.3	59.8	65.3	68.5	70.6
Sweden	1.4	2.4	5.5	5.3	6.9	8.1	9.1
Switzerland	3.9	10.6	17.5	20.2	20.6	21.4	25.3
United Kingdom	12.2	43.6	108.1	98.2	89.1	95.4	113.5
Other	0.6	2.7	7.9	9.3	9.6	8.4	15.3
Latin America and Other Western Hemisphere	7.0	16.8	19.7	18.9	21.1	20.3	24.0
Brazil	NA	.2	.4	.5	.6	.7	.8
Mexico	NA	.5	.6	.8	1.2	1.0	2.2
Panama	0.7	2.2	3.3	4.8	5.0	4.8	3.6
Bahamas	NA	.2	1.5	2.0	2.8	1.2	1.1
Bermuda	NA	1.7	2.2	1.4	1.5	1.4	1.2
Netherlands Antilles	NA	10.4	11.1	7.8	8.6	7.0	8.4
Other	NA	1.6	.6	1.6	1.4	4.2	6.7
Asia and Pacific	4.4	23.5	95.1	105.4	110.0	108.9	117.8
Australia	NA	3.3	8.4	6.4	7.1	7.3	7.9
Hong Kong	NA	.6	1.2	1.9	1.8	2.0	1.7
Japan	4.2	19.3	83.5	93.8	97.5	96.2	103.1
Other	NA	.3	2.0	3.3	3.6	3.4	5.1
Other countries	1.2	5.8	4.7	5.5	5.5	5.9	6.5

Note: NA = not available.
Sources: U.S. Department of Commerce, Bureau of Economic Affairs, *Survey of Current Business* (various issues).

Many changes have taken place in FDI in the United States since the early 1980s. In 1985, Britain replaced the Netherlands as the largest foreign direct investor in the United States. However, British direct investment was surpassed by that of Japan in 1992 and 1993. At the end of 1994, Britain regained its position as the largest supplier of FDI in the United States. British direct investment at that time was $113.5 billion, compared with $103.1 billion invested by Japanese enterprises. Other developed countries such as the Netherlands, Canada, Germany, and France also have substantial direct investment in the United States.

Table 2.9 shows the distribution of U.S. DIPs abroad and FDI positions in the United States by industry for 1994. About 10 percent ($65.7 billion) of U.S. DIP were in the petroleum industry and 36 percent ($220.3 billion) were invested in various manufacturing industries. Interestingly, about one-third ($204.5 billion) of U.S. DIP abroad in 1994 were in banking, finance, insurance, and real estate, and 11 percent ($67.4 billion) were invested in wholesale trade.

There were some similarities between the industry distribution of FDIPs in the United States and that for U.S. DIPs abroad. For example, 36.6 percent of FDIPs were in manufacturing industries and 6.7 percent were in the petroleum industry. About $141 billion (28 percent) of FDIPs were in banking, finance, insurance, and real estate. The table also shows that $65.8 billion (13.1 percent) of FDIPs were in wholesale trade. A study of the background statistics reveals that $20.0 billion of the $65.8 billion investment was actually used for the wholesale trade of motor vehicles and equipment, and $12.6 billion was used for the wholesale trade of electrical goods.

Profile of Foreign Affiliates of U.S. MNCs

Table 2.10 provides the following data by country for all majority-owned nonbank foreign affiliates (MOFAs) of U.S. parents for 1993:

—number of affiliates:

—total assets;

—sales;

—net income (NI);

—ratio of NI to sales; and

—number of employees.

These data were derived from the Annual Survey of U.S. Direct Investment conducted by the Bureau of Economic Analysis (BEA) for the year 1993. The table shows that there were 16,484 MOFAs in 1993, about 52 percent of which were located in the EU and other Western European countries. Eleven percent (or 1,837) of the MOFAs were in Canada, while 2,891 (18 percent) were located

Table 2.9

U.S. Direct Investment Position Abroad and Foreign Direct Investment Position in the United States by Industry, 1993 (Billions of U.S. Dollars)

U.S. Direct Investment Position (DIP) Abroad			Foreign Direct Investment (FDI) Position in the United States		
Industry	U.S. DIP	% of Total	Industry	FDI in the U.S.	% of Total
Petroleum	62.4	11.4	Petroleum	32.6	7.3
Manufacturing Total	199.5	36.4	Manufacturing Total	166.7	37.4
Food & Kindred Products	22.6	4.1	Food & Kindred Products	25.4	5.7
Chemicals & Allied Products	46.1	8.4	Chemicals & Allied Products	57.7	13.0
Primary & Fabricated Materials	9.9	1.8	Primary & Fabricated Materials	13.0	2.9
Machinery, Except Electrical	29.7	5.4	Machinery, Except Electrical	10.6	2.1
Electric and Electronic Equipment	18.4	3.4	Electric and Electronic Equipment	20.2	4.0
Transportation Equipment	26.2	4.8	Transportation Equipment	5.0	0.1
Other Manufacturing	46.5	8.5	Other Manufacturing	40.9	9.2
			Retail Trade	10.4	2.3
Wholesale Trade	57.6	10.5	Wholesale Trade	59.3	13.3
Banking	26.7	4.9	Banking	31.0	7.0
Finance (except banking, insurance, and real estate	155.6	28.4	Finance (except banking, insurance, and real estate	94.3	21.1
Services	18.1	3.3	Services	33.8	7.6
Other Industries	28.7	5.2	Other Industries	17.1	3.8
Total for All Industries	548.6	100.0	Total for All Industries	445.3	100.0

Note: Percentages do not add up to 100 due to rounding.

Sources: U.S. Department of Commerce, Bureau of Economic Affairs, *Survey of Current Business* (various issues).

Table 2.10
Selected Data for Majority-Owned Nonbank Foreign Affiliates of Nonbank U.S. Parents, 1993

Country	No. of affiliates	Total assets (Million $)	Sales (Million $)	Net income (Million $)	Ratio of NI to sales	Number of employees (Thousands)
All countries	16,484	1,742,826	1,279,119	67,148	5.3%	5,259.9
Canada	1,837	193,153	193,153	3,026	1.6%	830.2
Europe	8,496	1,033,120	716,003	36,817	5.1%	2,418.5
Belgium	532	43,060	35,160	1,584	4.5%	103.1
France	1,024	73,391	92,300	1,461	1.6%	358.1
Germany	1,104	129,681	147,832	3,609	2.4%	520.6
Ireland	260	23,996	16,154	3,646	22.6%	43.8
Italy	617	36,403	50,022	1,905	3.8%	153.1
Netherlands	846	91,663	60,389	4,087	6.8%	127.5
Spain	442	22,785	28,001	104	0.4%	130.0
Switzerland	466	73,768	47,109	5,090	10.8%	40.1
United Kingdom	2,050	486,713	186,552	13,802	7.4%	738.2
Other	1,155	51,690	52,514	1,529	2.9%	204.0
Latin America & Other Western Hemisphere	2,500	185,706	120,471	12,285	10.2%	1,006.4
Argentina	140	7,813	8,256	508	6.2%	47.2
Brazil	385	28,765	31,960	3,039	9.5%	280.6
Chile	104	5,808	3,876	187	4.8%	25.9
Columbia	124	5,242	5,681	223	3.9%	37.2
Venezuela	151	3,596	4,755	416	8.8%	52.1
Mexico	458	25,284	32,671	2,233	6.8%	411.7
Bahamas	59	3,699	1,125	101	9.0%	8.2
Bermuda	283	51,273	10,712	2,556	23.9%	2.6
Netherlands Antilles	137	19,126	1,167	856	73.4%	.5
Other	659	35,100	20,268	2,166	10.7%	140.4
Asia and Pacific	2,891	291,496	232,510	12,752	5.5%	876.9
Australia	672	44,465	36,406	2,353	6.5%	189.8
Hong Kong	381	29,159	24,016	1,876	7.8%	66.4
Indonesia	129	11,135	7,809	1,497	19.2%	42.3
Japan	523	137,732	81,992	1,937	2.4%	157.5
Malaysia	121	9,644	9,586	883	9.2%	82.0
Singapore	321	25,178	38,298	2,474	6.5%	93.5
Taiwan	158	9,763	10,336	534	5.2%	47.5
Thailand	97	7,887	8,188	551	6.7%	49.2
Other	489	16,533	15,879	647	4.1%	148.7
Other countries	760	39,351	16,982	2,268	13.4%	127.9

Source: U.S. Department of Commerce, 1995b.

in the Asian Pacific region. Another 2,500 affiliates (15 percent) were in Latin America and other Western Hemisphere countries.

Together, those 16,484 MOFAs had combined total assets of $1.7 trillion in 1993. About 60 percent of total assets ($1 trillion) belonged to MOFAs in Western Europe, while 11 percent ($193 billion) were owned by MOFAs in Canada. MOFAs in Latin America and other Western Hemisphere countries had about $186 billion (11 percent) in assets. The total assets of MOFAs in the Asian Pacific region was $291 billion (17 percent). Britain was the country with the greatest number of MOFAs (2,050) and the greatest total assets ($487 billion). Background statistics indicate that about 70 percent of the total assets of MOFAs in Britain belonged to the category of finance (except banking), insurance, and real estate.

MOFAs of U.S. MNCs generated total sales revenue of $1.3 trillion in 1993. This amount was larger than the U.S. merchandise trade total (about $1 trillion) for 1993 and is another strong indicator of the globalization of U.S. business. MOFAs in Europe had $716 billion (56 percent) of sales revenue, while MOFAs in Canada generated $193 billion (15 percent) of sales. Other MOFAs in Latin America and the Asian Pacific region also generated significant amounts of sales revenue in 1993.

The statistics on net income (NI) and ratios of NI to sales in Table 2.10 are good profitability indicators of MOFAs located in various countries. Together, all MOFAs produced a net income of $67 billion in 1993, and the overall ratio of NI to sales (NI ratio) was 5.3 percent. However, the profitability of MOFAs varies substantially from one country to another. For example, the average NI ratio of MOFAs in Canada was only 1.6 percent, while at the other end of the scale, the NI ratio of MOFAs in Switzerland was 10.8 percent, for MOFAs in Netherlands Antilles, 73.4 percent. Both Bermuda and Netherlands Antilles are well-known tax havens and popular among MNCs for setting up holding companies for international operations. As of July 1996, no income tax was imposed on corporations in Bermuda. It is a financial center with the presence of more than 6,000 MNCs. In Netherlands Antilles, holding companies pay only 2.4 to 3 percent on net income (Barber 1993).

The last column of Table 2.10 provides the number of employees of MOFAs located in each country. Together, all MOFAs had a total of about 5.3 million employees. MOFAs in Canada provided the most jobs (830,200), while MOFAs in the United Kingdom employed about 738,200 workers in 1993. MOFAs with large numbers of employees are also located in Germany (520,600), Mexico (411,700), France (358,100), Brazil (280,600), Australia (189,800), and Japan (157,500).

For comparative purposes, a profile of U.S. affiliates of non-American MNCs in 1993 is provided in Table 2.11. We can observe that there were 12,207 U.S. affiliates of non-American MNCs with combined assets of about $2 trillion in the United States. Together, these affiliates generated sales revenue of $1.3 trillion in 1993 but produced a net loss of $9.9 billion. Their overall ratio of net

Table 2.11
A Profile of U.S. Affiliates of Non-American MNCs, 1993

Country	No. of affiliates (1)	Total assets (billion $) (2)	Sales (billion $) (3)	Net income (NI) in billion $ (4)	Ratio of NI to sales (5)	No. of employees in thousands (6)
All Countries	12,207	2,049	1,302	-9.9	-0.8%	4,722.3
Canada	1,293	260	135.9	1.3	1.0%	663.0
Europe	5,266	1,070	678.8	-2.9	-0.4%	2,869.6
France	621	214	101.6	-1.5	-1.5%	361.1
Germany	1,255	148	135.0	-0.3	-0.3%	565.7
Italy	267	21	14.2	-0.7	-5.1%	47.3
Netherlands	389	126	78.4	0.1	0.2%	295.2
Switzerland	594	159	75.9	0.0	0.0%	245.0
United Kingdom	1,216	323	201.5	1.2	0.6%	977.2
Others	924	79	72.2	-2.6	-4.0%	387.1
Latin America & Other Western Hemisphere	1,049	45	38.5	.2	0.4%	143.5
Mexico	232	8	5.4	-0.3	-5.7%	27.6
Panama	117	5	4.5	-0.2	-4.5%	24.4
Others	700	32	28.6	0.7	2.0%	91.5
Asia and Pacific	4,097	568	411.2	-10.1	-2.5%	947.3
Hong Kong	269	10	5.0	-0.3	-6.8%	28.0
Japan	3,216	487	352.2	-8.0	-2.3%	723.9
South Korea	99	8	11.2	-0.2	-2.2%	10.5
Taiwan	106	8	3.7	-0.2	-4.5%	14.9
Others	407	55	39.1	-8.6	-2.2%	170.0
Addenda:						
European Union	4,158	863	562.5	-1.8	-3.2%	2,466.3
OPEC	326	28	30.3	0.7	2.2%	67.1
Other Countries	502	106	37.6	1.6	4.0%	98.9

Source: U.S. Department of Commerce (1995a).

income to sales was −.8 percent. These 12,207 affiliates had about 4.7 million employees in the United States.

Countries from the European Union had a total of 4,158 affiliates, with a combined total assets of $863 billion. They generated sales of $562.5 billion; however, their ratio of net income to sales was −3.2 percent. Statistics of major

EU countries are also provided in Table 2.11. Most EU countries had negative NI to sales ratios in 1993, with the exception of the Netherlands and the United Kingdom.

Japan had 3,216 affiliates with total assets of $487 billion. These 3,216 affiliates generated sales of $352 billion but had a combined net loss of about $8 billion. Their ratio of NI to sales was −2.3 percent.

As a whole, the profitability ratio of U.S. affiliates in 1993 was considerably lower than that of the MOFAs of U.S. MNCs. This is not a new phenomenon. Statistics of the late 1980s and early 1990s showed similar findings on the low profitability ratios of U.S. affiliates of foreign corporations. Both the IRS and U.S. Congress have expressed great concern with the low levels of U.S. taxable income reported by U.S. subsidiaries of non-American MNCs (Scholes and Wolfson, 1992). According to Sullivan (1996), "Many believed that the low profitability of foreign-controlled firms doing business in the United States was the result of high prices, fees, and royalties charged by foreign parents to their subsidiaries in the United States" (p. 93).

Intrafirm Trade between U.S. MNCs and Their Foreign Affiliates

In Table 2.12, we provide the intrafirm trade statistics between U.S. parents and their MOFAs from 1982 to 1993. Intrafirm trade between U.S. MNCs and their MOFAs increased steadily between 1982 and 1993. In 1993, the intrafirm trade total was about $200.9 billion, accounting for 19.2 percent of U.S. merchandise trade. Table 2.11 shows the details of intrafirm trade statistics by country of affiliates, and Table 2.12 provides the statistics for each industry type of MOFA.

From Table 2.12, we can observe that total U.S. exports shipped to MOFAs in 1993 totaled $122.8 billion. Of that amount, 85.5 percent (or $105 billion) were shipped by U.S. parents. Column 3 of Table 2.12 shows the intrafirm export percentages of MOFAs in various countries. The intrafirm export percentages for exports shipped to MOFAs in Canada was 78.9 percent, and for exports shipped to MOFAs in Latin America and other Western Hemisphere countries, 84.6 percent. The intrafirm export percentages for exports shipped to the EU countries, the Organization for Petroleum Exporting Countries (OPEC), and the Asian Pacific region were slightly above 90 percent each.

Column (4) of Table 2.12 shows that total U.S. imports shipped by MOFAs in 1993 were $111.3 billion, of which 86.2 percent ($95.9 billion) were shipped to U.S. parents. Column (6) shows the percentages of intrafirm imports of MOFAs of various countries. We can observe that the MOFAs of most countries had high intrafirm import percentages. Surprisingly, however, the intrafirm import percentage for the United Kingdom was only 62.3. This may be due to the fact that 48 percent of the U.S. DIP in Britain in 1993 was in finance (except banking), insurance, and real estate.

Table 2.12
U.S. Exports Shipped to Majority-Owned Foreign Affiliates (MOFAs) of Nonbank U.S. MNCs and Imports Shipped by Those Affiliates by Countries of Affiliates, 1993 (Millions of U.S. dollars)

Country	U.S. exports shipped to MOFA			U.S. imports shipped by MOFA		
	Total (1)	Shipped by U.S. parents (2)	Exports shipped by U.S. parents as a % of total (3) = (2) - 1	Total (4)	Shipped to U.S. parents (5)	Imports shipped to U.S. parents as a % of total (6) = (4) - (5)
All countries	122,757	104,987	85.5%	111,309	95,906	86.2%
Canada	43,220	34,078	78.9%	48,751	41,231	84.6%
Europe	36,074	32,709	90.7%	18,153	14,553	80.2%
Belgium	2,456	2,201	89.6%	828	792	95.7%
France	4,024	3,689	91.7%	1,986	1,905	95.9%
Germany	7,431	6,955	93.6%	2,814	2,605	92.6%
Italy	1,569	1,403	89.4%	752	697	92.7%
Netherlands	5,139	4,611	89.7%	1,125	1,017	90.4%
Spain	1,072	963	89.8%	391	355	90.8%
Switzerland	2,562	2,509	97.9%	486	414	85.2%
United Kingdom	9,003	7,927	88.1%	7,222	4,502	62.3%
Other	2,818	2,451	87.0%	2,549	2,266	88.9%
Latin America & Other Western Hemisphere	18,293	15,480	84.6%	17,523	16,182	92.4%
Argentina	571	528	92.5%	85	76	89.4%
Brazil	1,641	1,421	86.6%	1,845	1,730	93.8%
Venezuela	1,163	1,105	95.0%	27	16	59.3%
Mexico	12,680	10,761	84.9%	11,921	11,807	99.0%
Other	2,238	1,665	74.4%	3,645	2,553	70.0%
Asia and Pacific	24,441	22,193	90.8%	23,308	20,785	89.2%
Australia	3,184	2,958	92.9%	839	592	70.6%
Hong Kong	3,553	3,352	94.3%	4,192	3,701	88.3%
Japan	8,556	8,125	95.0%	2,742	2,671	97.4%
South Korea	889	846	95.2%	360	359	99.7%
Malaysia	944	926	98.1%	2,800	2,173	77.6%
Singapore	4,010	3,136	78.2%	9,099	8,117	89.2%
Taiwan	1,245	1,190	95.6%	1,050	1,025	97.6%
Thailand	915	701	76.6%	920	902	98.0%
Other	1,145	959	83.8%	1,306	1,245	95.3%
Addenda:						
European Union	32,055	28,931	90.3%	17,126	13,787	80.5%
OPEC	1,667	1,531	91.8%	2,379	2,314	97.3%

Source: U.S. Department of Commerce (1995b).

Cho (1988) hypothesized that "countries with larger U.S. foreign direct investment presence tend to have larger intrafirm trade between U.S. parents and their foreign affiliates there, with the notable exception of Japan and Brazil" (p. 180). After comparing the statistics of Table 2.12 with the data on U.S. direct investment abroad in Table 2.7, we have to add more exceptions to the rule hypothesized by Cho (1988). For example, at the end of 1992 and 1993, U.S. direct investment positions in the United Kingdom ($82.6 billion and $96.4 billion, respectively) were higher than those in Canada for the same year-ends ($68.8 billion and $70.4 billion, respectively), and yet the intrafirm trade between U.S. MNCs and their Canadian MOFAs in 1993 ($75.3 billion) was substantially higher than that between U.S. MNCs and their British MOFAs ($15.1 billion). Another notable exception is Bermuda. At the end of 1992, U.S. DIP in Bermuda was $25.7 billion; however, the intrafirm trade between U.S. parents and their MOFAs was less than $500 million.

Table 2.13 provides statistics on U.S. exports shipped to MOFAs and imports shipped by those MOFAs, by industries of affiliates, in 1993. From column (2), we can observe that $66.5 billion (63 percent) of U.S. exports shipped to MOFAs were shipped by parent firms in the manufacturing industries, while 32 percent ($34.1 billion) were shipped by parents in wholesale trade. Intrafirm trade for companies in the service industries and in finance (except banking), insurance, and real estate were minimal. As indicated by column (5), about 81 percent ($77.4 billion) of U.S. imports shipped by MOFAs were for U.S. parents in manufacturing industries. Among the manufacturing industries, the motor vehicle and equipment industry had the largest volume of intrafirm trade ($60.2 billion) between U.S. parents and their MOFAs. After checking some background statistics, we discovered that $45 billion of the $60.2 billion intrafirm trade in the motor vehicle and equipment industry was carried out by U.S. parents and their MOFAs in Canada. Other industries that had substantial intrafirm trade volumes included "durable goods" ($32.7 billion) for wholesale trade, "machinery except electrical" ($30.2 billion), and "electric and electronic equipment" ($23.2 billion).

Intrafirm trade between U.S. MNCs and their MOFAs in Mexico is expanding rapidly. In 1993, their intrafirm trade reached a total of $22.6 billion, most of which occurred in manufacturing industries. This has a lot to do with the Maquiladora program in Mexico. (We will discuss more details of that program in Chapter 6.)

SUMMARY AND CONCLUSIONS

This chapter reviews recent literature and trends in international intrafirm trade from a U.S. perspective. We also examined international investment activities related to the United States and a profile of foreign affiliates of U.S. MNCs, since these topics are related to intrafirm trade. Intrafirm trade data

Table 2.13

U.S. Exports Shipped to Majority-Owned Affiliates (MOFAs) of Nonbank American MNCs and Imports Shipped by Those Affiliates by Industries of Affiliates, 1993 (Money Amounts in Millions of U.S. Dollars)

Country	U.S. exports shipped to MOFAs			U.S. imports shipped by MOFAs		
	Total (1)	Shipped by U.S. parents (2)	Exports shipped by U.S. parents as a % of total $(3)=\frac{(2)}{(1)}$	Total (4)	Shipped to U.S. parents (5)	Imports shipped to U.S. parents as a % of total $(6)=\frac{(4)}{(5)}$
All industries	122,757	104,987	85.5%	111,309	95,906	86.2%
Petroleum	2,559	1,940	75.8%	12,839	8,575	66.8%
Manufacturing	80,706	66,546	82.5%	86,991	77,388	89.0%
Food & Kindred Products	2,382	1,890	79.4%	1,704	1,224	71.8%
Chemicals & Allied Products	9,102	7,860	86.4%	4,486	3,901	87.0%
Primary & Fabricated Materials	1,803	1,234	68.4%	1,933	1,002	51.8%
Machinery, except electrical	13,854	12,054	87.0%	18,143	16,397	90.4%
Electric & Electronic Equipment	10,220	9,522	93.2%	13,638	12,443	91.2%
Motor Vehicle & Equipment	32,403	24,876	76.8%	36,485	35,327	96.8%
Other Transportation Equipment	586	235	40.1%	1,463	773	52.8%
Other Manufacturing	10,356	8,875	85.7%	9,137	6,320	69.2%
Wholesale trade	36,476	34,081	93.4%	9,996	9,003	90.1%
Durable goods	26,870	25,635	95.4%	7,022	6,664	94.9%
Nondurable goods	9,606	8,447	87.9%	2,974	2,339	78.7%
Services	1,347	1,259	93.5%	122	113	92.6%
Other Industries	1,668	1,162	69.7%	1,360	827	60.8%

Source: U.S. Department of Commerce (1995b).

between U.S. MNCs and their foreign affiliates were analyzed by country and by industry of affiliate.

Recent literature has provided many insights into various aspects of intrafirm trade related to the United States. The studies by Lall (1978a), Helleiner and Lavergne (1979), and the OECD (1993) identified some variables that may explain some of the variations in intrafirm trade for certain industries. Cho (1988) provided a useful framework for the analysis of major determinants of intrafirm trade. Little (1986, 1987) noted many significant differences between intrafirm trade and unaffiliated trade. Hipple (1990, 1995) has reminded us that intrafirm trade (especially trade between U.S. affiliates and their foreign parent groups) contributed to the deficit pressure on the U.S. trade balance. However, much remains to be learned on the impact of tax and legal environmental factors on intrafirm trade and transfer pricing. Corporate transfer pricing practices have to adapt to the new laws and guidelines released by tax authorities in many countries and the OECD (1995). These new laws and guidelines and their implications will be examined from Chapters 3 through 8 of this book.

Intrafirm trade data published by the U.S. Department of Commerce were used to analyze record trends of intrafirm trade related to the United States. We noted that intrafirm trade of U.S. MNCs and non-U.S. MNCs continued to expand in the 1980s and early 1990s. In 1993, intrafirm trade between U.S. parents and their MOFAs amounted to $200.9 billion. Intrafirm trade between U.S. affiliates and their foreign parent groups totaled $195.7 billion in 1993. Together, international intrafirm trade of U.S. and non-U.S. MNCs accounted for about 37.9 percent of U.S. merchandise trade. In 1993, the United States had a surplus of $9.1 billion in intrafirm trade between U.S. parents and their majority-owned foreign affiliates. During the same year, the United States experienced a huge deficit, of $101.4 billion, in intrafirm trade between U.S. affiliates and their parent groups.

We also noted that international direct investment activities related to the United States were expanding rapidly in the 1980s and early 1990s. At the end of 1994, the U.S. DIP abroad was $612.1 billion, compared with $504.4 billion of foreign DIP in the United States. Most of the U.S. DIP abroad in 1994 involved investments in developed countries such as Canada, the EU member countries, Japan, and Australia. Countries with large amounts of direct investment in the United States include the United Kingdom, Japan, the Netherlands, Canada, Germany, and France.

In 1993, U.S. MNCs had 16,484 MOFAs abroad, most of which were located in Canada, the EU countries, and Japan. Together, these MOFAs had combined total assets of $1.7 trillion and generated sales revenue of $1.3 trillion in 1993. This amount is larger than the U.S. merchandise trade total in 1993. These MOFAs produced a total net income of $67 billion in 1993, and the average net income to sales ratio was 5.3 percent. However, the NI ratio varies significantly from one country to another. The average NI to sales ratio of MOFAs of

U.S. MNCs was considerably higher than that of U.S. affiliates of foreign corporations in 1993.

We also examined intrafirm trade between U.S. MNCs and their MOFAs by MOFA country and industry. We noted that about 37.5 percent (or $75.3 billion) of intrafirm trade related to U.S. MNCs involved trade between these MNCs and their MOFAs in Canada. The greatest amount of intrafirm trade between Canada and the United States was in motor vehicles and related equipment which amounted to $60.2 billion in 1993. Intrafirm trade between U.S. MNCs and their Mexican MOFAs reached a total of $22 billion in 1993, most of which occurred in the manufacturing industries. Intrafirm trade between U.S. MNCs and their MOFAs in the EU countries totaled $42.7 billion in 1993. U.S. firms had especially strong intrafirm trade relationships with their MOFAs in the United Kingdom, Germany, the Netherlands and France.

With the globalization of U.S. business and the expansion of foreign trade and international investment, we can expect intrafirm trade to grow further in the future. The stakes are high as the volume of intrafirm trade becomes larger. Tax authorities in many countries are releasing new transfer pricing regulations to ensure that they collect their ''fair'' shares of tax revenue. In the next two chapters, we will examine U.S. transfer pricing regulations and programs related to transfer pricing. The new OECD Guidelines will be reviewed in Chapter 5. Intrafirm trade and transfer pricing regulations of other selected countries in North America, Europe and the Asian Pacific region will be discussed in Chapters 6 through 8.

REFERENCES

Anderson, Andrew D. M., and Kazuo Noguchi. 1995. An Analysis of the Intra-Firm Sales Activities of Japanese Multinational Enterprises in the United States: 1977 to 1989. *Asia Pacific Journal of Management* (Vol. 12, No. 1): 69–89.

Baker, George. 1995. Don't Count on Exports. *Business Mexico* (March): 30–33.

Barber, Hoytl. 1993. *Tax Havens*. New York: McGraw-Hill.

Benvignati, Anita M. 1990. Industry Determinants and ''Differences'' in U.S. Intrafirm and Arm's Length Exports. *Review of Economics and Statistics* (August): 481–488.

Bisat, Talal A. 1967. An Evaluation of International Intercompany Transactions. Ph.D. dissertation, American University, Washington, D.C.

Cho, Kang Rae. 1988. Determinants of Intra-firm Trade: A Research for a Theoretical Framework. *International Trade Journal* (Winter): 167–185.

———. 1990. The Role of Product-specific Factors in Intra-firm Trade of U.S. Manufacturing Multinational Corporations. *Journal of International Business Studies* (second quarter): 319–330.

Graham, Edward M., and Paul R. Krugman. 1989. *Foreign Direct Investment in the United States*. Washington, D.C.: Institute for International Economics.

Greene, James, and Michael G. Duerr. 1970. *Intercompany Transactions in the Multinational Firm*. New York: Conference Board.

Helleiner, Gerald K. 1981. *Intra-firm Trade and the Developing Countries*. New York: St. Martin's Press.

Helleiner, Gerald K., and Real Lavergne. 1979. Intra-firm Trade and Industrial Exports to the United States. *Oxford Bulletin of Economics and Statistics* (November): 209–222.

Hipple, F. Steb. 1990. Multinational Companies and International Trade: The Impact of Intrafirm Shipments on U.S. Foreign Trade 1977–1982. *Journal of International Business Studies* (third quarter): 495–504.

———. 1995. *Multinational Companies in United States International Trade: A Statistical and Analytical Source book*. Westport, Conn.: Quorum Books.

Kobrin, Stephen J. 1991. An Empirical Analysis of the Determinants of Global Integration. *Strategic Management Journal* (Vol. 12): 17–31.

Krajewski, Stephen. 1992. *Intrafirm Trade and the New North American Business Dynamic*. Ottawa: Conference Board of Canada.

Lall, Sanjaya. 1973. Transfer-Pricing by Multinational Manufacturing Firms. *Oxford Bulletin of Economics and Statistics* (August): 173–193.

———. 1978a. The Pattern of Intra-firm Exports by U.S. Multinationals. *Oxford Bulletin of Economics and Statistics* (August): 209–223.

———. 1978b. Transfer-Pricing and LDCs: Some Problems of Investigation. *World Development* (Vol. 7): 59–71.

Little, Jane Sneddon. 1986. Intra-Firm Trade and U.S. Protectionism: Thoughts Based on a Small Survey. *New England Economic Review* (January/February): 42–51.

———. 1987. Intra-Firm Trade: An Update. *New England Economic Review* (May/June): 46–51.

Organization for Economic Cooperation and Development (OECD). 1993. *Intra-firm Trade*. Paris: OECD.

———. 1995. *Transfer Pricing Guidelines for Multiuational Enterprises and Tax Administrations*. Paris: OECD.

Price Waterhouse. 1995. *Corporate Taxes: A Worldwide Summary*. New York: Price Waterhouse.

Scholes, Myron S., and Mark. A. Wolfson. 1992. *Taxes and Business Strategy*. Englewood Cliffs, N.J.: Prentice-Hall.

Siddharthan, N. S., and M. Kumar. 1990. The Determinants of Inter-Industry Variations in the Proportion of Intra-Firm Trade: The Behavior of U.S. Multinationals. *Weltwirtschaftliches Archive* (Vol. 126): 581–590.

Sullivan, Martin A. 1996. Transfer Pricing: Trouble Waiting to Happen? *Tax Notes International* (July 8): 93–95.

Tang, Roger Y. W. 1981. *Multinational Transfer Pricing: Canadian and British Perspectives*. Toronto: Butterworths.

———. 1993. *Transfer Pricing in the 1990s: Tax and Management Perspectives*. Westport, Conn.: Quorum.

U.S. Department of Commerce. Economics and Statistics Administration. Bureau of Economic Affairs. 1995a. *Foreign Direct Investment in the United States: Preliminary 1993 Estimates*. Washington, D.C.: U.S. Government Printing Office.

———. 1995b. *U.S. Direct Investment Abroad: Preliminary 1993 Estimates*. Washington, D.C.: U.S. Government Printing Office.

U.S. Tariff Commission. 1973. *Implications of Multinational Firms for World Trade and*

Investment and for U.S. Trade and Labor. Washington, D.C.: U.S. Government Printing Office.

Whitman, Marina V. 1995. Domestic Myths on Globalization. *Wall Street Journal* (October 27): A14.

Wyckoff, Andrew W. 1993. The International Expansion of Productive Networks. *OECD Observer* (February/March): 8–11.

Zeile, William J. 1993. Merchandise Trade of U.S. Affiliates of Foreign Companies. *Survey of Current Business* (October): 52–65.

3

Transfer Pricing Regulations in the United States

In Chapter 1, in the discussion of the stakeholders of intrafirm transactions and transfer pricing, we mentioned that there are many stakeholders in addition to the corporate management of U.S. multinational companies (MNCs). These stakeholders include the U.S. Congress, Treasury Department, and Internal Revenue Service (IRS); tax authorities of foreign governments; the Organization for Economic Cooperation and Development (OECD); the European Union (EU); and the United Nations (UN). Most of these stakeholders endorse the use of arm's-length prices to account for intrafirm transactions. Arm's-length prices are defined as ''prices which would have been agreed upon between unrelated parties engaged in the same or similar transactions under the same or similar conditions in the open market'' (OECD, 1979, p. 7). In Chapters 3 and 4 of this book, we will provide an overview of the transfer pricing regulations and related programs of the United States. Transfer pricing guidelines and regulations issued by the OECD, the EU, and other selected countries will be reviewed in Chapters 5 through 8.

Transfer pricing legislation and regulations in the United States have changed many times over the past three decades, and the pace of changes accelerated during the 1990s. In Chapter 3, we will provide some historical perspectives on transfer pricing regulations in the United States. Final regulations of section 482 of the Internal Revenue Code will be discussed in detail. Also discussed in Chapter 3 are final cost-sharing regulations and section 6662 regulations on the imposition of the accuracy-related penalty. In Chapter 4, we will discuss such transfer pricing programs as the advance-pricing agreement (APA) programs, the competent authority procedure, and transfer pricing arbitrations.

HISTORICAL DEVELOPMENTS OF SECTION 482 REGULATIONS

Section 482 and the 1968 Regulations

Section 482 of the U.S. Internal Revenue Code authorizes the Internal Revenue Service to allocate income or expenses among related companies when it is necessary to prevent tax evasion or to clearly reflect the income of each company. The original version of section 482 is composed of only one sentence, as follows:

In any case of two or more organizations, trades, or businesses (whether or not incorporated, whether or not organized in the United States, and whether or not affiliated) owned or controlled directly or indirectly by the same interests, the Secretary or his delegate may distribute, apportion, or allocate gross income, deductions, credits, or allowances between or among such organizations, trades, or businesses, if he determines that such distribution, apportionment, or allocation is necessary in order to prevent evasion of taxes or clearly to reflect the income of any such organizations, trades, or businesses.

The regulations issued in 1968 (Treasury Regulations 1.482–2[e][1]) allow the use of the following three methods, in order of precedence, for establishing transfer prices for sales and transfers of tangible property:

—the comparable uncontrolled price method (CUP);

—the resale price method (RPM); and

—the cost plus method (CPLM).

Under the CUP, the arm's-length price is equal to the price paid in comparable uncontrolled sales when adjusted for differences in circumstances. Uncontrolled sales are sales between two businesses that are not members of the same controlled group. Under the RPM, the arm's-length price is equal to the applicable resale price less an appropriate gross profit. The regulations stated that the RPM should be used in cases where no CUP existed and the buyer will not add substantially to the value of the product. Following the CPLM, the transfer price is the cost of producing the product plus an appropriate gross profit markup, such as realized in comparable uncontrolled transactions. The CPLM should be used when neither the CUP nor the RPM can be applied. In addition, the 1968 regulations also allowed the use of any other reasonable method if none of the three methods above was applicable.

The 1968 regulations also required the use of comparable uncontrolled transactions to establish an arm's-length rate for the transfer and use of intangible property. When comparable uncontrolled transactions are not available, Treasury

Regulation 1.482–2(d)(2)(iii) states that the following 12 factors may be considered in establishing an arm's-length rate:

1. the prevailing rates in the same industry or for similar property in a different industry;

2. the offer of competing transferors or the bids of competing transferees;

3. the terms of the transfer, including limitations on the geographic area covered and the exclusive or nonexclusive character of any rights granted;

4. the uniqueness of the property and the period for which it is likely to remain unique;

5. the degree and duration of protection afforded to the property under the laws of the relevant countries;

6. value of services rendered by the transferor to the transferee in connection with the transfer within the meaning of paragraph (b)(8) of this section (services rendered in connection with the transfer of property);

7. prospective profits to be realized or costs to be saved by the transferee through its use or subsequent transfer of the property;

8. the capital investment and start-up expenses required of the transferee;

9. the availability of substitutes for the property transferred;

10. the arm's-length rates and prices paid by unrelated parties where the property is resold or sublicensed to such parties;

11. the costs incurred by the transferor in developing the property; and

12. any other fact or circumstance which unrelated parties would have been likely to consider in determining the amount of an arm's-length consideration for the property.

The 1968 regulations and the administration of activities related to section 482 of the Internal Revenue Code have been criticized by many sectors, including the U.S. Congress. For example, in a report to the chair of the House Ways and Means Committee of the U. S. Congress, the General Accounting Office (U.S. GAO, 1981, p. i) stated that the "IRS often has difficulty identifying a true arm's length price on which to base adjustments of corporate transfer prices." In its review of IRS examination data on 519 U.S. MNCs, each having assets over $250 million and engaged in transactions with its foreign subsidiaries, the GAO found that only 3 percent of the IRS's total recommended section 482 adjustments to reported income were based on a true arm's-length price. The GAO also criticized the Treasury guidelines for causing administrative burdens and uncertainty both for IRS and taxpayers. On the administration of section 482, the U.S. GAO (1981, p. i) stated that "the IRS has no sound basis for determining the amount of audit resources to be assigned to address the problem, nor for gauging the success of those resources that are applied to it." In the early 1980s, several other reports and studies were published to comment on the IRS's "use and misuse" of section 482. To respond to the GAO's report and other criticisms, the IRS prepared its own study (U.S. IRS, 1984) using section 482 cases completed during fiscal years 1980 and 1981.

The IRS claimed that tax examiners used the comparable uncontrolled price method at a rate of 21.2 percent (225 of 1,062 cases). The report of the IRS (1984) concluded that "the IRS is protecting the United States interests through its international enforcement of section 482, and is applying the regulations in such a manner as to offer consistency and predictability for corporations in their international planning."

In 1986, Congress added the "super-royalty provision" to section 482 through the Tax Reform Act of 1986. This new provision is as follows: "In the case of any transfer (or license) of intangible property (within the meaning of section 935(h)(3)(B)), the income with respect to such transfer or license shall be commensurate with the income attributable to the intangible."

The complete and updated version of section 482 is reprinted in Appendix A. Section 93b(h)(3)(B) defines intangible property to include the following:

1. patent, invention, formula, process, design, pattern, or know-how;

2. copyright, literary, musical, or artistic composition;

3. trademark, trade name, or brand name;

4. franchise, license, or contract;

5. method, program, system, procedure, campaign, survey, study, forecast, estimate, customer list, or technical data; and

6. any similar item that has substantial value independent of the services of any individual.

The super royalty provision was designed to provide the Internal Revenue Service with the tools to collect royalties commensurate with the economic values of intangibles. The IRS believed that many U.S. parent companies were transferring intangibles to related foreign subsidiaries at less than their true value. It was estimated by the Treasury Department that the 1986 act would raise $410 million over five years.

As part of the Tax Reform Act of 1986, Congress directed the Treasury Department and the IRS to study transfer pricing issues to determine whether, and how, existing regulations should be modified. On October 18, 1988, the Treasury Department issued a white paper titled, *A Study on Intercompany Pricing* (U.S. IRS, 1988). The white paper contains the Treasury Department's proposed interpretation of the 1986 amendment to section 482, which provides that the transferor or licensor of intangible property to a related person shall receive consideration commensurate with the income attributable to the intangibles. The proposals would require stricter documentation of the pricing for intercompany transfers of intangibles. The white paper suggested several new methods for the transfers and licensing of intangible property. These methods included the basic arm's-length return method (BALRM) and the BALRM plus profit split. These methods focused on the income generated by the intangibles rather than on comparable products and transactions. On the sales and transfers of tangible property, the white paper did not recommend any significant changes from the 1968 regulations. However, the study did propose eliminating the priority of the RPM over the cost plus method.

In 1992, the IRS published the *Report on the Application and Administration of Section 482* (U.S. IRS, 1992). Following the direction of Congress, the study examined:

1. the effect of recent legislative amendments in increasing compliance with section 482;

2. the use of advance pricing agreements to address issues under section 482;

3. possible legislative or administrative changes that would assist the IRS in enforcing section 482; and

4. the coordination of the administration of section 482 with similar provisions of foreign tax laws and domestic nontax laws.

The main conclusions of the study are as follows:

—Preliminary data suggest that the recent legislative amendments will have an important positive effect in increasing compliance with section 482.

—The IRS successfully developed and implemented a detailed procedure for obtaining advance-pricing agreements (APAs) under section 482. The APA procedure is an important new tool, which is reducing controversies and promoting reasonable transfer prices.

—Additional legislative changes would be premature at this time. The IRS is aggressively pursuing administrative steps to assist in section 482 enforcement.

—The IRS has been successful in initiating measures to coordinate section 482 issues with foreign treaty partners and to identify domestic nontax laws that may enhance compliance efforts.

The IRS (U.S. IRS, 1992) also stated that it is:

dedicated to improving its current practices and to developing new approaches to simplify and to intensify the enforcement of section 482. To this end, the IRS must encourage greater voluntary compliance, strengthen the examination process, and prepare more effectively for litigation. (p. vii)

The 1992 Proposed Regulations

On January 24, 1992, the U.S. Treasury Department issued the 1992 proposed regulations dealing with intangibles, cost-sharing arrangements for the development of intangibles, and new rules for intangible property. These regulations are related to the super-royalty provision added to section 482. The proposed regulations would have allowed three pricing methods, presented in order of highest to lowest priority (Burge and Dildine, 1992; Turro, 1992):

1. Matching transaction method (MTM): this method parallels the exact comparable method outlined by the IRS in the white paper. Under this method, the arm's-length consideration for a controlled transfer of an intangible is determined by reference to the consideration charged in an uncontrolled transfer of the same intangible property.

2. Comparable adjustable transaction (CAT) method: this is similar to the inexact comparable method as explained in the white paper. Under this approach, the arm's-length price for an intangible is determined by reference to the consideration charged in an uncontrolled transfer involving the same or similar intangible under adjustable economic conditions and contractual terms, subject to verification by the comparable profit interval (CPI). CPI is a profit range determined by analyzing comparable uncontrolled entities using a six-step process, outlined as follows:

   —select the tested party (a controlled entity);

   —match its tested operations to those of uncontrolled parties;

   —compute its constructive operating income using reliable data and selected profit-level indicators;

   —Determine the comparable profit interval;

   —Determine the most appropriate point in the interval, if necessary; and

   —compute the appropriate transfer price.

3. Comparable profit method (CPM): under this method, the arm's-length consideration for the controlled transfer is determined by reference to the CPI of the tested party. If the reported operating profit of a controlled entity (the tested party) is within the comparable interval, the price of the intangible property will be deemed arm's length. If the reported income is far outside the range, an adjustment would be made to bring the tested party's results to the most appropriate point in the range.

The 1992 proposed regulations generated lively debates among IRS officials, corporate tax executives of MNCs, and tax partners of public accounting firms. Many tax executives are concerned with the depth of quantitative and qualitative analysis necessary to comply with the regulations. As Mogle (1993) explained, there were many basic problems with the 1992 proposed regulation:

—The proposed regulations could be characterized as an abandonment of the arm's-length standard as they reflected no coherent theme or strategy for improving compliance with the standard.

—The regulations adopted several procedural rules that were problematic and sometimes unrealistic.

—The proposed regulations were found to be unacceptable by nearly everyone but the drafters, inspiring negative commentary from taxpayers, practitioners, and foreign governments.

The OECD Committee on Fiscal Affairs also had serious reservations about the regulations. In a report published by the OECD (1993), a special task force of the Committee on Fiscal Affairs concluded that "the implementation of the proposed section 482 Regulations in their present form could risk undermining the consensus that has been built up over a number of years on the application of the arm's-length principle and thereby increase the risk of economic double taxation'' (p. vii). The task force recommended that ''the proposed Regulations should be substantially amended according to the suggestions set out in the OECD report and, even after such amendments, they should ideally be implemented on a temporary basis'' (p. xvi).

In July 1992, the U.S. Treasury Department decided to change the focus of its enforcement strategy under section 482. The basic goal of the new strategy was to balance the need to restore congressional confidence in the IRS's ability to enforce the statutory mandate of section 482 and taxpayers' need for regulations that are fair and flexible in their applications. Another objective was to minimize the risk of double taxation. On January 13, 1993, the Treasury Department issued temporary regulations under section 482.

The 1993 Temporary Regulations

The 1993 regulations superseded the proposed regulations issued in January 1992. One of the most significant changes in the 1993 temporary regulations was to eliminate the strict hierarchy of various pricing methods and adopt instead the ''best method'' rule. The best method was defined as the method that provides ''the most accurate measure of an arm's length result'' (p. xvi). The temporary regulations encouraged companies to use more than one transfer pricing method. When two or more methods provided inconsistent results, the best method rule was to be used to select the most accurate method. The following three factors were to be used in selecting the best method:

1. the completeness and accuracy of the data used to apply each method;

2. the degree of comparability between controlled and uncontrolled transactions; and

3. the number, magnitude, and accuracy of the adjustments required to select the method.

Another major change in the 1993 regulations was to delete the mandatory CPI check required in the 1992 regulations. Under the temporary regulations, the methods allowable for determining an arm's length price for the transfer of tangible property were the CUP method, the RPM, the CPLM, the comparable profits method (CPM), and any other method that was reasonable under the circumstances. For the transfer of intangible property, the 1993 regulations allowed the use of the following methods subject to the best method rule: the comparable uncontrolled transaction method (CUT), the CPM, and any other suitable method.

Public reactions to the 1993 temporary regulations were generally favorable. However, some taxpayers felt that the regulations continued to place undue emphasis on profit-based, as opposed to transactional-based, methods (Hirsh,

Lederman, and Hughes, 1994). Many commenters asserted that because operating profit can be affected by factors other than transfer pricing, the CPM would not provide a reliable measure of an arm's-length result and was therefore not consistent with that standard.

THE FINAL REGULATIONS OF SECTION 482

General Principles and Guidelines

The final regulations of section 482 were released on July 1, 1994, replacing the 1993 temporary regulations. The final regulations were effective for taxable years beginning 90 days after publication in the *Federal Register* (for taxable years beginning after October 6, 1994). However, taxpayers could elect to apply the new regulations retroactively for any open year and all subsequent years.

In the final regulations, the IRS made many changes in response to comments and criticisms regarding the 1993 regulations. However, both the format and the substance of the final regulations are, for the most part, consistent with the 1993 regulations. Like the proposed 1993 regulations, the final regulations also emphasize comparability (i.e., the degree of similarity between the controlled and uncontrolled transaction) and flexibility.

The final regulations contain general principles and guidelines that are mandatory. The principles and guidelines require the application of three related standards: (1) the arm's-length standard; (2) the best method rule; and (3) comparability analysis. The arm's-length standard is defined by Treasury Regulations 1.482–1(b) as follows:

A controlled transaction meets the arm's-length standard if the results of that transaction are consistent with the results that would have been realized if uncontrolled taxpayers had engaged in the same transaction under the circumstances (arm's-length result). However, because identical transactions can rarely be located, whether a transaction produces an arm's-length result generally will be determined by reference to the results of comparable transactions under comparable circumstances.

The arm's-length standard is also endorsed by the OECD (1979, 1995) guidelines. The main purpose is to place a controlled taxpayer on a tax parity with an uncontrolled taxpayer in determining the taxable income of the controlled taxpayer.

In the final regulations, the ''best method rule'' is redefined as the best transfer pricing method that provides the most reliable measure of an arm's-length result, given the facts and circumstances of the business activity. Two primary factors should be considered in deciding which method provides the most reliable measure of an arm's-length result:

1. the degree of comparability between the controlled transaction (or taxpayer) and any uncontrolled comparables; and

2. the quality of the data and assumptions used in the analysis.

The regulations state that the comparability of transactions and circumstances must be evaluated by considering all factors that could affect prices or profits in arm's-length dealings. Such factors may include the following: (1) functions; (2) contract terms; (3) risks; (4) economic conditions; and (5) property or services. Detailed components that must be analyzed for each of these five factors are listed in Table 3.1.

The quality of the data and assumptions depends upon the completeness and accuracy of the underlying data, the reliability of the assumptions, and the sensitivity of the results to possible deficiencies in the data and assumptions.

In addition, the final regulations also provide guidelines for selecting the best method for sales and transfers of tangible and intangible property. These guidelines and others for the transfers of services will be discussed in detail in the following sections.

Transfer Pricing Methods for Sales and Transfer of Tangible Property

For sales and transfers of tangible property, the regulations allow the use of one of the following six methods, subject to the best method rule:

1. the comparable uncontrolled price method (CUP);

2. the resale price method (RPM);

3. the cost plus method (CPLM);

4. the comparable profits method (CPM);

5. the profit split method (PSM); and

6. unspecified methods that might be applicable to the facts and circumstances of a particular transaction.

Under the CUP method, the arm's-length price is equal to the price paid in comparable uncontrolled sales, adjusted for differences in the following:

—quality of the product;

—contractual terms (e.g., scope and terms of warranties provided, sales or purchase volume, credit terms, transport terms etc.);

—level of the market (wholesale, retail, etc.);

—geographic market in which the transaction takes place;

—date of the transaction;

—intangible property associated with the sale;

Table 3.1

Detailed Factors for Determining the Comparability of Two Transactions

1. Functions performed and associated resources employed by taxpayers in each transaction:
   - Research and development;
   - Product design and engineering;
   - Manufacturing, production and process engineering;
   - Product fabrication, extraction, and assembly;
   - Purchasing and materials management;
   - Marketing and distribution functions, including inventory management, warranty administration, and advertising activities;
   - Transportation and warehousing; and
   - Managerial, legal, accounting and finance, credit and collection, training, and personnel management services.

2. Contractual terms:
   - The form of consideration charged or paid;
   - Sales or purchase volume;
   - The scope and terms of warranties provided;
   - Rights to updates, revisions, or modifications;
   - The duration of relevant license, contract, or other agreements and termination or renegotiation rights;
   - Collateral transactions or ongoing business relationships between the buyer and the seller, including arrangements for the provision of ancillary or subsidiary services; and
   - Extension of credit and payment terms.

3. Significant risk that could affect the prices that would be charged or paid or the profit that would be earned:
   - Market risks, including fluctuations in cost, demand, pricing, and inventory levels;
   - Risks associated with the success or failure of research and development activities;
   - Financial risks, including fluctuations in foreign currency rates of exchange and interest rates;
   - Credit and collection risks;
   - Product liability risks; and
   - General business risks related to the ownership of property, plant, and equipment.

4. Significant economic conditions that could affect the prices that would be charged or paid or the profit that would be earned in each of the transactions:
   - The similarity of geographic markets;
   - The relative size of each market and the extent of the overall economic development in each market;
   - The level of the market (e.g., wholesale, retail, etc.);
   - The relevant market shares for the products, properties, or services transferred or provided;

Table 3.1 (continued)

- The location-specific costs of the factors of production and distribution;
- The extent of competition in each market with regard to the property or services under review;
- The economic condition of the particular industry, including whether the market is in contraction or expansion; and
- The alternatives realistically available to the buyer and seller.

5. Property or services transferred in the transactions. These may include any intangibles that are embedded in tangible property or services being transferred.

Source: U.S. Treasury Regulations, section 1.482–1.

—foreign currency risks; and

—alternatives realistically available to the buyer and seller.

We may use data from public exchanges or quotation media to calculate a comparable uncontrolled price if the following three requirements are met:

1. the data are widely and routinely used in the ordinary course of business in the industry to negotiate prices for uncontrolled sales;
2. the data derived from public exchanges or quotation media are used to set prices in the controlled transaction in the same way they are used by uncontrolled taxpayers in the industry; and
3. the amount charged in the controlled transaction is adjusted to reflect differences in product quality and quantity, contractual terms, transportation costs, market conditions, risks borne, and other factors that affect the price that would be agreed to by uncontrolled taxpayers.

Under the RPM, the arm's-length price is equal to the applicable resale price less an appropriate gross profit. This gross profit is computed by multiplying the applicable resale price by the gross profit margin percentage earned in comparable uncontrolled transactions. According to Feinschreiber (1996), the following six basic characteristics of RPM should be considered before its application:

1. The resale price is the price from the distributor (or reseller) to the customer. The transfer price is the price to the customer, less the applicable gross margin earned by the distributor.
2. The applicable gross margin is based on the gross profit margin realized in comparable uncontrolled transactions, subtracting the appropriate gross profit from the applicable resale price.
3. The RPM measures the value of functions performed by a distributor.

4. The RPM is normally used in the purchase and sale of tangible property.

5. The RPM assumes that the reseller has not added substantial value to the tangible goods.

6. The RPM should not be used when the distributor uses its intangible property to add substantial value to the tangible goods.

Under CPLM, the arm's-length price is the cost of producing the product (or other property) plus an appropriate gross profit markup, as is realized in comparable uncontrolled transactions. This method is normally used in cases involving the manufacture, assembly, or other production of goods that are sold to related parties.

Before adopting the CPLM, the taxpayer must analyze the functions performed and the risks assumed in the noncontrolled transactions. When making adjustments for differences between controlled and uncontrolled transactions, we have to consider the following and other similar factors:

—the complexity of manufacturing or assembly;

—manufacturing, production, and process engineering;

—procurement, purchasing, and inventory control activities;

—testing functions;

—selling, general, and administrative expenses;

—foreign currency risks; and

—contractual terms.

Both the comparable profits method (CPM) and the profit split method (PSM) are transactional profit methods that examine the profits resulting from particular transactions between related companies. According to the regulations, the CPM evaluates whether the amount charged in a controlled transaction is arm's-length based on objective measures of profitability (profit-level indicators) derived from uncontrolled taxpayers that engage in similar business activities under similar circumstances. Profit-level indicators are ratios that measure relationships between profits and costs incurred or resources employed. Some examples of acceptable profit-level indicators are the following:

—rate of return on capital employed: the ratio of operating profit to operating assets;

—ratio of operating profit to sales; and

—ratio of gross profit to operating expenses, which normally include advertising and promotional expenses, sales and marketing expenses, warehousing and distribution, administration, and a reasonable allowance for depreciation and amortization.

The regulations also state that the profit-level indicators should be derived from a sufficient number of years to reasonably measure returns that accrue to uncontrolled comparables. Usually, such a period should include the taxable year under review and the preceding two taxable years.

The standard of comparability also applies to the CPM. Adjustments must be made for significant differences in the functions performed, risk assumed, foreign currency differences, and other factors that affect profitability.

The basic approach of a profit split method (PSM) is defined by the regulations (1.482–6[a]), as follows:

The profit split method evaluates whether the allocation of the combined operating profit or loss attributable to one or more controlled transactions is arm's-length by preference to the relative value of each controlled taxpayer's contribution to that combined operating profit or loss. The combined operating profit or loss must be derived from the most narrowly identifiable business activity of the controlled taxpayers from which data is available that includes the controlled transactions (relevant business activity).

The regulations provide two profit split methods: the comparable profit split and the residual profit split. Under the comparable profit split method, the combined profit of the controlled parties is allocated to each party in accordance with the percentage allocation of the combined profits of uncontrolled parties whose transactions and activities are similar to those of the controlled parties.

Under the residual profit split method, the combined operating profit or loss from the relevant business activity is allocated between the controlled taxpayers in two steps:

1. Allocate operating income to each party to the controlled transactions to provide a market return for its routine contributions to the relevant business activity.

2. Allocate residual profit among the controlled taxpayers based on the relative value of their contributions of intangible property to the relevant business activity that was not accounted for as a routine contribution.

When neither method can reasonably be applied to a transaction, the taxpayer can use another, unspecified, method that is reasonable under the facts and circumstances. As with any other method, an unspecified method cannot be applied unless it provides the most reliable measure of an arm's-length result based on the best method rule.

Transfer Pricing Methods for the Transfer and Use of Intangible Property

According to the final regulations, an intangible (or intangible property) is defined as an asset that comprises any of the following items and has substantial value independent of the services of any individual:

—patents, inventions, formulae, processes, designs, patterns, or know-how;

—copyrights and literary, musical, or artistic compositions;

—trademarks, trade names, or brand names;

—franchises, licenses, or contracts;

—methods, programs, systems, procedures, campaigns, survey, studies, forecasts, estimates, customer lists, or technical data; and

—other, similar items.

Four transfer pricing methods were provided in the regulations for a transfer of intangible property:

1. the comparable uncontrolled transaction method (CUT);
2. the comparable profit method (CPM);
3. the profit split method (PSM); and
4. unspecified methods.

Under the comparable uncontrolled transaction method, the arm's-length price is determined by reference to the amount charged in a comparable uncontrolled transaction. When evaluating the comparability of the circumstances of the controlled and uncontrolled transactions involving intangible property, one must also consider the factors listed in Table 3.1. In addition, the following factors may have to be considered:

—the terms of the transfer, including the exploitation rights granted in the intangible, the exclusive or nonexclusive character of any rights granted, any restrictions on use, or any limitations on the geographic area in which the rights may be exploited;

—the stage of development of the intangible in the market in which it is to be used;

—rights to receive updates, revisions, or modifications of the intangible;

—the uniqueness of the property and the period for which it remains unique, including the degree and duration of protection afforded to the property under the laws of the relevant countries;

—the duration of the license, contract, or other agreement and any termination or renegotiation rights;

—any economic and product liability risks to be assumed by the transferee;

—the existence and extent of any collateral transactions or ongoing business relationships between the transferee and transferor; and

—the functions to be performed by the transferor and transferee, including any ancillary or subsidiary services.

Both the comparable profit method (CPM) and the profit split method (PSM) applicable to tangible property can also be applied to intangibles. The best

Table 3.2
A Summary of Transfer Pricing Methods Allowable by Section 482 and Related Regulations

For transfer of tangible property—select one of the following six methods according to the best method rule (see reg. section 1.482-1):

1. The comparable uncontrolled price method
   (reg. section 1.482-3[b]);
2. The resale price method (reg. section 1.482-3[c]);
3. The cost plus method (reg. section 1.482-3[d]);
4. The comparable profit method (reg. section 1.482-5);
5. The profit split method (reg section 1.482-6); and
6. Unspecified methods (reg. section 1.482-3[e])

For transfer and use of intangible property—select one of the following four methods according to the best method rule (reg. section 1.482-1):

1. The comparable uncontrolled transaction method
   (reg. section 1.482-4[c]);
2. The comparable profit method (reg. section 1.482-5);
3. The profit split method (reg. section 1.482-6); and
4. Unspecified methods (reg. section 1.482-4[d]).

Source: U.S. Treasury Regulations, section 482.

method rule also applies to a transaction involving intangible property when an unspecified method is adopted.

All the transfer pricing methods applicable to tangible and intangible property are summarized in Table 3.2. Related sections of the regulations are also indicated.

Transfer Pricing Methods for the Transfer of Services

Despite the increasing importance of intrafirm trade in services, the transfer pricing of services has received far less attention from the Internal Revenue Service than has the transfer pricing for tangible and intangible goods. The types of services transferred may include marketing, managerial, administrative, technical, logistics, and other services. Applying the arm's-length standard to these services can be difficult for two reasons (Klein and Karter, 1996):

—it is difficult to find third-party comparable transactions, and

—in many instances, the performance of intracompany service may involve the use or transfer of tangible or intangible property.

In determining the transfer pricing method for services, Klein and Karter (1996) suggest that the following issues be analyzed:

1. Who is doing what for whom?
2. Where are they doing it?
3. Why are they doing it?
4. How are they doing it?
5. What property is being used or transferred in connection therewith?

Such an analysis is useful in determining the type of services being performed and the pricing method that should be used. Under normal circumstances, the three general principles and guidelines (the arm's-length standard, the best method rules and comparability analysis) that apply to the pricing of tangible and intangible properties also apply to the pricing of services. In addition, the technical advice memorandum (TAM) 8806002, issued by the IRS on September 24, 1987, also provides some useful guidelines for cost allocation for services transferred.

When services are provided with the sales or transfer of an intangible property, separate transfer pricing analyses must be performed for the services and the property (Treasury Regulations 1.482–1[b][2][ii]). However, if the services provided are merely ancillary and subsidiary to the sale or transfer of the property or the commencement of the effective use of the property, a separate allocation for services is not required (Treasury Regulations 1.482–2[b][8]).

FINAL COST-SHARING REGULATIONS

Formulating a cost-sharing arrangement (CSA) is one of several approaches for an MNC to structure the development, ownership, and utilization of intangible property with other affiliates or independent companies (Dolan, 1996). Other approaches include partnerships, joint venture arrangements, and licensing. In recent years, however, many U.S. and foreign-based MNCs have adopted CSAs as practical alternatives to licensing (or joint venture arrangements) to manage the development and cross-border transfer of intangibles (Dodge et al., 1996). By agreeing to share the development and maintenance costs of an intangible property, the parties to a CSA become coowners of the intangible, with each entitled to the income generated from its use without paying any royalties (Lewis, 1992).

The cost-sharing regulations in the United States have changed several times in the past 30 years. In the 1968 regulations under section 482, brief and simple rules regulated cost sharing arrangements. The old regulations contain only one paragraph, as follows (1.482–2[d][4]):

Sharing of costs and risks. Where a member of a group controlled entities acquires an interest in intangible property as a participating party in a bona fide cost sharing arrangement with respect to the development of such intangible property, the district director shall not make allocations with respect to such acquisition except as may be appropriate to reflect each participant's arm's-length share of the costs and risks of developing the property. A bona fide cost sharing arrangement is an agreement, in writing, between two or more members of a group of controlled entities providing for the sharing of the costs and risks of developing intangible property in return for a specified interest in the intangible property that may be produced. In order for the arrangement to qualify as a bona fide arrangement, it must reflect an effort in good faith by the participating members to bear their respective shares of all the costs and risks of development on an arm's-length basis. In order for the sharing of costs and risk to be considered on an arm's-length basis, the terms and conditions must be comparable to those which would have been adopted by unrelated parties similarly situated had they entered into such an arrangement. If an oral cost sharing arrangement, entered into prior to April 16, 1968, and continued in effect after that date, is otherwise in compliance with the standards prescribed in this subparagraph, it shall constitute a bona fide cost sharing arrangement if it is reduced to writing prior to January 1, 1969.

The Tax Reform Act of 1986 amended section 482 to require that consideration for intangible property transferred in a controlled transaction "be commensurate with the income attributable to the intangible." Later, the Conference Committee of the U.S. Congress reporting on the act recommended that the IRS conduct a comprehensive study and consider whether the 1968 regulations should be modified in any respect. It took the IRS about two years to conduct such a study. On October 18, 1988, the Treasury Department and the IRS issued a white paper that recommended some drastic changes to cost-sharing regulations. For example, the white paper suggested that "most product areas covered by cost-sharing arrangements should be within three-digit Standard Industrial Classification codes, that most participants should be assigned exclusive geographic rights in developed intangibles and that marketing intangibles should be excluded from bona fide cost-sharing arrangements." Comments from many taxpayers indicated that such rules would unduly restrict the use of many other bona fide cost-sharing arrangements.

On January 30, 1992, the IRS issued proposed cost-sharing regulations that allowed more flexibility than had been recommended by the white paper. The proposed regulations established the following five criteria for a qualified cost-sharing arrangement:

—the arrangement had to have two or more eligible participants;

—the arrangement had to be recorded in writing contemporaneously with the formation of the cost-sharing arrangement;

—the eligible participants had to share the costs and risks of intangible development in return for a specified interest in any intangible produced;

—the arrangement had to reflect a reasonable effort by each eligible participant to share costs and risks in proportion to anticipated benefits from using developed intangibles; and

—the arrangement had to meet certain administrative requirements, with the key requirements being that participants had to be eligible and that costs and risks had to be proportionate to benefits.

The 1992 proposed cost-sharing regulations had other provisions on the allocation of costs and income from a cost-sharing arrangement. The proposed regulations also have some accounting and administrative requirements for a qualified CSA. Responses from commentators were mixed. Some parts of the proposed regulations were well received, but some writers criticized the profit-based guidelines and procedural requirements of the regulations (Levey, O'Haver, and Clancy, 1992).

On December 20, 1995, the IRS issued the final regulations (section 1.482-7) on CSAs. The regulations are effective for taxable years beginning on or after January 1, 1996. Important guidelines and criteria are provided for the following areas:

—definition of a CSA;

—criteria for a qualified CSA;

—definition and criteria for an eligible participant;

—rules for allocating costs and benefits derived from a CSA; and

—accountancy and administrative requirements for a CSA.

According to the final regulations, a cost-sharing arrangement is an agreement under which the parties agree to share the costs of development of one or more intangibles in proportion to their shares of reasonably anticipated benefits from their individual exploitation of the interests in the intangibles assigned to them under the arrangement (section 1.482–7[a]). To be a qualified cost-sharing arrangement, a CSA must meet the following criteria (1.482–7[b]):

1. include two or more participants;

2. provide a method to calculate each controlled participant's share of intangible development costs, based on factors that can reasonably be expected to reflect that participant's share of anticipated benefits;

3. provide for adjustment to the controlled participants' shares of intangible development costs to account for changes in economic conditions, the business operations and practices of the participants, and the ongoing development of intangibles under the arrangement; and

4. be recorded in a document that is contemporaneous with the formation (and any revision) of the costs-sharing arrangement and that includes:

   i. A list of the arrangement's participants, and any other member of the controlled group that will benefit from the use of intangibles developed under the cost sharing arrangement:

ii. The information described in paragraphs (b)(2) and (b)(3) of this section;

iii. A description of the scope of the research and development to be undertaken, including the intangible or class of intangibles intended to be developed;

iv. A description of each participant's interest in any covered intangibles. A covered intangible is any intangible property that is developed as a result of the research and development undertaken under the cost-sharing arrangement (intangible development areas);

v. The duration of the arrangement; and

vi. The conditions under which the arrangement may be modified or terminated and the consequences of such modification or termination, such as the interest that each participant will receive in any covered intangibles.

These above criteria are more specific than those included in the 1992 proposed regulations.

Regulation 1.482–7(c) defines an eligible participant of a CSA as a controlled taxpayer who meets the requirements for a controlled participant or an uncontrolled taxpayer who is a party to the CSA (uncontrolled participant). A controlled taxpayer can be a controlled participant only if that party:

—uses, or reasonably expects to use, covered intangibles in the active conduct of a trade or business; and

—substantially complies with the accounting requirements and administrative requirements of the regulations.

Before explaining the rules for allocating costs and benefits related to a CSA, the final regulations define the intangible development costs, benefits, and reasonably anticipated benefits as follows:

—A controlled participant's costs of developing intangibles for a taxable year mean all of the costs incurred by that participant related to the intangible development area, plus all of the cost sharing payments it makes to other controlled and uncontrolled participants, minus all of the cost-sharing payments it receives from other controlled and uncontrolled participants.

—Benefits are additional income generated or costs saved by the use of covered intangibles.

—A controlled participant's reasonably anticipated benefits are the aggregate benefits that it reasonably anticipates that it will derive from covered intangibles.

A controlled participant's share of intangible development costs for a taxable year is equal to its intangible development costs for the taxable year (as defined here), divided by the sum of the intangible development costs for the taxable year of all the controlled participants. On the other hand, a controlled participant's share of reasonably anticipated benefits under a qualified CSA is equal to the reasonably anticipated benefits (as defined here), divided by the sum of the reasonably anticipated benefits of all the controlled participants. The final regulations regarding accounting requirements state that the controlled participants in a qualified CSA must use a consistent method of accounting to measure costs and benefits and translate foreign currencies on a consistent basis.

There are two types of administrative requirements for a qualified CSA: documentation and reporting. A controlled participant must maintain sufficient documentation to establish that the criteria for a qualified CSA and those for eligible participants have been met. A controlled participant must provide such documentation to the IRS within 30 days of a request. In addition, the taxpayer must also maintain the following records:

—the total amount of costs incurred pursuant to the arrangement;

—the costs borne by each controlled participant;

—a description of the method used to determine each controlled participant's share of the intangible development costs, including the projections used to estimate benefits and an explanation of why that method was selected;

—the accounting method used to determine the costs and benefits of the intangible development (including the method used to translate foreign currencies) and, to the extent that the method materially differs from U.S. generally accepted accounting principles, an explanation of such material differences; and

—prior research, if any, undertaken in the intangible development area, any tangible or intangible property made available for use in the arrangement, by each controlled participant, and any information used to establish the value of preexisting and covered intangibles.

For reporting requirements, a controlled participant must attach to its U.S. income tax return a statement indicating that it is a participant in a qualified cost-sharing arrangement and listing the other controlled participants in the arrangement. A controlled participant who is not required to file a U.S. income tax return must ensure that such a statement is attached to Schedule M of any Form 5471 or to any Form 5472 filed with respect to that participant. (Form 5471, "Information Return of U.S. Persons with Respect to Certain Foreign Corporations"; Form 5472, "Information Return of a 25% Foreign-Owned U.S. Corporation or a Foreign Corporation Engaged in a U.S. Trade or Business"; and Schedule M, "Transactions between Controlled Foreign Corporation and Shareholders or Other Related Persons"; may be obtained from the IRS district offices.)

The final regulations of CSAs follow the internationally recognized principle that cost shares should be in proportion to anticipated benefits received. However, it is still too early to tell whether the major trading partners of the United

States will accept all the final regulations. The OECD was expected to issue its final guidelines on CSAs before the end of the 1990s.

SECTION 6662 REGULATIONS ON THE IMPOSITION OF THE ACCURACY-RELATED PENALTY

Section 6662 was first enacted by the Revenue Reconciliation Act of 1990. Later, the section was amended by the Omnibus Budget Reconciliation Act of 1993. The regulations relating to section 6662 have also been revised several times. Proposed amendments to regulations under sections 6662 and 6664 relating to the imposition of accuracy-related penalties were issued by the IRS on January 21, 1993. After considering all comments received and pursuant to statutory changes in 1993, the IRS withdrew the 1993 proposed regulations and issued temporary regulations on February 2, 1994. On July 8, 1994, the temporary regulations were amended to conform with the final section 482 regulations issued in July 1994. On February 9, 1996, the IRS issued the final regulations for section 6662. According to the preamble to the final regulations under section 6662, the regulations "provide guidance on the imposition of the accuracy related penalty under Internal Revenue Code section 6662(e) for net section 482 transfer price adjustments. This action implements changes to the applicable tax laws made by the Omnibus Budget Reconciliation Act of 1993." These regulations were effective as of February 9, 1996. At the election of the taxpayer, the final regulations may be applied to all open taxable years beginning after December 31, 1993.

Section 6662 imposes a penalty of 20 percent with respect to underpayment of taxes attributable to one or more of the following five items:

1. negligence or disregard of rules of regulations;
2. any substantial understatement of income tax;
3. any substantial valuation misstatement;
4. any substantial overstatement of pension liabilities; or
5. any substantial estate or gift tax valuation understatement.

Only item (3) is related to the transfer pricing penalty; it is further defined in section 6662(e) of the Internal Revenue Code. The objective of section 6662(e) is "to improve compliance with the arm's length standard by encouraging taxpayers to make reasonable efforts to determine and document arm's length prices for their intercompany transactions" according to the preamble to the final regulations under section 6662.

There are two different penalty schemes under sections 6662(e) and 6662(h): (1) the transactional penalty; and (2) the net adjustment penalty. Under section 6662(e), the 20 percent transactional penalty is to be assessed if:

1. the price for any property or services (or for the use of property) claimed on any such return in connection with any transaction between persons described in section 482 is 200 percent or more (or 50 percent or less) of the amount determined under section 482 to be the correct price; or

2. the net section 482 transfer price adjustment for the taxable year exceeds the lesser of $5 million or 10 percent of the taxpayer's gross receipts.

According to the final regulations for section 6662, the term, ''net section 482 adjustment,'' means the sum of all increases in the taxable income of a taxpayer for a taxable year resulting from allocations under section 482 less any decreases in taxable income attributable to collateral adjustments.

Under section 6662(h), the penalty will be increased to 40 percent if there is a ''gross value misstatement.'' The 40 percent penalty applied if:

1. the transfer price or adjusted basis of the property or services exceeds 400 percent or more (or 25 percent or less) of the correct amount determined under section 482; or

2. the net section 482 transfer pricing adjustment for the taxable year exceeds the lesser of $20 million or 20 percent of the taxpayer's gross receipts.

However, pursuant to section 6664(c), the transactional penalty will not be imposed on any portion of an underpayment if the taxpayer meets the requirements in regulation section 1.6664–4. Basically, the taxpayer has to demonstrate reasonable cause and good faith in applying rules stated in section 482 regulations. In addition, amounts that meet both the specified method and documentation requirements described in the final regulations of section 6662 are not subject to the net section 482 adjustment penalty. The specified method requirement is met if the taxpayer selects and applies a specified method in a reasonable manner. The taxpayer's selection and application of a specified method is reasonable if, given the available data and the applicable pricing methods, the taxpayer reasonably concluded that the method provides the most reliable measure of an arm's-length result under the best method rule. The documentation requirement is met if the taxpayer maintains sufficient documentation to establish having reasonably concluded that the method provided the most accurate measure of an arm's-length result under the best market rule and provides that documentation to the IRS within 30 days of a request. According to the final regulations, the principal documents must include the following:

1. an overview of the taxpayer's business, including an analysis of the economic and legal factors that affect the pricing of its property or services;

2. a description of the taxpayer's organizational structure covering all related parties engaged in transactions potentially relevant under section 482, including foreign affiliates whose transactions directly or indirectly affect the pricing of property or services in the United States;

3. any documentation explicitly required by the regulations under section 482;

4. a description of the method selected and an explanation of why that method was selected;

5. a description of the alternative methods that were considered and an explanation of why they were not selected:

6. a description of the controlled transactions (including the terms of sale) and any internal data used to analyze those transactions. For example, if a profit split method is applied, the documentation must include a schedule providing the total income, costs and assets (with adjustments for different accounting practices and currencies) for each controlled taxpayer participating in the relevant business activity and detailing the allocations of such items to that activity;

7. a description of the comparables that were used, how comparability was evaluated, and what (if any) adjustments were made;

8. an explanation of the economic analysis and projections relied upon in developing the method;

9. a description or summary of any relevant data that the taxpayer obtained after the end of the tax year and before filing a tax return, and that would help determine if the selection and application of a specified method had been done in a reasonable manner; and

10. a general index of the principal and background documents and a description of the record-keeping system used for cataloging and accessing those documents.

Background documents such as those presenting the assumptions, conclusions, and positions contained in principal documents must also be provided. If a taxpayer uses an unspecified method, then he or she has to meet both the unspecified method and document requirements to avoid the net adjustment penalty. Essentially, the taxpayer has to demonstrate that none of the specified methods are likely to provide a reliable measure of an arm's-length result and that the selection and application of an unspecified method was done in a way that would likely provide a reliable measure of an arm's-length result. The document requirements for unspecified methods are similar to those described for specified methods.

In order to ensure uniform application of the reasonableness standard and documentation requirements on a nationwide basis, the IRS recently formed the Transfer Pricing Penalty Oversight Committee. According to IRS Announcement 96–16 issued in early 1996, the committee will review all cases in which a district director is considering assertion of the penalty. The committee will also collect data on cases in which the statutory thresholds for imposition of the penalty were met but the penalty was not imposed. The committee members will include personnel from International, Examination, Appeals, and Chief Counsel.

SUMMARY AND CONCLUSIONS

This chapter summarizes several important transfer pricing legislation and regulations in the United States: section 482 and related regulations; final cost-sharing regulations; and section 6662 and its final regulations. We also reviewed some historical developments of section 482 regulations, including the 1968 regulations, the white paper, the 1992 regulations, the proposed 1993 regulations, and the final regulations of 1994. It has taken about ten years to revise all major regulations on transfer pricing in the United States.

Transfer pricing methods acceptable to the IRS for a transfer of tangible property include the comparable uncontrolled price method (CUP), the resale price method (RPM), the cost plus method (CPLM), the comparable profits method (CPM), the profit split method (PSM), and unspecified methods. Each of these methods must be applied in accordance with all the provisions of regulation section 1.482–1, including the best method rule, comparability analysis, and the arm's-length range.

The approved transfer pricing methods for a transfer of intangible property include the comparable uncontrolled transaction method (CUT), the comparable profits method (CPM), the profit split method (PSM), and unspecified methods. The application of each of these must also follow all of the provisions of regulation section 1.482–1.

The final cost-sharing regulations are effective for taxable years beginning on or after January 1, 1996. The regulations provide definitions and criteria for a qualified cost-sharing arrangement and eligible participants. Rules for sharing costs and benefits as well as documentation requirements are also clarified.

Final regulations for section 6662 on the imposition of the accuracy-related penalty were issued in February 1996. This section imposes accuracy-related penalties in several situations, including cases where there is a substantial misstatement of the valuation of transfer prices for property or services. Transactional penalties and net transfer pricing adjustment penalties up to 40 percent may be imposed if the threshold requirements for imposition of the penalty are met. However, these penalties can be avoided if a taxpayer complies with the specified (or unspecified) method requirements and documentation requirements described in the final regulations.

Many proposed transfer pricing regulations issued by the U.S. government over the past ten years have generated controversies and intense debates among tax authorities, MNCs, tax practitioners, and other transfer pricing researchers. Thanks to the debates and cooperation among most transfer pricing stakeholders, as of 1996, all of the key transfer pricing legislation and regulations are now in place. These new regulations should provide badly needed stability and certainty in intrafirm trade and transfer pricing in the future.

The legal and tax environments of transfer pricing have changed enormously since the mid-1980s. The stakes are extremely high because more than $500 billion of U.S. foreign trade in 1995 represents intrafirm trade. All of the final regulations discussed in this chapter have significant tax-planning implications for MNCs. To reduce their compliance costs, multinational taxpayers should review their transfer pricing policies, strategies, and documentation to make sure that these elements are in compliance with current U.S. regulations and the OECD guidelines.

REFERENCES

Abel, William, and Peter J. Connors. 1994. International Tax Planning in the New Environment. *Practical Accountant* (January): 44–50.

Arnold, Brian J., and Thomas E. McDonnell. 1993. Report on the Invitational Conference on Transfer Pricing: The Allocation of Income and Expenses among Countries. *Tax Notes International* (December 13): 1507–1520.

Aud, Ernest F., Jr., and James P. Fuller. 1994. The Final Section 482 Regulations. *Tax Notes International* (July 25): 265–277.

Birnkrant, Henry J., and James E. Croker, Jr. 1994a. Transfer Pricing Final Regulations Increase Flexibility, But Not Certainty, in Choice of Method. *Journal of Taxation* (November): 268–273.

———. 1994b. Despite Improvements, Transfer Pricing Regulations Still Carry a Risk of Double Taxation. *Journal of Taxation* (December): 332–337.

Burge, Marianne, and Larry Dildine. 1992. U.S. Issues Proposed Transfer Pricing Regulations for Intangibles; Tangible Property Also Affected. *International Tax Review* (January/February): 10–11.

Careccia, Frank P., and Lincoln A. Terzian. 1995. Section 6662 Penalty Quarterly: More Regulations, More Compliance, and Less Logic. *International Tax Journal* (Winter): 1–14.

Carlson, George N., Laurie J. Dicker, Gerald M. Godshaw, Margaretha C. Haeussler, Brian C. Becker, Michael A. Murphy, and Mary P. Comerford. 1994. The U.S. Final Transfer Pricing Regulations: The More Things Change, the More They Stay the Same. *Tax Notes International* (August 1): 333–348.

Crow, Stephen, and Eugene Sauls. 1994. Setting the Right Transfer Price. *Management Accounting* (December): 41–47.

Culbertson, Robert E. 1995. Speaking Softly and Carrying a Big Stick: The Interplay between Substantive and Penalty Rules in the U.S. Transfer Pricing Regulations. *Tax Notes International* (December 4): 1509–1529.

Dodge, William G., Julie Joy, Edward Maguire, and Alan Shapiro. 1996. Final Cost Sharing Regulations: Do They Solve the Intangibles Puzzle? *Journal of Taxation* (May): 270–278.

Dolan, D. Kevin. 1996. Final Cost Sharing Regulations. *Tax Management International Journal* (March 8): 147–156.

Feinschreiber, Robert, ed. 1993. *Transfer Pricing Handbook*. New York: John Wiley and Sons.

———. 1996. *Transfer Pricing Handbook: 1996 Cumulative Supplement #1*. New York: John Wiley and Sons.

Gianni, Monica Brown. 1996. Transfer Pricing and Formulary Apportionment. *Taxes* (March): 169–182.

Harper, Lucinda. 1994. New Tax Rules Expand Multinationals' Flexibility in Dealing with U.S. Units. *Wall Street Journal* (July 6).

Hershey, Robert D., Jr. 1994. U.S. Sets New Tax Rules on Pricing. *New York Times* (July 5).

Hirsh, Bobbe, Alan S. Lederman, and John M. Hughes. 1994. Final Transfer Pricing Regulations Restate Arm's Length Principle. *Taxes* (October): 587–604.

Klein, Kenneth, and Philip Karter. 1996. Transfer Pricing for Services. In Robert Feinschreiber, ed., *Transfer Pricing Handbook: 1996 Cumulative Supplement #1.* New York: John Wiley and Sons.

Lassar, Sharon S., and Terrance R. Skautz. 1995. New Transfer Pricing Documentation Requirements and Penalties. *CPA Journal* (April): 36–39.

Levey, Marc M., R. Russ O'Haver, and James P. Clancy. 1992. Application of 482 Prop. Regs. to Transfer of Intangibles Is Likely to Create Problems. *Journal of Taxation* (November): 308–315.

Lewis, Patricia Gimbel. 1992. Strategic Choices for Transfer Pricing Controversies. *Tax Executive* (September–October): 349–358.

Lowell, Cym H. 1996. Relationship of Section 482 to International Corporate Tax Planning. *Journal of Corporate Taxation* (January): 36–56.

Lowell, Cym H., Marianne Burge, and Peter L. Briger. 1994a. International Transfer Pricing—Planning for the Section 482 Penalty. *Tax Notes International* (August 1): 349–374.

———. 1994b. *U.S. International Transfer Pricing.* Boston: Warren, Gorham and Lamont.

Matthews, Kathleen. 1994. Major U.S. Trading Partners Respond to U.S. Transfer Pricing Regulations. *Tax Notes International* (October 24): 1275–1278.

Mogle, James R. 1993. Introduction to Intercompany Transfer Pricing. In Robert Feinschreiber, ed., *Transfer Pricing Handbook.* New York: John Wiley and Sons.

O'Grady, John E. 1992. Cost-Sharing Arrangements under the New Proposed Section 482 Regulation. *Tax Notes International* (February 24): 381–392.

Organization for Economic Cooperation and Development (OECD). 1979. *Transfer Pricing and Multinational Enterprises.* Paris: OECD.

———. 1993. *Tax Aspects of Transfer Pricing within Multinational Enterprises: The United States Proposed Regulations.* Paris: OECD.

———. 1995. *Transfer Pricing Guidelines for Multinational Enterprises and Tax Administrations.* Paris: OECD.

Sherman, W. Richard, and Jennifer L. McBride. 1995. International Transfer Pricing: Application and Analysis. *Ohio CPA Journal* (August): 29–35.

Smith, Carlton M. Documentation Needed to Avoid Penalties Specified by Transfer Pricing Temporary Regulations. *Journal of Taxation* (May): 304–308.

Tang, Roger Y. W. 1993. *Transfer Pricing in the 1990s: Tax and Management Perspectives.* Westport, Conn.: Quorum Books.

Turro, John. 1992. Section 482 Regulations Issued at Long Last; "Comparable Profit" Analysis Introduced. *Tax Notes International* (February 3): 207–210.

———. 1994. U.S. Releases Final Transfer Pricing Regulations under Section 482. *Tax Notes International* (July 11): 79–102.

U.S. Chamber of Commerce. Economics and Statistics Administration. Bureau of Economic Affairs. 1995. *Foreign Direct Investment in the United States: Preliminary 1993 Estimates.* Washington D.C.: U.S. Government Printing Office.

U.S. General Accounting Office (GAO). 1981. *IRS Could Better Protect U.S. Tax Interests in Determining the Income of Multinational Corporations: Report to the Chairman of the House Committee on Ways and Means.* Washington, D.C.: GAO.

———. 1995. *International Taxation, Transfer Pricing and Information on Nonpayment of Tax*. Washington, D.C.: GAO.

U.S. Treasury Department. Internal Revenue Service (IRS). 1988. *A Study of Intercompany Pricing*. Washington, D.C.: IRS.

———. 1992. *Report on the Application and Administration of Section 482*. Washington, D.C.: IRS.

———. 1994. *IRS Examination Data Reveal an Effective Administration of Section 482 Regulations: Report to the Associate Commissioner (Operations) by the Assistant Commissioner (Examination)*. Washington, D.C.: IRS.

4

Advance-Pricing Agreements and Other U.S. Programs Related to Transfer Pricing

In Chapter 3, we explained many major changes to section 482 of the Internal Revenue Code over the past three decades. Changes in legislation and regulations should facilitate the administration and enforcement of section 482. However, the new legislation and regulations will not resolve all the controversies concerning transfer pricing and international taxation. Over the past seven years, the U.S. Treasury Department and the IRS have initiated several innovative programs that have helped reduce controversy and uncertainty in multinational transfer pricing. In this chapter, we will discuss three of those programs: advance-pricing agreements (APAs), competent authority procedure, and transfer pricing arbitration.

THE ADVANCE-PRICING AGREEMENT (APA) PROGRAM

On March 1, 1991, the IRS released the official procedures for obtaining an APA in Revenue Procedure 91–22. The program was designed as a dispute resolution process, supplementing the traditional administrative, judicial, and treaty mechanisms for resolving intercompany pricing issues. That Revenue Procedure incorporated extensive comments received from tax practitioners, taxpayers and professional organizations, numerous functions within the IRS, and several U.S. treaty partners. The document also reflected the IRS experience with four experimental APAs. Shortly after the Revenue Procedure was released, the first APA was completed between the Apple Computer Company and the IRS. That APA covered the sales of goods to an Australian affiliate, and the agreement was between the Apple Company, the IRS, and the Australian Taxation Office. The duration of the initial agreement was for four years.

Since April 1991, many other APAs have been completed. As of June 30,

1996, there were 129 pending APAs at various stages of development. Of these, about half involved U.S. parent corporations and the other half, parent companies of various foreign nations. These cases involved business operations in Puerto Rico and 21 foreign countries. Also, as of June 30, 1996, there have been 64 APAs completed, many of which included bilateral agreements with treaty partners. In addition, various taxpayers have held preliminary talks with the IRS on 50 new APA matters. Many industries are involved in the APA process. These industries include automotive, beverages, chemicals, consumer products, electronics, financial products, oil and oil products, pharmaceuticals, retail, and services.

On May 25, 1995, the IRS issued Announcement 95–49 as a proposed update of Revenve procedure 91–22. The new revenue procedure restates the rules currently contained in Revenue Procedure 91–22 and makes some substantial changes (Patton and Wood, 1995).

In the following sections, we will explain the major objectives of the APA program, the nature and legal effect of an APA, the system of program administrators used at the IRS, the APA process and information required, potential benefits and risks of the process, and possible IRS audits after the APA is in effect. Major changes that have been proposed to update the APA Revenue Procedure will also be presented.

Major Objectives of the APA Program

In the proposed Revenue Procedure, published on May 24, 1995, the IRS explains that "the APA process is designed to be a flexible problem-solving process, based on cooperative and principled negotiations between taxpayers and the [Internal Revenue] Service." In its description of the APA program, the IRS also spells out the general objectives of the APA program as follows:

1. to enable taxpayers to arrive at an understanding with the IRS on three basic issues:
   i. the factual nature of the intercompany transactions to which the APA applies;
   ii. an appropriate transfer pricing methodology (TPM) applicable to those transactions; and
   iii. the expected range of results from applying the TPM to the transactions. However, in appropriate cases, the IRS will consider APAs that set forth a TPM without the specification of any range;
2. to do so in an environment that encourages common understanding and cooperation between the taxpayer and the IRS and that harmonizes and incorporates the opinions and views of all the IRS functions involved with the taxpayer;
3. to come to an agreement in an expedited fashion, as compared with the traditional method, which entails separate and distinct dealings with the Examination, Appeals, and Competent Authority functions and/or possible subsequent litigation; and
4. to come to an agreement in a cost-effective fashion for both the taxpayer and the IRS.

Therefore, the APA program is a mechanism to promote voluntary compliance and reduce the administrative burden on both the IRS and taxpayers. The program is designed to lessen the uncertainties and enhance the predictability of the tax consequences of international intrafirm transactions.

The Nature and Legal Effect of an APA

An APA is a binding agreement between the IRS and the taxpayer on the prospective application of a TPM, consistent with the arm-length standard, for the taxpayer's transfer pricing practices. An APA may or may not cover all of the taxpayer's pricing arrangements. Revenue Procedure 91–22 allows a taxpayer the flexibility to limit its APA to "specified prospective tax years," "specified affiliates," and "specified intercompany transactions." The APA may be applied to prior tax years with the consent of the IRS. In addition, the pricing procedure applies only to international intercompany transactions and is designed to determine both intercompany transfer pricing and resulting inventory costs (Feinschreiber, 1993).

An APA is a renewable agreement that can be unilateral (agreed to by the IRS), bilateral (agreed to by the IRS and one foreign tax authority), or multilateral (including two or more foreign tax authorities). The APA reduces the burden on the taxpayer of dealing separately with the various functions of the IRS involved with transfer pricing issues. The agreement also simplifies the procedures for dealing with different tax authorities in cases of bilateral and multilateral APAs. Many countries, including Australia, Canada, Japan, and the Netherlands, have enacted legislation and established organizations for their APA programs. (The program guidelines released by foreign tax authorities will be discussed in subsequent chapters, where we explain their transfer pricing regulations.)

Revenue Procedure 91–22 requires the taxpayer applying for an APA to indicate the functional currency of each party and the currency in which the payment is to be made (section 5.03[6]). The taxpayer also has to describe the "significant financial accounting methods" that have a "direct bearing" on the proposed transfer pricing methodology (TPM)." If there are significant financial and accounting differences between the United States and foreign countries that have "a direct bearing" on the proposed TPM, the taxpayer has to explain them as well.

An APA has to specify the critical assumptions under which the APA can be applied. Revenue Procedure 91–22 defines a critical assumption as "any fact about the taxpayer, a third party, or an industry that would significantly affect the substantive terms of the APA if it changed" (section 5.07). A critical assumption may change as a result of uncontrollable changes in economic circumstances (such as substantial devaluation of a foreign currency). It may also be altered by a taxpayer's action due to changes in business strategies. Therefore, taxpayers must be careful in selecting the critical assumptions. As Feinschreiber

(1993) points out, "Selecting a critical assumption that is too broad may invalidate the APA *ab initio*, but selecting a critical assumption that is too narrow may invalidate the APA because even the most minor change in the facts might be limited by the critical assumptions"(pp. 579–580).

The APA Program Administration at the IRS

The IRS has organized a multifunctional team to administer the APA program. The team is composed of personnel from District Office Examination, Appeals, the Office of the Assistant Commissioner (International), and the Office of the Associate Chief Counsel (International), who join as a partnership to represent the IRS. According to the IRS, the involvement of all interested parties from the start provides great certainty and reduces compliance costs for taxpayers seeking APAs. The APA program has a director, a prefiling coordinator and many other full-time staff. The official address of the program is: APA Program, Office of the Associate Chief Counsel (International), Internal Revenue Service, P.O. Box 23764, Washington, D.C. 20026–3764.

The program has a Policy Board whose members include the associate chief counsel (international), assistant commissioner (international), and assistant commissioner (examination). The board establishes policy on matters of substantial general importance pertaining to the APA Program and resolves issues of special importance that arise in connection with particular APA requests or renewals.

In an address to the public on October 11, 1994, Director Michael C. Durst noted that "the pace of growth [of the APA program] will pick up more dramatically as the APA process continues to gain acceptance among treaty partners." He stressed the need for good case management and reasonably prompt resolution of cases. In the future, Durst stated, "We need to use the special procedural advantages of the APA approach—namely, streamlined access to taxpayer information and the less-adversarial nature of APA proceedings—to reach workable and fair agreements as promptly as possible."

The APA Process and Information Required

The process of applying for, and obtaining, an APA can be long and expensive. However, a successful APA may replace the need for costly and time-consuming examinations of transfer pricing practices. The major steps of an APA process are shown in Figure 4.1. Step 1 begins with an economic analysis for a chosen TPM and testing of the TPM with existing cases. According to Olson, Boykin, and Schwartz (1994), "An economic analysis is key in deciding whether to pursue an APA, in choosing the TPM to be employed in the APA, and in ensuring that the ultimate agreement will allow the taxpayer adequate flexibility to adjust to changes in markets and competitive conditions" (p. 1325). Based on the results of the economic analysis, in step 2, a decision should be

Figure 4.1
Major Steps of an APA Process

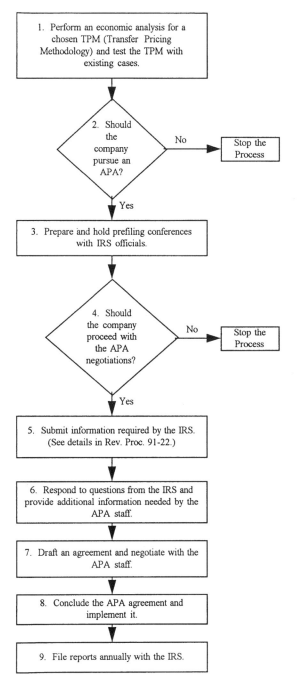

made as to whether to pursue an APA. If the decision is made to pursue an APA, the taxpayer should make an appointment to hold a prefiling conference with IRS officials. More than one prefiling conference may be arranged if necessary. The conference is usually held with representatives of the Office of the Associate Chief Counsel (International) in Washington, D.C., and there is no charge. The main purpose of the prefiling conferences is to assess the situation to determine whether an APA is appropriate for the taxpayer. Some authors (e.g., Feinschreiber, 1993; Fallon, 1995) have suggested that the taxpayers should be prepared to discuss the following issues at the prefiling conference(s):

—the types of data, documentation, and economic analysis needed;

—the need for an independent expert;

—the appropriateness of the proposed transfer pricing methodology;

—the parties to the APA and the transactions and businesses to be covered;

—whether the APA will be prospective only or will include a rollback to prior years;

—the possibility of agreement with competent authorities; and

—IRS scheduling, coordination, and evaluation.

After the prefiling conference(s), the taxpayer should have some idea about the data, documentation, and analyses the IRS requires; the suitability of the proposed TPM; whether an independent consultant is needed; and the likelihood that the agreement may be approved for all parties involved. At this point, the taxpayer can decide whether to proceed with the formal APA request (step 4). If a decision is made to apply for an APA, the taxpayer may have to submit detailed information required by the IRS. The formal APA application includes a $5,000 fee and submission of the following types of information (the original and seven copies) according to Revenue Procedure 91–22:

—general factual background information;

—information about the proposed transfer pricing methodology (TPM) that does not involve a cost-sharing arrangement; and

—specific information for a cost-sharing APA.

In the proposed update of APA revenue procedure, the user fee for each request and each renewal is to be increased to $10,000, except as reduced pursuant to the procedure for certain U.S. citizens with sales revenue of less than $100 million (Section 5.14). The general factual information includes the following items, unless agreed otherwise in the prefiling conference(s):

1. names of the organizations, trades, businesses, and transactions that will be subject to the APA;

2. names, addresses, telephone numbers, and taxpayer identification numbers of all parties to the requested APA;

3. completed Form 2848 for all persons authorized to represent the parties in the APA request;

4. a brief description of the general history of business operations, worldwide organizational structure, ownership, capitalization, financial arrangements, principal businesses, the places where such businesses are conducted, and major transaction flows of the parties;

5. representative financial and tax data of the parties for the past three years, along with other relevant data and supporting documents. These documents include, but are not limited to, the following:

   a. Form 5471 (''Information Return of U.S. Persons with Respect to certain Foreign Corporations'');

   b. Form 5472 (''Information Return of a 25% Foreign-Owned) U.S. Corporation or a Foreign Corporation Engaged in a U.S. Trade or Business'');

   c. tax returns, financial statements, and annual reports;

   d. pertinent U.S. and foreign government filings such as customs reports, Security and Exchange Commission (SEC) filings, and so forth;

   e. existing pricing, distribution, or licensing agreements;

   f. marketing and financial studies; and

   g. companywide accounting procedures, business segment reports, budgets, projections, business plans, and worldwide product line or business segment profitability reports.

6. the functional currency used by each party and the currency with which payment between parties will be made for the transactions covered by the APA;

7. the tax year for each party;

8. a description of financial and accounting methods having a direct bearing on the proposed TPM;

9. an explanation of any significant financial and tax accounting difference, if any, between the United States and the foreign countries involved that have a direct bearing on the proposed TPM;

10. a discussion of any relevant statutory provisions, tax treaties, court decisions, regulations, revenue rulings, or revenue procedures that relate to the proposed TPM;

11. an explanation of the taxpayer's and the government's positions on previous and current issues at the examination, appeals, judicial, or competent authority levels that relate to the proposed TPM. Similar information may be required for foreign tax authorities.

Taxpayers are required to follow the final section 482 regulations in developing the proposed TPM. The specific factual items needed for a proposed TPM include the following:

1. pertinent measurements of profitability and return on investment to provide a basis for comparison to similar businesses;

2. a functional analysis of each party, showing the economic activities performed, the assets employed, the economic costs incurred, and the risks assumed;

3. an economic analysis of the general industry pricing practices and economic functions performed within the markets and geographical areas to be covered by the agreement;

4. a list of the taxpayer's competitors and a discussion of any businesses that may be comparable or similar to the taxpayer's; and

5. a detailed presentation of criteria used to identify possible independent comparable or similar businesses.

For an APA involving a cost-sharing arrangement, the taxpayer has to submit the following 17 specific factual items to establish that the cost sharing arrangement is bona fide (Viehe, 1991):

1. the original date of the arrangement, the date that it was written, and the date each participant entered into the agreement;

2. the text of the arrangement, along with any agreements, amendments, addenda, exhibits, and previous agreements for which the current agreement is a successor;

3. the history of business operations, the geographic locations, and the principal business activities of each of the participants;

4. each participant's original contribution to the arrangement, both tangible and intangible;

5. details of royalties or other amounts paid to any participants who contributed intangibles and the method used to compute the amount of such payments;

6. documentation of provision for research and development to be conducted in general product areas, processes, or services for further research and development of specific products;

7. how each participant's benefit or expected benefit can be measured;

8. which costs are to be shared or excluded and how the division of cost is based;

9. the ownership rights of each participant in developed intangibles;

10. whether participants have an established procedure for periodically estimating the expected benefits that each will receive from the research and development and for adjusting each participant's share of costs accordingly;

11. the accounting procedures used to determine each entity's contribution and whether these procedures have been uniformly followed;

12. how the cost-sharing payments made and received have been treated for U.S. income tax purposes;

13. each participant's gross and net profitability with regard to the product area covered by the arrangement;

14. whether new participants may join the arrangement and, if so, the mechanism used

to determine how and when they will pay for any partially or fully developed intangible property; how the arrangement provides for the expansion of an existing participant's rights; the mechanism used to repurchase the rights of a participant that withdraws from the arrangement or of a participant that will not be using its rights in the active conduct of its trade or business; and an explanation of the financing arrangements for these matters;

15. whether any payments are made for contract research, the manner in which such payments are accounted for by the participants, and how such payments are treated for U.S. income tax purposes;

16. whether any payments are received from third parties for the licensing or selling of intangible property developed through the arrangement and how such payments are treated for U.S. income tax purposes; and

17. representative internal manuals, directives, guidelines, and similar documents prepared for accounting, financial, or managerial personnel for the purposes of implementing or operating the cost-sharing arrangement.

To complete the APA request, the taxpayer must include a perjury statement (section 5.11) and the signature(s) of the taxpayer or its authorized representative (section 5.12). Then the request can be submitted to the office of the associate chief counsel (international).

After receiving the APA request, the IRS will evaluate the taxpayer's proposal by reviewing all the information submitted. Within 60 days after receiving the APA request, the IRS's APA team will contact the taxpayer to discuss the proposal or request any additional information that the team may need. Most of these actions are done in writing. The taxpayer not only has to respond to those questions but also has to provide additional information needed by the APA program staff (step 6). If the taxpayer does not provide the necessary information by the date specified by the IRS, the APA request is considered withdrawn.

Normally, it takes the IRS two to six months to complete the evaluation process. The IRS expects to reach an informal decision on the APA request within six to nine months after the taxpayer submits a request.

After the APA is approved by the IRS and other tax authorities involved, step 8 is to sign the APA agreement and implement it. The last step is to file annual reports with the IRS.

The main purpose of the annual report is to ensure that the taxpayer is complying with the terms of the agreement. The report may include, but need not be limited to, the following items:

1. A description of the actual operations and the transfer pricing methodology used during the year.

2. Changes in critical assumptions, if any, and the reasons for such changes.

3. A description of any compensating adjustments that have been made during the year. A compensating adjustment may be required for a number of reasons other than a change in any critical assumption. For example, inflation, currency fluctuations, and

sudden changes in market conditions may affect the range of arm's-length results from applying the proposed TPM. These types of adjustments apply to both the taxable income of the taxpayer and the earnings and profits of the related foreign entity.

Potential Benefits and Risks of the APA Process

The APA process is long and tedious. However, it may provide the following benefits, as explained in the program description released by the IRS:

1. By obtaining an APA, a taxpayer gains substantial certainty with respect to how the desired transfer pricing activities will be treated for U.S. tax purposes and, in the case of a bilateral APA, how U.S. transfer pricing activities will be treated by foreign tax authorities as well.

2. The APA process provides an environment in which the taxpayer, the IRS, and, where appropriate, the competent authorities cooperate to determine which transfer pricing method should apply to transfer pricing activities. The APA process stimulates a free flow of information between all parties involved in the process so as to come to a legally correct and practically workable result.

3. The APA can reduce the taxpayer's record-keeping burden. Taxpayers will have to keep records to substantiate only one reasonable methodology (the TPM agreed upon), and generally do not have the burden of keeping all documents potentially relevant to other methodologies that the IRS could consider in an examination.

4. The APA process may help taxpayers avoid extended litigation, subjects the TPM to extensive review, and retains legal merit.

5. The APA process provides the opportunity to resolve open years by rolling back the APA pricing methodology to resolve transfer pricing issues in prior years, with consent of the appropriate district, appeals, or competent authority.

Conversely, the taxpayer exposes itself to the following risks by applying for an APA:

1. The IRS may scrutinize the detailed industry and taxpayer-specific information submitted and the annual reports for each taxable year covered by the APA.

2. An APA does not shelter the taxpayer from the IRS's subsequent scrutiny regarding transfer pricing activities of the entity. In addition, the taxpayer is not sheltered from normal and routine audits by the district director on other issues.

3. The critical assumptions may change. What appeared to be a reasonable TPM at the time the APA was signed may seem quite disadvantageous later.

4. The cost of obtaining an APA may be significant. In addition to the $5,000 filing fee, payments to consultants and independent experts may range from $50,000 for a simple APA to $1 million for one requiring the services of many lawyers and accountants (Fallon, 1995). A taxpayer needs to weigh the direct and indirect costs of the APA against the expenses of undergoing transfer pricing audits in several jurisdictions (Ryan and Patton, 1991).

In a recent study done by Borkowski (1996), only 10 percent of the U.S. MNCs responding had APAs or planned to have APAs in the future. In the United Kingdom, about 29 percent of respondent British MNCs stated that they had APAs or planned to apply for APAs in the future. The principal reasons cited by many MNCs for nonparticipation in APAs involve documentation, the cost involved, and confidentiality concerns with the information contained in the documentation. However, as the IRS and taxpayers gain experience from the ongoing APA processes, the popularity of the program will more than likely increase in the future. In the past, many writers (Viehe 1991; Olson, Boykin, and Schwartz, 1994; Fallon, 1995; Schwartz, Olson, and Boykin, 1995) praised the APA program for providing certainty in international intercompany trans-actions and reducing compliance costs for both the IRS and taxpayers. In the new *Transfer Pricing Guidelines for Multinational Enterprises and Tax Admin-istrations*, released in July 1995 (OECD, 1995), the Organization for Economic Cooperation and Development has also given its qualified support for the use of APAs:

There are some continuing issues regarding the form and scope of APAs that require greater experience for full resolution and agreement among Member countries, such as the question of unilateral APAs. While it is too early to make a final recommendation whether the expansion of such programs should be encouraged, it seems likely that in certain circumstances they will aid in resolving transfer pricing disputes. The Commit-tee on Fiscal Affairs intends to monitor carefully any expanded use of APAs and to pro-mote greater consistency in practice among those countries that choose to use them. (p. IV-52)

IRS Audits after the APA Is in Effect

The IRS can still carry out three types of tax audits for a taxpayer with an APA. These include an audit of transfer pricing methodology (TPM), the ex-amination of five substantive issues, and normal and routine audit adjustments.

The IRS district director may not reevaluate the TPM stated in the APA; however, other substantive aspects of the APA may be investigated. According to Fallon (1995), the five substantive issues that may be subject to IRS audits are as follows:

1. Has the taxpayer complied in good faith with the terms and conditions of the APA?

2. Are the material representations in the APA and the annual report accurate, and do they remain valid?

3. Are the data and supporting computations correct in all material aspects?

4. Are the critical assumptions underlying the APA valid?

5. Have the transfer pricing methodology and the critical assumptions been consistently applied?

After the examination, the IRS may conclude that the taxpayer has or has not performed satisfactorily on one or more of these substantive issues. The IRS district director will submit any of the unfulfilled issues to the chief counsel (international) or his or her delegate for resolution. After consideration, the chief counsel will instruct the district director to take one of the following actions (Fallon, 1995):

—apply the APA;

—revise the APA;

—cancel the APA; or

—revoke the APA.

In addition, the IRS district director may use normal and routine audit adjustments to monitor the computation of the operating results of the taxpayer's TPM during the taxable year or years under examination. This type of audit or adjustment does not affect the validity or applicability of the APA.

Major Changes in the Proposed Update of the APA Revenue Procedure

In 1995 the IRS issued a proposed update of the APA Revenue Procedure through Announcement 95–49, which restates both the language and substance of Revenue Procedure 91–22 and proposes new procedures and statements of applicable principles. Many of these new procedures and principles have already been incorporated in the APA process in response to taxpayers' demand. They are designed to achieve the following two objectives:

—to ensure that the views of the taxpayer and of all involved IRS personnel are represented effectively; and

—to resolve cases fairly and promptly.

Some significant changes to Revenue Procedure 91–22 are summarized as follows:

—Section 3.06 of the update describes the composition and function of the APA Policy Board.

—Section 3.07 emphasizes the IRS policy that the TPM should be used to resolve outstanding transfer pricing issues for prior taxable years.

—Section 5.01(3) has been revised to eliminate the requirement that taxpayers provide "certified" translations of foreign language documents. Noncertified translations will now be acceptable.

—Section 5.04(6) requires that the taxpayer describe the nature of the comparables search used in formulating a request. Taxpayers must explain why particular comparables were either accepted or rejected.

—The use fee for each request and each renewal has been increased to $10,000.

—Section 6.05 provides rules for "Case Plans and Schedules" and sets forth other procedures designed to ensure the prompt and careful resolution of APA cases.

—Section 7 was revised to reflect recent movement toward the use of bilateral and multilateral APAs when treaty countries are involved.

—Section 10.08 revises the provisions for "renewal of APAs" to eliminate the possible implication that the IRS is bound by the method used in the original APA.

Taxpayers interested in applying for an APA should contact the IRS APA Program to obtain copies of application forms and current regulations.

THE COMPETENT AUTHORITY PROCEDURE AND U.S. GUIDELINES

As of January 31, 1996, the United States has entered into 58 income tax treaties and 17 estate and gift tax treaties with other countries. These tax treaties are designed to achieve the following three objectives:

1. to prevent the double taxation of income, property, or property transfers by allocating or limiting the right of the source or the residence country to tax income or property;

2. to avoid discriminatory tax treatment of residents of the contracting states: and

3. to provide reciprocal administrative assistance in the prevention of tax avoidance and tax evasion.

Under the terms of most of these tax treaties, a mechanism exists to relieve international double taxation and to handle complaints that one treaty partner is taxing a resident of the other treaty partner in a manner inconsistent with the provisions of the tax treaty (Rooney and Fortunato, 1993). Each treaty country may designate a representative (the competent authority) to assist taxpayers in resolving transfer pricing or other disputes between taxing jurisdictions. In the United States, the IRS assistant commissioner (international) acts as competent authority in administering the operating provisions of tax treaties and in applying these treaties. Most U.S. treaty partners have also identified their competent authorities. Some examples are shown below:

—Canada: minister of national revenue (Revenue Canada);

—France: minister of economy and finance;

—Germany: federal minister of finance;

—Japan: minister of finance;

—United Kingdom: commissioner of the Inland Revenue.

The competent authorities in various countries can be important players in the APA process. U.S. regulations and guidelines for requesting competent authority assistance are stated in Revenue Procedure 91–23, released on March 18, 1991. In 1995, the IRS issued a proposed competent authority revenue procedure in Announcement 95–9. This proposed revenue procedure, if adopted, would supersede Revenue Procedure 91–23. In the following sections, we will describe some important roles of the competent authority and major guidelines in Revenue Procedure 91-23. Important changes in the proposed revenue procedure will also be discussed.

The Role of the Competent Authority

One important role of the competent authority is to act as the official liaison with counterparts in other countries. Besides administering all functions derived from the operating provisions of the tax treaties and tax information exchange agreements, the assistant commissioner (international) is responsible for interpreting and applying the tax treaties and determining the proper allocation of income between multijurisdictional taxpayers.

An eligible U.S. taxpayer can request competent authority assistance by following the procedures described in Revenue Procedure 91–23. No user fees are required for a request for competent authority assistance pursuant to Revenue Procedure 91–23. After receiving a request for assistance, the U.S. competent authority will notify the taxpayer as to whether the facts provide a basis for assistance.

Besides handling taxpayers' requests, the U.S. competent authority may initiate competent authority negotiations in any situation to protect U.S. interests. The U.S. competent authority can also conclude a bilateral or multilateral APA with the consent of the taxpayer.

Important Guidelines for Using the Competent Authority Procedure

When a U.S. taxpayer considers that the actions of the United States, the treaty country, or both may result in double taxation or deny or improperly restrict a benefit or safeguard to which the taxpayer is entitled under the terms of a tax treaty, the taxpayer may request assistance from the U.S. competent authority. According to section 2.02 of Revenue Procedure 91–23, if the taxpayer's request for competent authority consideration provides a basis for competent authority assistance, the U.S. competent authority will consult with the appropriate foreign competent authority for the purpose of avoiding taxation contrary to the provisions of the treaty. However, the U.S. competent authority generally will not accept a request for assistance or will cease providing assistance to the taxpayer under the following situations:

1. The taxpayer is not entitled to the treaty benefit or safeguard in question or to the assistance requested:

2. The taxpayer is only willing to accept a competent authority agreement under conditions that are unreasonable or prejudicial to the interests of the United States:

3. The taxpayer does not agree that competent authority negotiations are a government to government activity that does not include the taxpayer's participation in the negotiation proceedings:

4. The taxpayer does not furnish, upon request, sufficient information to determine whether the treaty applies to the taxpayer's facts and circumstances:

5. The taxpayer was found, in the course of the examination of its tax return, to have acquiesced in a foreign-initiated adjustment that involved significant legal or factual issues that otherwise would be properly handled through the competent authority process, and then unilaterally made a corresponding correlative adjustment or claimed an increased foreign tax credit on its U.S. tax return, without initially seeking U.S. competent authority assistance:

6. The taxpayer fails to comply with the revenue procedure; fails to cooperate with the U.S. competent authority; or failed to cooperate with the Internal Revenue Service during the examination of the years in issue, such that the ability of the U.S. competent authority to negotiate and conclude an agreement is significantly impeded.

In addition, the assistant Commissioner (international) will not, without the consent of the associate chief counsel (international), accept any request for assistance involving a case that has been designated for litigation.

With respect to requests for competent authority assistance involving the allocation of income and deductions between a U.S. taxpayer and a related party, the U.S. competent authority, in seeking to arrive at an agreement with a treaty country, will be guided by the arm's-length standards under the section 482 regulations and equivalent standards applicable to transactions between independent persons (Venuti, Gordon, and Fogarasi, 1995). Under section 3.03 of Revenue Procedure 91–23, the U.S. competent authority will also take into account all the facts and circumstances and the purpose of the income tax treaty to avoid double taxation.

After processing the taxpayer's request for assistance, the U.S. competent authority will notify the taxpayer of any agreement or partial agreement that is reached on the request. If the agreement is acceptable to the taxpayer, the agreement is not subject to administrative or judicial review. If the agreement is not acceptable to the taxpayer, the taxpayer may withdraw the request for assistance and may pursue all rights to review otherwise remaining available under U.S. or foreign laws.

Revenue Procedure 91–23 (section 7.01) requires the taxpayer to take protective measures or, if necessary, to advise a related person to take the protective measures that are necessary with the U.S. or foreign tax authorities so that the implementation of any agreement reached by the competent authorities is not barred by administrative, legal, or procedural barriers. This may include, but not be limited to, the filing of amended returns or protective claims for refund or credit, the staying of the expiration of any period of limitations on the making of a refund or other tax adjustment, avoiding the lapse or termination of the taxpayer's right to appeal any tax determination, complying with all applicable procedures for invoking competent authority consideration, and contesting an adjustment or seeking an appropriate correlative adjustment with respect to the U.S. or treaty country tax.

From the taxpayer's point of view, the competent authority procedures in the United States have a satisfactory record. For example, in 1992, IRS statistics show that full or partial tax relief was provided in nearly all competent authority cases (Feinschreiber, 1993; Lowell, Burge, and Briger, 1994). Full relief included correlative adjustments provided in 40.25 percent of the cases and adjustments withdrawn in 52.93 percent of the cases in 1992. Partial relief was provided in 3.65 percent of the cases during the same year, while no relief was granted in only 3.17 percent. One major complaint against the competent authority procedure is that it takes too long to resolve the cases. For example, the average time for completion of U.S.-initiated adjustments in 1991 was about 3.7 years, and for adjustments initiated by treaty partners, 2.4 years (Lowell, Burge, and Briger, 1994). However, Matthews (1994) reported that the number of days needed to complete a competent case has decreased substantially in recent years. For all competent authority cases, the number of days to complete a case was reduced from 1,201 days in 1990 to 552 days in 1994. The reduction in days needed to complete a U.S.-initiated case is very dramatic: from 1,577 days in 1990 to 439 days in 1994.

Major Changes in the Proposed Revenue Procedure

The proposed competent authority revenue procedure does not make any fundamental changes to the current procedure. The proposed procedure clarifies the existing process, expands the scope of the small-case competent authority procedure and provides for a new "simultaneous appeals procedure" and an "accelerated competent authority procedure" (Venuti, Gordon, and Fogarasi, 1995, p. 229). Major changes proposed in the new revenue procedure are summarized as follows:

—It consolidates provisions in Revenue Procedure 91–23 for rules to be followed when a treaty country proposes an adjustment and when the United States proposes an adjustment.

—It increases the maximum adjustment allowable under the small-case filing procedure to permit more taxpayers access to the simplified procedure. Under Revenue Procedure 91–23, the competent authority "small-case procedure" can be used by individuals and corporations if both the total proposed adjustment and total U.S. tax involved are not greater than the following:

Taxpayer	Proposed Adjustment	Proposed Tax
Individual	$50,000	$10,000
Corporation	$100,000	$25,000

The proposed procedure increases the thresholds for small-case procedure as follows:

Taxpayer	Proposed Adjustment
Individual	$100,000
Corporation	$200,000
Other	$200,000

—It establishes a new accelerated competent authority procedure, under which a taxpayer requesting competent authority assistance on an issue may also request that the competent authority attempt to resolve the same issue for subsequent filed return periods. The process should apply only to the extent that the substantially identical facts and issues exist for subsequent years.

—When a taxpayer disagrees with a proposed IRS adjustment, the taxpayer has three alternatives:

a. Pursue his or her right of administrative review with appeals before requesting competent authority assistance;

b. Request competent authority assistance; or

c. Request a simultaneous appeal procedure as described in section 7.02.

Changes in the proposed procedure, if implemented, will accelerate the competent authority procedure and clarify many issues faced by taxpayers seeking assistance.

TRANSFER PRICING ARBITRATION

Arbitration of Transfer Pricing Disputes and Rule 124

Arbitration is another approach to resolve transfer pricing disputes between the taxpayer and the IRS. In March 1992, Apple Computer, Inc., and the IRS entered into the first agreement to arbitrate a section 482 case. At about the same time, a signed stipulation ordering arbitration was presented to the U.S. Tax Court. This case was related to the transfer prices charged by Apple's Singapore subsidiary to Apple during the 1984–1986 fiscal years. The products involved were printed circuit boards for personal computers and other computer systems. Before this case entered the arbitration process, Apple and the IRS also settled an earlier transfer pricing case involving the same subsidiary for the fiscal years of 1981–1983. The arbitration decision on the Apple Computer case was handed down within 18 months from the time the stipulation was filed. According to a *Wall Street Journal* (''Apple Loses a Battle,'' 1993) report, ''Originally, Apple put its costs [for the printed circuit boards] at $131 million. The IRS argued that the fair value was only $16.3 million; that would make Apple's taxable income from resales in the U.S. far higher." At the end, the three panelists chose "IRS numbers over Apple Computer's." However, the actual numbers proposed by the arbitration panel were never disclosed. Other details of that case are described in Bergquist and Clark (1993) and Clolery (1993).

In the fall of 1993, the tax court used arbitration under Rule 124 of the U.S. Tax Court Rules of Practice and Procedure in the Apple Computer case. A similar case of the same magnitude could have taken five years or longer to finally resolve through traditional litigation (Richardson, 1994). Therefore, transfer pricing arbitration is a more efficient and cost-effective dispute resolution process than is conventional litigation.

As shown in Table 4.1, Rule 124 is an established procedure for voluntary binding arbitration. It is a straightforward procedure that has been used in a number of Tax Court cases related to valuation issues. In many respects, a binding arbitration award is similar to a final judgment rendered in a civil trial (Bergquist and Clark, 1993). However, binding arbitration awards (unlike judgments) typically do not require lengthy discussion of reasons or rationale for the decision. On the other hand, a nonbinding arbitration would allow parties to either accept the arbitration decision or return to litigation.

Arbitration Panel and Arbitration Procedure

The arbitration can be handled by an arbitrator or an arbitration panel. The Apple Computer case was handled by a three-person arbitration panel. The panel comprised one retired federal judge, one economist, and one industry expert. The IRS and Apple also agreed to split the costs equally. Bergquist and Clark (1993) suggested that the use of more than one arbitrator "because multiple decision makers may lower the chances of an award being inappropriately based on one particular argument or piece of evidence" (p. 561).

Typically, an arbitration procedure includes four types of activities: (1) prehearing activities; (2) discovery; (3) the arbitration hearing; and (4) posthearing and decision. The prehearing activities may include such activities as the identification of expert witnesses and exchange of relevant information between the parties involved. In the Apple Computer case, both the IRS and Apple agreed to set aside one day to educate the panel about the computer industry in the prehearing phase. In the discovery phase, the parties involved try to gather all relevant information and respond to formal and informal discovery requests made by other parties. The discovery rules are usually governed by the Tax Court Rules of Practice and Procedure. According to Bergquist and Clark (1993), taxpayers generally have an incentive to limit the invasiveness of discovery, whereas the IRS would like to have broad discovery powers.

Arbitration hearings for transfer pricing disputes can range from informal affairs with relaxed rules of evidence to procedures more closely akin to a trial (Bergquist and Clark, 1993). The parties involved can also set the rules and

Table 4.1
Rule 124 of the U.S. Tax Court Rules of Practice and Procedure

---

Rule 124. Voluntary Binding Arbitration
(a) Availability: The parties may move that any factual issue in controversy be resolved through voluntary binding arbitration. Such a motion may be made at any time after a case is at issue and before trial. Upon the filing of such a motion, the Chief Judge will assign the case to a Judge or Special Trial Judge for deposition of the motion and supervision of any subsequent arbitration.
(b) Procedure:
    (1) Stipulation Required: The parties shall attach to any motion filed under paragraph (a) a stipulation executed by each party or counsel for each party. Such stipulation shall include the matters specified in subparagraph (2).
    (2) Content of Stipulation: The stipulation required by subparagraph (1) shall include the following:
        (A)   a statement of the issues to be resolved by the arbitrator;
        (B)   an agreement by the parties to be bound by the findings of the arbitrator in respect of the issues to be resolved;
        (C)   the identity of the arbitrator or the procedure to be used to select the arbitrator;
        (D)   the manner in which payment of the arbitrator's compensation and expenses, as well as any related fees and costs, is to be allocated among the parties;
        (E)   a prohibition against ex parte communication with the arbitrator; and
        (F)   such other matters as the parties deem to be appropriate.
    (3) Order by Court: The arbitrator will be appointed by order of the Court, which order may contain such directions to the arbitrator and to the parties as the Judge or Special Trial Judge considers to be appropriate.
    (4) Report by the Parties: The parties shall promptly report to the Court the findings made by the arbitrator and shall attach to their report any written report or summary that the arbitrator may have prepared.

---

time limit for arbitration hearings. Presentations of evidence and witnesses will be done at the arbitration hearings. At the posthearing and decision phase, the panel will present its findings after examining all evidence and testimonies presented at the hearing, and will provide a final decision. The decision reached by the arbitrator(s) would be binding in a binding arbitration.

Arbitration to Resolve Impasses between Competent Authorities

In the past, arbitration procedures have been used extensively to resolve international trade disputes. The General Agreement on Tariffs and Trade (GATT) and its successor, the World Trade Organization, have developed sophisticated procedures and institutions for international trade arbitration. The North American Free Trade Agreement (NAFTA) also provides for an arbitration panel procedure to resolve disputes concerning antidumping or countervailing duty issues (OECD, 1995).

Arbitration can also be used to resolve impasses between competent authorities on transfer pricing and other issues. Most recently concluded U.S. tax treaties have provision for an arbitration procedure. These include the U.S.-German Income Tax Treaty, the U.S.-Netherlands Income Tax Treaty, and the U.S.-Mexico Income Tax Treaty (Rooney and Fortunato, 1993). The following is the arbitration procedure stated in Article 25(5) of the U.S.-German Income Tax Treaty:

Disagreements between the Contracting States regarding the interpretation or application of this convention shall, as far as possible, be settled by the competent authorities. If a disagreement cannot be resolved by the competent authorities it may, if both competent authorities agree, be submitted for arbitration. The procedures shall be agreed upon and shall be established between the Contracting States by notes to be exchanged through diplomatic channels.

The European Union has a transfer pricing arbitration convention to resolve transfer pricing disputes among member states. This convention became effective on January 1, 1995. If a case is submitted for arbitration, the decision of the arbitration board is binding.

In the 1995 OECD *Transfer Pricing Guidelines for Multinational Enterprises and Tax Administrations*, the OECD Committee on Fiscal Affairs agreed to undertake a study on tax arbitration procedure and to supplement the OECD guidelines (1995) with the conclusions of the study when it is completed.

SUMMARY AND CONCLUSIONS

This chapter describes three U.S. programs to resolve (or prevent) disputes in multinational transfer pricing: the APA program, competent authority procedure, and transfer pricing arbitration. The APA program was launched by the IRS in 1991. The APA process is a flexible problem-solving process based on cooperative and principled negotiations between taxpayers and the IRS. As of June 30, 1996, there were 129 pending APAs at various stages of development. Sixty-four APAs have been completed by June 30, 1996, many of which included bilateral agreements with treaty partners. Revenue Procedure 91–22 on the APA program is being updated by a proposed revenue procedure through Announcement 95–49. There are many potential benefits and risks associated with the APA process. The process can be lengthy and expensive; however, it is still a cost-effective mechanism to promote voluntary compliance and to reduce the administrative burden on both the IRS and taxpayers.

Competent authority procedure is another useful program to resolve transfer pricing disputes or other disputes between taxing jurisdictions. In the United States, the IRS's assistant commissioner (international) acts as the competent authority in administering the operating provisions of tax treaties and in applying those treaties. The competent authority procedure and major guidelines are provided in Revenue Procedure 91–23, released on March 18, 1991. Revenue Procedure 91–23 is also being revised by a proposed revenue procedure included in Announcement 95–9.

The competent authority procedure has had a successful record over the past five years. However, the time needed to complete the procedure is still too long (averaging 552 days in 1994). The expansion of the small-case-filing procedure should allow more taxpayers access to the simplified and more efficient procedure.

Arbitration procedures have been used extensively to resolve international trade disputes in the past. However, the use of arbitration to handle transfer pricing disputes between taxpayers and the IRS is a more recent phenomenon. We can learn a great deal from the arbitration proceedings for the Apple Computer case. Moreover, the new transfer pricing arbitration convention of the European Union should provide some impetus for adopting the transfer pricing arbitration procedure in the future.

REFERENCES

Apple Loses a Battle in Tax Arbitration, But Wins the War, the Judge Says. 1993. *Wall Street Journal* (September 6): A1.

Bergquist, Philip J., and Kenneth B. Clark. 1993. In Robert Feinschreiber, ed. *Transfer Pricing Handbook*. New York: John Wiley and Sons.

Boidman, Nathan, 1992. The Effect of the APA and Other U.S. Transfer Pricing Initiatives in Canada and Other Countries. *Tax Executive* (July–August): 254–261.

Borkowski, Susan C. 1992. Section 482, Revenue Procedure 91–22, and the Realities of Multinational Transfer Pricing. *International Tax Journal* (Spring): 59–68.

———. 1996. Advance Pricing (Dis)Agreements: Differences in Tax Authority and Transnational Corporation Opinions. *International Tax Journal* (Summer): 23–34.

Clolery, Paul. 1993. Apple Computer, IRS Mum on First Tax Arbitration. *Practical Accountant* (December): 10.

Cole, Robert T. 1995. Advance Pricing Agreement Practice under the New Rules. *Journal of Taxation* (October): 215–222.

Cox, Timothy W. 1994. Australian Tax Office Releases Draft Ruling on Advance Pricing Agreements. *Tax Notes International* (October 24): 1279–1280.

Ernst & Young. 1995. Transfer Pricing: Risk Reeducation and Advance Pricing Agreements. *Tax Notes International* (July 31): 293–310.

Fallon, Geralyn M. 1995. Advance Pricing Agreements: Policy and Practice. *Taxes* (September): 490–513.

Feinschreiber, Robert. 1992. Advance Pricing Agreements: Advantageous or Not? *CPA Journal* (June): 58–61.

———. 1993. *Transfer Pricing Handbook*. New York: John Wiley and Sons.

Lowell, Cym H., Marianne Burge, and Peter L. Briger. 1994. *U.S. International Transfer Pricing*. Boston: Warren, Goham and Lamont.

Matthews, Kathleen. 1994. Major U.S. Trading Partners Respond to U.S. Transfer Pricing Regulations. *Tax Notes International* (October 24): 1275–1278.

———. 1995. Non-U.S. Bank Gets APA for Interbranch Foreign Exchange Transactions. *Tax Notes International* (March 13): 891–893.

Olson, Lawrence S., Richard A. Boykin, and Michael N. Schwartz. 1994. Advance Pricing Agreements: The Role of the Economic Study. *Tax Notes International* (October 24): 1325–1330.

Organization for Economic Cooperation and Development (OECD). 1995. *Transfer Pricing Guidelines for Multinational Enterprises and Tax Administrations*. Paris: OECD.

Patton, Michael F., and Kenneth W. Wood. 1995. The APA Program Lifecycle Moves from Start-Up to Growth Stage: Proposed Update of Rev. Proc. 91–22. *Tax Management International Journal* (August 11): 363–370.

Richardson, Margaret M. 1994. Remarks of Margaret Milner Richardson. *Taxes* (December): 717–721.

Rooney, Paul C., Jr., and Darren R. Fortunato. 1993. Competent Authority. In Robert Feinschreiber, ed., *Transfer Pricing Handbook*. John Wiley and Sons.

Rubinstein, Aaron A., and Todd Tuckner. 1994. Should a Bank Enter into an Advance Pricing Agreement with the IRS? *Journal of Bank Taxation* (Fall): 22–30.

Ryan, Eric D., and Michael F. Patton. 1991. IRS Advance Pricing Agreements: Are They a Practical Means to Resolve Potential International Transfer Pricing Disputes? *Tax Management International Journal* (March 8): 115–123.

Schwartz, Michael N., Lawrence S. Olson, and Richard A. Boykin. 1994. Working with the APA Process. *Tax Notes* (June 6): 1359–1364.

———. 1995. APAs: Successfully Reaching Agreement. *Tax Notes International* (March 13): 957–960.

Shaughnessy, Scott. 1995. U.S. APA Program Offers "One-Stop Shoping!" *Tax Notes International* (August 14): 402–407.

Smith, Carlton M. 1991. Use of Advance Pricing Agreements Enhanced by New Revenue Procedure. *Journal of Taxation* (June): 374–378.

Tax Executive Institute (TEI). 1993. Comments on Rev. Proc. 91–22: Advance Pricing Agreements. *Tax Executive* (May–June): 247–250.

———. 1995. Announcement 95–49: Procedures for Securing an Advance Pricing Agreement. *Tax Executive* (September—October): 407–411.

Turro, John. 1994a. Netherlands Formalizes APA Procedures. *Tax Notes International* (November 14): 1531–1532.

———. 1994b. Pacific Association of Tax Administrators Reaches Consensus on Common APA Guidelines. *Tax Notes International* (November 7): 1431–1432.

Venuti, John, Richard A. Gordon, and Andre Fogarasi. 1995. Requesting Competent Authority Assistance: IRS Proposes New Procedure. *Tax Management International Journal* (May 12): 229–235.

Viehe, Karl William. 1991. Advance Pricing Agreement: Stability for Transfer Pricing. *International Tax Journal* (Winter): 46–71.

Wood, Robert W. 1991. Advance Rulings on Transfer Pricing Agreements Now Available. *Corporate Taxation* (May/June): 37–38, 48.

5

The OECD Reports and Guidelines
for Transfer Pricing

In Chapters 3 and 4, we reviewed many different aspects of transfer pricing regulations in the United States. We noted that U.S. regulations have changed substantially in the 1980s and the early 1990s. During the same period, many other countries and the Organization for Economic Co-operation and Development (OECD) have also issued new guidelines and regulations on transfer pricing. In this chapter, we will review the OECD reports and guidelines. Chapter 6 will discuss the transfer pricing regulations of Canada and Mexico, the two North American Free Trade Agreement (NAFTA) partners of the United States. Regulations of selected European countries will be discussed in Chapter 7, and similar regulations of selected countries in the Asian-Pacific Region will be covered in Chapter 8. The balance of Chapter 5 is divided into the following sections:

—the role of the OECD in establishing transfer pricing guidelines;

—the 1979 OECD report, *Transfer Pricing and Multinational Enterprises* (OECD 1979);

—the 1984 OECD report, *Transfer Pricing and Multinational Enterprises. Three Taxation Issues* (OECD 1984);

—the 1995 OECD *Transfer Pricing Guidelines for Multinational Enterprises and Tax Administrations* (OECD 1995); and

—a comparison between the OECD 1995 guidelines and the final regulations of Section 482 of the U.S. Internal Revenue Code.

In this chapter, we will focus our discussion primarily on the 1995 guidelines, the most current document. Most member countries of the OECD and many nonmember countries have adopted the OECD guidelines for transfer pricing.

THE ROLE OF THE OECD IN ESTABLISHING TRANSFER PRICING GUIDELINES

The OECD was established under a convention signed in Paris on December 14, 1960, to promote polices for achieving the following three broad objectives:

—to achieve the highest sustainable economic growth and employment and a rising standard of living in member countries, while maintaining financial stability, and thus to contribute to the development of the world economy;

—to contribute to sound economic expansion in member as well as nonmember countries in the process of economic development; and

—to contribute to the expansion of world trade on a multilateral, nondiscriminatory basis in accordance with international obligations.

As of July 1995, members of the OECD include Australia, Austria, Belgium, Canada, Denmark, Finland, France, Germany, Greece, Iceland, Ireland, Italy, Japan, Luxembourg, Mexico, the Netherlands, New Zealand, Norway, Portugal, Spain, Sweden, Switzerland, Turkey, the United Kingdom, and the United States. The OECD has long been active in promoting uniformity and consistency in regulations for avoiding double taxation and for achieving an equitable system of international taxation. Over the past two decades, the Committee on Fiscal Affairs of the OECD has issued a number of reports or guidelines in the areas of transfer pricing and international taxation.

The OECD takes the leadership role in developing international taxation principles and transfer pricing guidelines to the fulfill its mission "to contribute to the expansion of world trade on a multilateral, non-discriminatory basis and to achieve the highest sustainable economic growth in member countries" (OECD 1995, p. ii). In the past, this role has been performed mainly by the Committee on Fiscal Affairs of the OECD. One key objective is to build a consensus on international taxation principles and transfer pricing guidelines so as to avoid unilateral responses to these international and multilateral problems.

THE 1979 OECD REPORT

The 1979 report, *Transfer Pricing and Multinational Enterprises*, was prepared by the OECD Committee on Fiscal Affairs. The main objectives were "to set out as far as possible the considerations to be taken into account and to describe, where possible, generally agreed practices in determining transfer prices for tax purposes" (p. 9). The report also offered detailed guidelines for determining arm's-length prices for intrafirm trade of goods, technology and trademarks, intragroup services, and loans.

The 1979 report recommended the use of the following pricing methods for the transfer of tangible goods: (1) the comparable uncontrolled price method;

(2) the resale price method; (3) the cost plus method; and (4) other approaches when none of the first three methods could be applied satisfactorily. These methods were very similar to the ones suggested in the 1968 regulations for section 482 of the U.S. Internal Revenue Code. However, the 1979 OECD report did not require a mandatory order of priority as the section 482 regulations did. The views of the OECD Committee on Fiscal Affairs on the priority of the four methods were stated in paragraph 46 of the report:

The question arises whether it is possible to lay down any order of priority in using these methods. Clearly the comparable uncontrolled price method is basically preferable to other methods since it uses evidence most closely related to an arm's length price, but there may be cases where the evidence of resale profit mark-ups, production costs or other data may be more complete, more conclusive and more easily obtained than undisputable evidence of open market prices. There should always be the possibility, therefore, of selecting the method which provides the most cogent evidence in a particular case. It has to be recognized that an arm's length price will in many cases not be precisely ascertainable and that in such circumstances it will be necessary to seek for a reasonable approximation to it. Frequently, it may be useful to take account of more than one method of reaching a satisfactory approximation to an arm's length price in the light of the evidence available.

On the transfer prices between associated enterprises under contracts for licensing patents or know-how, the 1979 OECD report recommended that "the prices should be those which would be paid between independent enterprises acting at arm's length" (paragraph 91). The report also provided general guidelines for establishing transfer prices for the use of trademarks, intragroup services, and loans. All the guidelines recommended in the 1979 OECD report have been superseded by the 1995 guidelines (OECD, 1995), after the new guidelines were approved by the Committee on Fiscal Affairs on June 27, 1995, and by the OECD Council for publication on July 13, 1995.

THE 1984 OECD REPORT

The title of the 1984 report is *Transfer Pricing and Multinational Enterprises: Three Taxation Issues* (OECD, 1984). The 1984 report dealt with three taxation issues: (1) transfer pricing, corresponding adjustments, and the mutual agreement procedure; (2) the taxation of multinational banking enterprises; and (3) the allocation of central management and service costs. These three issues are discussed separately in three parts of the 1984 report.

On the first issue, corresponding adjustments "covers a broad area of problems which arise if the transfer prices or allocations of profit adopted by an enterprise in its dealing with an associated enterprise in another country are not accepted by the tax authorities of one or other of the countries concerned" (paragraph 1). If an adjustment to prices or allocations are proposed in one of the countries, the question arises as to whether a corresponding adjustment should be made in the other country or whether the original adjustment should be modified, with or without a corresponding adjustment in the other country.

In the first part of the report, the OECD Committee on Fiscal Affairs discussed the experience with procedures currently available for avoiding or relieving double taxation including corresponding adjustments and mutual agreement procedure. The report discussed the possibility of mandatory corresponding adjustments subject to arbitration. Some important conclusions and recommendations on corresponding adjustments and the mutual agreement procedure are shown below:

—The responsibility for minimizing the likelihood of double taxation arising from transfer pricing adjustments is, in the first place, that of the multinational company itself, which should arrange its transfer prices to conform with the arm's-length principle.

—The committee recommends that tax authorities do all they can to reach agreement on disputed transfer pricing adjustments or corresponding adjustments to eliminate double taxation.

—The committee regards the existing mutual agreement procedure provided by Article 25 of the 1977 OECD Model Convention as being a useful and, in general, very effective machinery for resolving disputes between tax authorities, not withstanding the criticisms that have been leveled at it.

—The committee does not recommend the adoption of a compulsory arbitration procedure to supersede or supplement the mutual agreement procedure.

—In the course of mutual agreement proceedings on transfer pricing matters, the taxpayers concerned should be given every reasonable opportunity to present the relevant facts and arguments to the competent authorities, both in writing and orally.

—Competent authorities should, where appropriate, develop and publicize domestic rules, guidelines and procedures relating to the use of mutual agreement (or competent authority) procedure. (In the 1995 report (OECD, 1995), the Committee on Fiscal Affairs provided revised guidelines on corresponding adjustments and the mutual agreement procedure.)

The second part of the 1984 report discusses the issues of taxation and transfer pricing of multinational banking enterprises. The report noted that the arm's-length principle is "as suitable for application in the case of banking enterprises as well as in the case of other enterprises, and no special problems arise in the case of operations conducted through subsidiaries and other affiliated companies" (paragraph 33 on p. 52). The appropriate arm's length rate of interest for a loan between associated banking or financial enterprises is the rate that would be charged in similar circumstances in a transaction between unrelated parties (paragraph 53 on p. 58).

The last part of the 1984 report dealt with issues on the allocation of central management and service costs. The report distinguished between the following types of central management services:

—administrative services, including planning, coordination, budgetary control, financial advice, computer services;

—assistance in the field of production, buying, distribution and marketing;

—services in staff matters such as recruitment and training; and

—research and development and the protection of intangible property for the entire company or parts of it.

The report noted that the following methods have been used in practice for charging group members for costs incurred by parent companies or group service centers for services provided to associated enterprises:

—charging directly for individualized services;

—allocating and apportioning costs to each of the associated enterprises (cost sharing);

—remunerating the group services center by a contribution from other parts of the enterprise related to some broad aspect of the business of the enterprises concerned; and

—the inclusion of a markup in the price of products sold to an affiliate by the company that incurs the central management and service costs.

The first method can be characterized as a direct method, whereas the others may be referred to as indirect methods. The report stated that "the arm's-length criterion is met under direct method as long as the amount charged is an arm's-length amount" (paragraph 56 on p. 85). On indirect methods, the report suggested that "the most appropriate indirect method is generally recognized to be one which is based on sharing among the beneficiaries, in proportion to the benefits received or expected, the actual costs incurred in providing the services" (paragraph 65 on p. 87).

THE 1995 OECD GUIDELINES

The 1995 OECD Guidelines, *Transfer Pricing Guidelines for Multinational Enterprises and Tax Administration*, is a long and comprehensive document. These 1995 guidelines are intended to be a revision and compilation of previous reports prepared by the OECD Committee on Fiscal Affairs addressing issues on transfer pricing and international taxation. These reports include the 1979 report, *Transfer Pricing and Multinational Enterprises* (OECD, 1979), and the 1984 report, *Transfer Pricing and Multinational Enterprises: Three Taxation Issues* (OECD, 1984). The 1995 guidelines also draw upon discussion from another OECD task force report (OECD, 1993) on the proposed 1992 section 482 regulations of the U.S. Internal Revenue Code. In that 1993 report, the OECD was very critical of the proposed 1992 Section 482 regulations. The report stated that "the implementation of the proposed 482 Regulations in their present form could risk undermining the consensus that has been built up over a number of years on the application of the arm's length principle and thereby increase the risk of economic double taxation'' (OECD, 1993 p. vii). However, in the same report, the OECD also provided many suggestions to improve the proposed Section 482 regulations. Some of these suggestions were adopted by the Internal Revenue Service in the final regulations issued on July 1, 1994.

On July 8, 1994, the OECD issued the discussion draft of Part I (''Principles and Methods'') of *Transfer Pricing Guidelines for Multinational Enterprises and Tax Administrations*. On March 8, 1995, the OECD released Part II of the discussion draft, dealing with documentation, cost contribution arrangements, special considerations related to intangibles and intragroup services, and other issues. Both parts of the draft report and public comments were reviewed by the OECD working committee on transfer pricing. The final guidelines were approved by the Committee on Fiscal Affairs on June 27, 1995; they were approved for publication by the OECD Council on July 13, 1995. The first five chapters of the final guidelines were released in July 1995, and Chapters VI and VII were published in March 1996. Chapter VIII, on cost contribution arrangements, was to be released in the future. One key objective of the 1995 guidelines is ''to help tax administrations and MNEs [Multinational Enterprises] by indicating ways to find mutually satisfactory solutions between tax administrations and MNEs and avoiding costly litigation'' (OECD, 1995, paragraph 19). Because the OECD committee intends to continue its work in transfer pricing, it issued the 1995 guidelines in looseleaf format.

The 1995 guidelines contain detailed discussions and guidelines for multinational companies and tax administrations in the following areas:

—the arm's-length principle and its application guidelines;

—various transfer pricing methods and application guidelines;

—administrative approaches for avoiding and resolving transfer pricing disputes. These include corresponding adjustments, mutual agreement procedure, simultaneous tax examinations, safe harbors, advance-pricing arrangements, and arbitration;

—general guidelines for tax administrations in developing rules and/or procedure on documentation required for a transfer pricing inquiry;

—special considerations for the transfer of intangible property; and

—special considerations for intragroup services.

All of these topics will be discussed in the following sections except simultaneous tax examinations and safe harbors, because the OECD guidelines in these two areas are intended mainly for tax administrations.

The Arm's-Length Principle and Application Guidelines

The authoritative statement of the arm's-length principle can be found in paragraph 1 of Article 9 of the OECD Model Tax Convention. This convention is the basis of bilateral tax treaties involving OECD member countries and some nonmember countries. Article 9 of the convention states:

[When] conditions are made or imposed between . . . two [associated] enterprises in their commercial or financial relations which differ from those which would be made between independent enterprises, then any profits which would, but for those conditions, have accrued to one of the enterprises, but, by reason of those conditions, have not accrued, may be included in the profits of that enterprise and taxed accordingly.

According to the 1995 OECD report, the arm's-length principle should be adopted for several reasons. The most important is that the principle provides broad parity of tax treatment for multinational companies and independent enterprises.

Because the arm's length principle puts associated and independent enterprises on a more equal footing for tax purposes, it avoids the creation of tax advantages and disadvantages that would otherwise distort the relative competitive positions of either type of entity. In so removing these tax considerations from economic decisions, the arm's length principle promotes the growth of international trade and investment. (paragraph 1.7)

Another reason is that a deviation from the principle would threaten the international consensus and substantially increase the risk of double taxation. Double taxation means "the inclusion of the same income in the tax base by more than one tax administration, when either the income is in the hands of different taxpayers (economic double taxation, for associated enterprises) or the income is in the hands of the same juridical entity (juridical double taxation, for permanent establishments)" (paragraph 4.2). Double taxation is undesirable because it is a potential barrier to international trade and cross-border investment. Therefore, it is the view of the OECD that the arm's-length principle should govern the evaluation of transfer prices among associated enterprises.

The OECD report also provides the following guidelines for applying the arm's-length principle (ALP):

1. The application of the ALP is generally based on a comparison of the conditions in a controlled transaction with the conditions in transactions between independent enterprises. In order for such comparisons to be useful, the economically relevant characteristics of the situations being compared must be sufficiently comparable (paragraph 1.15).

2. When comparing the conditions in a controlled transaction with those of uncontrolled transactions, material differences between the compared transactions should be taken into account. It is also necessary to compare attributes of the transactions or enterprises that would affect conditions in arm's-length dealings. We need to consider such important attributes as the characteristics of the property or services transferred, the functions performed by the parties, the contractual terms, the economic circumstances of the parties, and the business strategies the parties pursue.

3. The ALP does not require the application of more than one method. "While in some cases the choice of a method may not be straightforward and more than one method may be initially considered, generally it will be possible to select one method that is apt to provide the best estimation of an arm's length price" (paragraph 1.69).

The report also clarifies the factors that are essential in determining comparability between controlled and uncontrolled transactions. For example, the report identifies the important characteristics of property or services as follows:

In the case of transfers of tangible property, the physical features of the property, its quality and reliability, and the availability and volume of supply; in the case of provision of services, the nature and extent of the services; in the case of intangible property, the form of transaction (e.g., licensing or sale), the type of property (e.g., patent, trademark, or know-how), the duration and degree of protection, and the anticipated benefits from the use of the property. (paragraph 1.19)

On the functions that taxpayers and tax administrations may need to identify and compare, the report suggests the following: design, manufacturing, assembling, research and development, servicing, purchasing, distribution, marketing, advertising, transportation, financing, and management. The major functions performed by the parties involved should also be examined.

On economic circumstances that might be relevant in determining market comparability, the report provides a number of examples as follows:

—the geographic location;

—the size of the markets;

—the extent of competition in the markets and the relative competitive position of the buyers and sellers;

—the availability of substitute goods and services;

—the level of supply and demand in the market as a whole and in a particular region;

—consumer purchasing power;

—the nature and extent of government regulation of the market;

—costs of production, including the costs of land, labor, and capital;

—transport costs;

—the level of the market; and

—the date and time of transactions.

The report also suggests that we examine many components of business strategies, including innovation and new product development, degree of diversification, risk aversion, assessment of political changes, input of existing and planned labor laws, and market penetration strategies. In addition, the report recommends the use of multiple-year data to arrive at a single arm's-length price or a range of figures that can be used to evaluate a controlled transaction.

Transfer Pricing Methods and Application Guidelines

Chapters II and III of the 1995 report explain the following transfer pricing methods in detail: (1) The three traditional transaction methods that include comparable uncontrolled price method (CUP), resale price method (RPM), and cost plus method (CPLM); (2) transactional profit methods that include profit split method (PSM) and transactional net margin method (TNMM); and (3) global formulary apportionment method (GFA). Under many circumstances, the three traditional transaction methods (CUP, RPM, CPLM) and the two transactional profit methods can be used as arm's length prices. GFA however, is treated as a non–arm's-length approach and rejected by the OECD. Each of these methods is discussed separately.

The Comparable Uncontrolled Price Method (CUP). As defined in the report, the CUP method "compares the price charged for property or services transferred in a controlled transaction to the price charged for property or services transferred in a comparable uncontrolled transaction in comparable circumstances" (paragraph 2.6). The CUP method is considered "the most direct and reliable way to apply the arm's length principle" if a comparable uncontrolled transaction can be found (paragraph 2.7).

For the purpose of the CUP method, an uncontrolled transaction is comparable to a controlled transaction if one of the following two conditions is met:

1. none of the differences (if any) between the transactions being compared or between the enterprises undertaking those transactions could materially affect the price in the open market; or
2. reasonably accurate adjustments can be made to eliminate the material effects of such differences.

If a reasonably accurate adjustment cannot be made, it may be necessary to combine the CUP method with other, less direct methods or to use such methods instead.

The Resale Price Method (RPM). The OECD provides a rather long explanation for the RPM, as follows:

The resale price method begins with the price at which a product that has been purchased from an associated enterprise is resold to an independent enterprise. This price (the resale price) is then reduced by an appropriate gross margin (the "resale price margin") representing the amount out of which the reseller would seek to cover its selling and other operating expenses and, in the light of the functions performed (taking into account assets used and risks assumed), make an appropriate profit. What is left after subtracting the gross margin can be regarded, after adjustment for other costs associated with the purchase of the product (e.g., customs duties), as an arm's length price for the original transfer of property between the associated enterprises. (paragraph 2.14)

This method is most useful when it is applied to marketing operations. It may be difficult to use the RPM method if the intangible goods are further processed or incorporated into a more complicated product before resale. Additionally, a resale price margin is more accurate where it is realized within a short time of the reseller's purchase of the goods. For the purpose of the RPM method, an uncontrolled transaction is comparable to a controlled transaction if one of the following two conditions is met:

1. none of the differences (if any) between the transactions being compared or between the enterprises undertaking those transactions could materially affect the resale price margin in the open market; or
2. reasonably accurate adjustments can be made to eliminate the material effects of such differences.

The Cost Plus Method (CPLM). Under this method, the transfer price is the costs incurred by the supplier of property (or services) plus an appropriate profit in light of the functions performed and the market conditions. According to the report, the CPLM is most useful "where semifinished goods are sold between related parties, where related parties have concluded joint facility agreements or long-term buy-and-supply arrangements, or where the controlled transaction is the provision of service" (paragraph 2.32).

For the purpose of CPLM, an uncontrolled transaction is comparable to a controlled transaction if one of the following two conditions is met:

1. none of the differences (if any) between the transactions being compared or between the enterprises undertaking those transactions materially affect the cost plus mark up in the open market; or
2. reasonably accurate adjustments can be made to eliminate the material effects of such differences.

The OECD's definitions of the three traditional transaction methods (CUP, RPM, and CPLM) are very similar to those defined in the final regulations of Section 482 of the Internal Revenue Code. (Those definitions in the IRS final regulations can be found in Chapter 4 of this book.)

On the applications of transfer pricing methods, the OECD indicates its preference of traditional transaction methods over all other methods: "Traditional transaction methods are the most direct means of establishing whether conditions in the commercial and financial relations between associated enterprises are arm's length. As a result, traditional transaction methods are preferable to other methods" (paragraph 2.49).

However, the OECD acknowledges that complexities of real-life business situations may put practical difficulties in the way of the application of the traditional transaction methods. In such cases, taxpayers can apply the following two transactional profit methods: the profit split method and the transactional net margin method. A transactional profit method examines the profit from a controlled transaction to determine the transfer price for the controlled transaction. According to the OECD report, two conditions must be fulfilled in order to use a transactional profit method:

1. Transactional profit methods can be accepted only if they are compatible with Article 9 of the OECD Model Tax Convention, especially with regard to comparability. This can be achieved by applying the methods in a manner that approximates arm's length pricing, which requires that the profits arising from particular controlled transactions be compared to the profits arising from comparable transactions between independent enterprises (paragraph 3.3).

2. Transactional profit methods should not be used so as to result in overtaxing enterprises mainly because they make profits lower than the average or in undertaxing enterprises that make higher-than-average profits (paragraph 3.4).

The Profit Split Method (PSM). The PSM method first identifies the profit to be split for the related enterprises from a controlled transaction and then splits the profit between the related enterprises on an economically valid basis that approximates the division of profits that would have been reflected in an arm's-length agreement. The distribution of profit between related enterprises is usually based on the functions performed by each enterprise.

Like all other transfer pricing methods, the PSM has its share of strengths and weaknesses. The most important strength of the method is that it can be applied to cases where comparable transactions are not available. Another advantage of the method is that parties to the controlled transaction will not be left with extreme and improbable profit result because the contributions of both parties to the transaction are evaluated. However, a significant weakness of PSM is that the external market data used in valuing the contributions of the related enterprises may not be closely connected to the controlled transactions. As the report noted, ''The more tenuous the nature of the external market data used when applying the profit split method, the more subjective will be the resulting allocation of profits'' (paragraph 3.8).

Another problem for applying PSM is that it may be difficult to obtain information concerning foreign affiliates. In addition, it is not easy to combine revenue and costs of all the related enterprises involved in the controlled transactions when these enterprises are using different currencies and accounting principles.

There are two basic approaches in applying the PSM method: contribution analysis and residual analysis. These two approaches are not exhaustive or mutually exclusive. Under a contribution analysis approach, the combined profits of the controlled transactions would be divided between the related enterprises based upon the relative value of the functions performed by each party, and external market data indicating how independent enterprises would have divided profits in similar situations (paragraph 3.16).

Under a residual analysis approach, the combined profit from the controlled transactions is divided in two stages. In the first stage, each party is allocated sufficient profit to provide it with a basic return appropriate for the type of transactions involved. In the second stage, any residual profit (or loss) remaining would be allocated among the parties based on an analysis of the facts and circumstances that might indicate how this residual would have been divided between independent enterprises (paragraph 3.19). Some examples for dividing the residual profit (or loss) are provided in paragraphs 3.20 through 3.22 of the report.

Transactional Net Margin Method (TNMM). The TNMM examines the net profit margin (e.g., return on assets, return on sales, or other, similar measures) that a taxpayer realizes from a controlled transaction to derive a transfer price for the controlled transaction. A TNMM operates in a manner similar to the cost plus and resale price methods. The net margin of the taxpayer from the controlled transaction should be established by reference to the net margin that the taxpayer earns in comparable uncontrolled transactions.

The TNMM has several strengths and weaknesses. One strength is that the net margins are less affected by transactional differences than is the case with price, as used in the CUP or RPM methods. Moreover, because the TNMM typically applies to only one of the related enterprises, it is not necessary to determine the functions performed and responsibilities assumed by all parties involved. The most significant weakness of the method however, is that the net margin of a taxpayer can be influenced by factors that either do not have an effect or have a less substantial or direct effect on price or gross margins. This makes it difficult to determine reliable arm's-length net margins. In addition, information on uncontrolled transactions may not be available at the time the controlled transaction takes place. The OECD report noted that ''very few countries have much experience in the application of the transactional net margin method and most consider it experimental and therefore prefer to use the profit split method'' (paragraph 3.52).

The Global Formulary Apportionment (GFA) Method. Under the GFA approach, the consolidated global profit of a multinational company would be allocated among related enterprises in different countries on the basis of a predetermined and mechanistic formula. According to the OECD report, there are three essential components to applying the GFA method:

determining the unit to be taxed, i.e., which of the subsidiaries and branches of an multinational enterprise group should comprise the global taxable entity; accurately determining the global profits; and establishing the formula to be used to allocate the global profits of the unit. The formula would most likely be based on some combination of costs, assets, payroll, and sales. (paragraph 3.59)

The OECD report noted that the GFA method has not been applied as yet between countries, although it has been attempted by some local taxing jurisdictions (paragraph 3.58). Some proposals for formulary apportionment are discussed in Gianni (1996). Advocates of the GFA method often mention the following advantages:

1. As an alternative to the arm's-length principle, the method would provide greater administrative convenience and certainty for taxpayers.
2. The method considers a multinational company on a worldwide or consolidated basis to reflect the business realities of the relationships among the related enterprises.
3. The GFA method reduces compliance costs for taxpayers because in principle, only one set of accounts would be prepared for the company for domestic tax purposes.

However, the OECD does not accept the above propositions and does not consider the GFA method a realistic alternative to the arm's-length principle. The OECD report rejects the use of the GFA method mainly for the following reasons:

1. It is difficult to implement a system of GFA in a manner that both protects against double taxation and ensures single taxation. Achieving this would require substantial international coordination and consensus on the predetermined formulae to be used and on the composition of the group in question.
2. Any predetermined formulae are arbitrary and would ignore market conditions, the particular circumstances of the individual enterprises, and management's own allocation of resources and thus produce an allocation of profits that may bear no sound relationship to the specific facts and circumstances surrounding the transaction.
3. The documentation and compliance requirements for an application of the GFA method would be more burdensome than under the separate-entity approach of the arm's-length principle. The taxpayer has to present information about the entire corporate group to each jurisdiction on the basis of its currency and tax accounting rules.
4. By ignoring the intrafirm transactions for the sake of computing consolidated profits, the GFA method would ''raise questions about the relevance of imposing withholding taxes on cross-border payments between group members and would involve a rejection of a number of rules incorporated in bilateral tax treaties'' (paragraph 3.72).

The Mutual Agreement Procedure and Corresponding Adjustments

The mutual agreement procedure and corresponding adjustments are two of several administrative procedures available to resolve transfer pricing disputes between taxpayers and their tax authorities and between different tax authorities. Many basic issues on the mutual agreement procedure and corresponding adjustments have been discussed in the first section of the OECD 1984 report. The 1995 OECD guidelines provide more specific criteria for implementing these procedures.

The mutual agreement procedure was described and authorized by Article 25 of the OECD Model Tax Convention. It can be used to eliminate double taxation that may arise from transfer pricing adjustments. The mutual agreement procedure does not compel competent authorities to reach an agreement and resolve their differences. If the competent authorities cannot resolve their tax disputes, the cases may have recourse to arbitration. A multilateral Arbitration Convention was signed by the member states of the European Communities on July 23, 1990, and became effective on January 1, 1995.

The procedure for requesting corresponding adjustments is described in paragraph 2 of Article 9 of the OECD Model Tax Convention. The paragraph recommends that the competent authorities consult each other if necessary to determine corresponding adjustments. On the nature of corresponding adjustments, the OECD 1995 guidelines provide the following explanation:

A corresponding adjustment, which in practice may be undertaken as part of the mutual agreement procedure, can mitigate or eliminate double taxation in cases where one tax administration increases a company's taxable profits (i.e., makes a primary adjustment) as a result of applying the arm's length principle to transactions involving an associated enterprise in a second tax jurisdiction. The corresponding adjustment in such a case is a downward adjustment to the tax liability of that associated enterprise, made by the tax administration of the second jurisdiction, so that the allocation of profits between the two jurisdictions is consistent with the primary adjustment and no double taxation occurs. It is also possible that the first tax administration will agree to decrease (or eliminate) the primary adjustment as part of the consultative process with the second tax administration, in which case the corresponding adjustment would be smaller (or perhaps unnecessary). (paragraph 4.32)

There is some overlap between the mutual agreement procedure and corresponding adjustments because a corresponding adjustment can be undertaken as part of the mutual agreement procedure. Together, the two procedures can be very effective in providing relief from double taxation caused by transfer pricing adjustments.

Advance-Pricing Arrangements and Arbitration

The 1995 OECD report has an extensive discussion of the nature and procedure of advance-pricing arrangements or agreements (APAs). It defines APA as "an arrangement that determines, in advance of controlled transactions, an appropriate set of criteria (e.g., method, comparable and appropriate adjustments thereto, critical assumptions as to future events) for the determination of the transfer pricing for those transactions over a fixed period of time" (paragraph 4.124).

The guidelines also explain the advantages and disadvantages of an APA (discussed in Chapter 4) and provides some useful recommendations for taxpayers and tax administrations. These recommendations are summarized as follows:

1. When considering the scope of an APA, taxpayers and tax administrations need to pay close attention to the reliability of any predictions. Great care must be taken if the APA goes beyond the methodology, its application, and critical assumptions.

2. Wherever possible, an APA should be concluded on a bilateral or multilateral basis between competent authorities through the mutual agreement procedure of the relevant treaty.

3. Tax administrations should consider the possibility of adopting a streamlined access for small taxpayers. Tax authorities should also adapt their levels of inquiry, in evaluating APAs, to the side of the international transactions involved.

4. Tax administrations of those countries that have APA programs should develop working agreements between competent authorities to provide greater uniformity in APA practices.

Some of these recommendations have already been implemented by taxpayers and tax authorities. For example, of the 29 APAs concluded between U.S. taxpayers and the IRS as of March 31, 1995, 11 include bilateral agreements with treaty partners. In addition, some countries have concluded working agreements to coordinate the implementation of their APA programs. The Committee on Fiscal Affairs of the OECD has stated its intention to monitor any future expanded use of APAs and to promote greater consistency in APA programs and practices.

On arbitration procedures, the OECD 1995 guidelines noted that the General Agreement on Tariffs and Trade and its successor, the World Trade Organization, have developed sophisticated procedures and institutions to resolve international trade disputes. The use of arbitration in tax disputes has been recognized in the OECD Model Tax Convention. (Moreover, the transfer pricing arbitration convention signed by member states of the European Community became effective on January 1, 1995.)

In the past, the OECD has done some studies on arbitration in the context of transfer pricing. Early findings from another study were included in the 1984 report. The 1995 report considered it appropriate "to analyze again and in more detail whether the introduction of a tax arbitration procedure would be appropriate addition to international tax relations" (paragraph 4.171). The Committee on Fiscal Affairs of the OECD also agreed to undertake a study on this issue in the future.

Guidelines on Documentation

In Chapter V of the 1995 guidelines, the OECD provides extensive discussion on the documentation to be obtained from taxpayers in connection with a transfer pricing inquiry. The report also identified documentation that needs to be prepared by taxpayers to show that their controlled transactions satisfy the arm's-length principle and resolve transfer pricing issues and facilitating tax examinations. The following is a list of documentation suggested by the 1995 OECD guidelines:

1. information about the associated enterprises involved in the controlled transactions; the transactions at issue; the functions performed; information derived from independent enterprises engaged in similar transactions or businesses;

2. in specific transfer pricing cases, it may be useful to have the following information relating to each associated enterprise involved in the controlled transactions:

   —an outline of the business;

   —the structure of the organization;

   —ownership linkages within the corporate group;

   —the amount of sales and operating results from the last few years preceding the transactions; and

   —the level of the taxpayer's transactions with foreign associated enterprises, which may include the amount of sales of inventory assets, the rendering of services, the rent of tangible assets, the use and transfer of intangible property, and interest on loans;

3. information on pricing, including business strategies and special circumstances at issue. This may include factors that influenced the setting of prices or the establishment of any pricing policies for the taxpayer and the entire company;

4. general commercial and industry conditions affecting the taxpayer, which may include the current business environment and its forecasted changes and how the potential changes may influence the taxpayer's industry, market and competitive conditions, regulatory framework, technologies, and so forth;

5. information about functions performed that is useful for the functional analysis in applying the arm's-length principle. The functions include manufacturing, assemblage, management of purchase and materials, marketing, wholesale, stock control, warranty administration, advertising and marketing activities, carriage and warehousing activities, lending and payment terms, training, and personnel;

6. the possible risks assumed by parties involved, which may include risks of change in cost, price, or stack, risks relating to success or failure of research and development, financial risks including change in the foreign exchange and interest rates, risks of lending and payment terms, risks for manufacturing liability, and business risk related to ownership of assets or facilities;

7. financial information useful for comparing profit and loss between the associated enterprises with which the taxpayer has transactions subject to the transfer pricing rules. Other relevant information may include reports on manufacturing costs, research and development expenditure, and general and administrative expenses; and

8. documents showing the process of negotiations for determining or revising prices in controlled transactions.

The report suggests that taxpayers should make reasonable efforts at the time transfer pricing is established to determine whether the pricing is appropriate for tax purposes in accordance with the arm's-length principle. The OECD also recognizes that tax authorities should have the right to obtain the documentation to verify compliance with the arm's-length principle. The report emphasizes that the need for documentation should be balanced by the costs and administrative burdens for preparing maintaining such documentation. In the future, the Committee on Fiscal Affairs intends to study the issue of documentation to develop additional guidelines for assisting taxpayers and tax administrations.

Special Considerations for the Transfer of Intangible Property

In the 1995 guidelines, intangible property is divided into three categories as follows:

—the rights to use industrial assets such as patents, trademarks, trade names, designs, or models;

—literary and artistic property rights; and

—intellectual property such as know-how and trade secrets.

These assets may or may not have any book value on the corporate balance sheet, but many of them may be valuable to the company. Conversely, some of them may be associated with considerable risks (e.g., product liability or environmental damages).

In applying the arm's length principle to the transfer of intangible property the guidelines suggest the following:

—The general rules discussed in Chapter 1 (the arm's-length principle), Chapter 2 (traditional transaction methods), and Chapter 3 (other methods) of the guidelines also pertain to the determination of transfer prices for intangible property. However, the guidelines also noted that the arm's-length principle may be difficult to apply to controlled transactions involving intangible property "because such property may have a special character complicating the search for comparables and in some cases making value difficult to determine at the time of transaction" (paragraph 6.13).

—For the purpose of comparability, arm's-length pricing for the transfer of intangible property must take into account the perspectives of both the transferor of the property and the transferee. From the perspective of the transferor, the arm's-length principle should consider the pricing at which a comparable independent enterprise would be willing to transfer the property. From the perspective of the transferee, a comparable independent enterprise may or may not be willing to pay such a price, depending on the value and usefulness of the property to the transferee.

—Some factors relevant to comparability between the controlled and uncontrolled transactions should be considered. These factors include the expected benefits from the intangible property, limitations on the geographic area in which rights may be exercised, export restrictions on goods produced, the exclusive or nonexclusive character of any rights transferred, the capital investment, the startup expenses, the possibility of sublicensing, the licensee's distribution network, and whether the licensee has the right to participate in further developments of the property by the licensor (paragraph 6.20).

—In establishing arm's-length pricing in the case of a sale or license of intangible property, the CUP method is allowable if the same owner has transferred or licensed comparable intangible property under comparable circumstances to independent enterprises (paragraph 6.23).

—In the sale of goods incorporating intangible property, either the CUP or the resale price method is allowed (paragraph 6.24).

—In cases involving highly valuable intangible property, it may be difficult to apply the traditional transaction methods and the transactional net margin method, especially when both parties to the transaction own valuable intangible property or unique assets used in the transaction. In such cases, we can apply the profit split method.

—When the valuation of intangible property is highly uncertain at the time of the transaction, both the taxpayers and tax administrations should determine the arm's length price by reference to what independent enterprises would have done in comparable circumstances (paragraph 6.28).

Special Considerations for Intragroup Services

The 1995 guidelines identify two major issues relating to the transfer pricing for intragroup services. The first issue is to determine whether intragroup services have, in fact, been performed. Another issue is to calculate the appropriate transfer price(s) for intragroup services. Resolving these two issues may not be easy because some intragroup service arrangements are connected to the transfer of other goods or intangible property.

To determine whether intragroup services have been rendered, the OECD report offers the following guidelines and examples:

—If an activity performed by a group member for one or more other group members provides economic or commercial value to enhance the commercial position of the service recipient(s), then the intragroup service has been rendered.

—If an intragroup activity is performed because the service provider (e.g., the parent company or a regional holding company) has an ownership interest in the service recipient, it cannot be considered an intragroup service. It is instead considered as "shareholder activities." Other examples of shareholder activities include: (a) activities relating to the juridical structure of the parent company itself, such as meetings of shareholders of the parent and issuing of shares in the parent company; and (b) preparing consolidated financial statements for the entire company.

—Activities undertaken by one group member that merely duplicate a service that another group member is performing for itself, or that is being performed for such other group member by a third party, cannot be considered as intragroup services.

—Some centralized activities that independent enterprises would have been willing to pay for or to perform for themselves are considered as intragroup services. These include "administrative services such as planning, coordination, budgetary control, financial advice, accounting, auditing, legal, factoring, computer services; financial services such as supervision of cash flows and solvency, capital increases, loan contracts, management of interest and exchange rate risks, and refinancing; assistance in the fields of production, buying, distribution and marketing; and services in staff matters such as recruitment and training" (paragraph 7.14).

—The mere existence of a payment does not prove that an intracorporate service has been rendered. For example, a payment for a management fee is not strong evidence that such services have been rendered. On the other hand, the absence of payment or contractual agreements does not indicate that no intragroup services have been performed.

Once we determine that an intragroup service has been rendered, we have to calculate the transfer price according to the arm's-length principle. The general rule is that "the charge for intra-group services should be that which would have been made and accepted between independent enterprises in comparable circumstances" (paragraph 7.19). We also need to consider the pricing issue from the perspective of the service provider and from the perspective of the service recipient. Other factors that we should consider include the value of the service to the recipient; the amount a comparable independent company would be willing to pay for the service; and the costs to the service provider for performing the intragroup service.

In cases for the transfer of intangible property, the transfer pricing method to be used for intragroup services should be determined according to the general guidelines provided in Chapters I, II, and III of the 1995 report. The application of those guidelines usually leads to the selection of the CUP method or cost plus method for determining the transfer prices for intragroup services. The situations for using these two methods are explained in paragraph 7.31 of the report:

A CUP method is likely to be used where there is a comparable service provided between independent enterprises in the recipient's market, or by the associated enterprise providing the services to an independent enterprise in comparable circumstances. For example, this might be the case where accounting, auditing, legal, or computer services are being provided. A cost plus method would likely be appropriate in the absence of a CUP where the nature of the activities involved, assets used, and risks assumed are comparable to those undertaken by independent enterprises.

In exceptional cases where the CUP and the cost plus method cannot be applied, we may use more than one method to determine an arm's length price or use transactional profit methods as a last resort. For illustrative purposes, the 1995 report also recommends the pricing method(s) that should be used for three types of intragroup services:

—For the debt-factoring activities performed by a debt-factoring center of a multinational company, the CUP method could be appropriate.

—For contract manufacturing services provided by a related enterprise, the cost plus method should be used. In such cases, the risk to the producing enterprise is very low and its entire output will be purchased by another related company if quality requirements are met.

—For contract research services, the cost plus method may be appropriate, subject to the principles discussed in Chapter II of the 1995 report.

A COMPARISON BETWEEN THE OECD GUIDELINES AND THE FINAL U.S. REGULATIONS OF SECTION 482

Both the 1995 OECD guidelines and the final U.S. Regulations of section 482 are long and complex documents that cover a wide range of transfer pricing issues. A comparison between the provisions of the two documents shows that both the OECD and the U.S. Treasury Department are in agreement on many vital issues, including the arm's-length principle and acceptable transfer pricing methods for tangible property. For example, both the OECD and the U.S. government reaffirmed their commitment to the arm's-length principle, and both emphasize comparability and reliability in selecting an arm's-length price as the transfer price for tangible goods or intangible property. There is also substantial agreement between the two documents on the important factors that determine "comparability": functions performed, contractual terms, risks involved, economic conditions or circumstances, characteristics of property or services, and business strategies.

The list of transfer pricing methods acceptable by the OECD guidelines and the U.S. regulations for the transfer of tangible property are quite similar. The U.S. regulations accept the CUP method, the RPM method, the CPLM method, the comparable profits method (CPM), the PSM method, and other unspecified methods subject to the best-method rule. The OECD guidelines accept the CUP method, the RPM method, the CPLM method, the PSM method, and the TNMM method, but the OECD indicates its preference of traditional transaction methods (CUP, RPM, and CPLM) over all others. In the OECD final guidelines, the TNMM method was used (instead of the CPM method, as in the OECD draft guidelines) because several OECD countries strongly opposed the use of CPM (Hamaekers, 1996; Taly, 1996). Under the U.S. regulations, the CPM evaluates whether the amount charged in a controlled transaction is arm's length based on objective measure of profitability derived from uncontrolled taxpayers that engage in similar business activities under similar circumstances.

On the transfer pricing methods for intangible property, the OECD guidelines recommend the use of the CUP method, the RPM method, and the PSM method under different circumstances. However, the U.S. regulations allow the use of the CUP method, the CPM method, the PSM method, and unspecified methods subject to the best-method rule. In addition, the arm's-length consideration for the transfer of an intangible must be commensurate with the income attributable to the intangible (the super-royalty provision of section 482). This approach was not endorsed by the OECD guidelines.

We can find another area of slight disagreement between the OECD's recommendation and the IRS approach toward the APA program. The IRS is treating the program as an effective process to promote voluntary compliance and to reduce the administrative burden on both the IRS and taxpayers. However, the APA program is receiving only qualified support from the OECD. Its 1995 guidelines stated that "while it is too early to make a final recommendation whether the expansion of such programmes should be encouraged, it seems likely that in certain circumstances they will aid in resolving transfer pricing disputes" (paragraph 4.161).

SUMMARY AND CONCLUSIONS

This chapter summarizes the key provisions of three OECD reports and guidelines related to transfer pricing: the 1979 report, the 1984 report, and the 1995 transfer pricing guidelines for multinational enterprises and tax administrations. We noted that both the 1979 report and the 1984 report have been superseded by the 1995 guidelines. The OECD is taking a leadership role in developing transfer pricing guidelines to fulfill its mission and to prevent unilateral responses to international taxation and transfer pricing problems.

We also compared the key concepts and provisions of the OECD guidelines with those in the final U.S. section 482 regulations. We found that both documents reaffirm their commitment to the arm's-length principle and both recommend similar sets of transfer pricing methods for the transfers of tangible property. However, the transfer pricing methods recommended by the OECD for the transfer of intangible property are different from those acceptable under U.S. regulations. We also noted that the two documents recommend different sets of transfer pricing methods for the transfer of intangible property. The super-royalty approach required under U.S. regulations is not endorsed by the OECD.

Despite their remaining differences, the harmonization between the OECD guidelines and the U.S. section 482 regulations has significantly reduced the uncertainties in intrafirm trade and transfer pricing. Both sets of guidelines are more specific and yet more flexible than their predecessors: the 1979 OECD guidelines and the 1968 section 482 regulations. Multinational companies should benefit from these developments as they expand their international investment and intrafirm trade. On the other hand, multinational taxpayers should study the two sets of guidelines in detail to ensure that they are in compliance with the key provisions of the U.S. regulations and the OECD guidelines.

REFERENCES

Broadhurst, David G. 1995. The OECD Transfer Pricing Report. *Canadian Tax Journal* (Vol. 43, No. 1): 140–153.

Cheng, Dora K. 1995. Transfer Pricing: U.S. Regulations and OECD Discussion Draft Compared. *Tax Notes International* (January 16): 199–202.

Elliott, Jamie. 1994. Developments in Transfer Pricing. *British Tax Review* (July 8): 348–357.

Gianni, Monica Brown. 1996. Transfer Pricing and Formulary Apportionment. *Taxes* (March): 169–182.

Hamaekers, Hubert. 1996. The New OECD Transfer Pricing Guidelines for Multinational Enterprises and Tax Administrations. *Asia-Pacific Tax Bulletin* (January/February): 15–25.

Hay, Diane, Frances Horner, and Jeffrey Owens. 1994. Past and Present Work in the OECD on Transfer Pricing and Selected Issues. *Tax Notes International* (July 25): 249–264.

Organization for Economic Cooperation and Development (OECD). 1979. *Transfer Pricing and Multinational Enterprises*. Paris: OECD.

———. 1984. *Transfer Pricing and Multinational Enterprises: Three Taxation Issues*. Paris: OECD.

———. 1993. *Tax Aspects of Transfer Pricing within Multinational Enterprises: The United States Proposed Regulations*. Paris: OECD.

———. 1995. *Transfer Pricing Guidelines for Multinational Enterprises and Tax Administrations*. Paris: OECD.

Taly, Michel. 1996. Comparison of CPM and TNMM Transfer Pricing Methods: A Point of View. *Tax Notes International* (January 29): 351–353.

Tax Executive Institute. 1995. OECD Draft Transfer Pricing Guidelines for Multinational Enterprises and Tax Administrations. *Tax Executive* (January–February): 40–42.

6

Intrafirm Trade and Transfer Pricing Regulations in Canada and Mexico

Over the past ten years, there have been significant changes in the trilateral trade relationships between Canada, Mexico, and the United States. On January 1, 1989, the Free Trade Agreement (FTA) between the United States and Canada became effective. The FTA will eliminate all tariffs between the two countries by January 1, 1999, and it will also remove most nontariff barriers and investment restrictions. On January 1, 1993, the North American Free Trade Agreement (NAFTA), signed by Canada, Mexico, and the United States, went into effect. NAFTA will eventually create a free trade area that has more than 360 million customers and joint gross national products (GNP) of more than $6 trillion.

Since the signing of the FTA, the two-way trade between Canada and the United States has been expanding. In 1988, before the FTA became effective, the bilateral trade total between the U.S. and Canada was $157.1 billion, while by 1995, the bilateral trade between Canada and the United States had reached $275.5 billion (Bach, 1996). The merchandise trade between Mexico and the United States has also experienced significant growth in recent years. In 1995, the merchandise trade between the United States and Mexico was $108.6 billion (Bach, 1996). It makes Mexico the third largest trading partner of the United States. Over the past ten years, we have also witnessed significant increases in U.S. investment in Mexico and Canada. Because of NAFTA, we can expect the U.S. trade and investment relations with the two NAFTA partners to expand further in the future.

In this chapter, we will examine the transfer pricing regulations in Canada and Mexico. Because these regulations will have significant implications for bilateral trade and investment relations between the three countries, we will also review the changes in investment and trade relationships between the United

States, Canada, and Mexico in recent years. The Canadian advance-pricing agreement (APA) program, which began in 1993, will also be discussed. To facilitate our discussion, we will examine the transfer pricing issues concerning Canada before reviewing similar issues in Mexico.

TRANSFER PRICING ISSUES IN CANADA

In the past, Canadian transfer pricing issues have been the subjects of many studies and governmental inquiries in Canada (e.g., Chambers, 1976; Tang, 1980; Baxter and Konopka, 1985; Boidman, 1987, 1995; Humphreys, 1994, 1995). Several authors have also recognized the importance of transfer pricing to Canada. For example, Milburn made the following observation in 1976:

The Canadian economy may be more susceptible to international transfer pricing varia-bility than that of any other country in the world. This is because much of Canadian industry is foreign owned and also because there is a great deal of trade between Ca-nadian companies and their foreign associates. (p. 22)

Milburn's statement is still valid today, as many Canadian companies are con-trolled by investors from the United States, the United Kingdom, and Japan. For example, four of the ten largest Canadian firms in 1996 were invested by U.S. companies: General Motors of Canada, Ford Motor Co. of Canada; Chrysler Canada; and Imperial Oil. One of the firms (Imasco) was invested by BAT Industries from the United Kingdom. Many companies that appeared in the 1995 *Canadian Business* directory of the largest 500 corporations are invested by multinational companies (MNCs) from other countries (*Canadian Business*, 1995). On the other hand, Canadian companies have also invested heavily in the United States in recent years.

Table 6.1 presents statistics on bilateral investment positions between Canada and the United States from 1982 to 1993. Column (1) of the table shows that U.S. direct investment position (DIP) in Canada increased steadily from 1982 to 1991. However, in 1992, U.S. DIP experienced the first decrease since the early 1980s. This was followed by a slight increase in 1993. At the end of 1993, U.S. DIP in Canada totaled $70.4 billion.

Column (2) of the table shows the Canadian direct investment position (DIP) in the United States from 1982 to 1993. At the end of 1982, Canadian DIP in the United States was only $11.4 billion. There was a slight decrease in 1983. However, Canadian DIP in the United States has increased continuously since then. At the end of 1993, Canadian DIP in the United States was $39.4 billion.

The net U.S. investment positions from 1982 to 1993 are shown in column (3), which column indicates that the net U.S. investment positions during those years varied between $30 billion and $40 billion. The net U.S. investment po-sition has declined in recent years, as the increase in U.S. DIP (column 1) was less than that in Canadian DIP (column 2). As a result, Canadian DIP as a

Table 6.1
Bilateral Direct Investment Positions between Canada and the United States, 1982–1993 (Millions of U.S. Dollars)

Year	U.S. Direct Investment Position (DIP) in Canada (1)	Canadian Direct Investment Position (DIP) in the U.S. (2)	Net U.S. Investment Position (3)=(1)-(2)	Canadian DIP as % of U.S. DIP (4)
1982	43,511	11,435	32,076	26.3
1983	44,339	11,115	33,224	25.1
1984	46,730	15,286	31,444	32.7
1985	46,909	17,131	29,778	36.5
1986	50,629	20,318	30,311	40.1
1987	58,377	24,684	33,693	42.3
1988	62,656	26,566	36,090	42.4
1989	65,548	28,686	35,318	43.8
1990	69,508	30,037	39,471	43.2
1991	70,711	36,341	34,370	51.4
1992	68,832	37,845	30,987	55.0
1993	70,395	39,408	30,987	56.0

Sources: U.S. Department of Commerce, Bureau of Economic Analysis, *Survey of Current Business* (various issues).

Table 6.2
U.S. Merchandise Trade with Canada, 1980–1995 (Millions of U.S. Dollars)

Year	Exports to Canada (1)	Imports from Canada (2)	Trade Total (3)=(1)+(2)	Balance of Trade (4)=(1)-(2)
1980	41,389	42,434	83,823	- 1,045
1981	45,250	47,316	92,566	- 2,066
1982	39,275	48,473	87,748	- 9,198
1983	43,812	54,360	98,172	-10,548
1984	53,135	69,515	122,650	-16,380
1985	53,879	71,173	125,052	-17,294
1986	56,984	70,315	127,299	-13,331
1987	61,092	73,647	134,739	-12,555
1988	73,116	84,078	157,194	-10,962
1989	80,451	88,960	169,411	- 8,509
1990	83,572	93,026	176,598	- 9,454
1991	85,104	93,080	178,184	- 7,976
1992	91,146	100,871	192,017	-9,725
1993	101,155	113,310	214,465	-12,155
1994	114,869	131,115	245,984	-16,246
1995	127,589	147,870	275,459	-20,281

Sources: U.S. Department of Commerce, Bureau of Economic Analysis, *Survey of Current Business* (various issues).

percentage of U.S. DIP (see column 4) has increased by more than 50 percent in recent years.

Besides bilateral investments, bilateral trade between the United States and Canada also played an important role in transfer pricing for Canada. Significant trends and statistics on U.S.-Canadian bilateral trade will be discussed in the following section.

Bilateral and Intrafirm Trade between Canada and the United States

Canada is the largest trading partner of the United States. Table 6.2 provides the merchandise trade statistics between Canada and the United States from 1980 to 1995. Columns (1) and (2) show that both U.S. exports to Canada (column 1) and imports from Canada (column 2) increased steadily from the mid-1980s to 1995. The bilateral trade totals for those years are shown in column (3). We can observe that bilateral trade between the two countries has more than doubled

Table 6.3
Intrafirm Trade between U.S. MNCs and Their Majority-Owned Nonbank Canadian Affiliates, 1982–1993 (Millions of U.S. Dollars)

Year	U.S. Exports Shipped to Majority-Owned Canadian Affiliates by U.S. Parents (1)	U.S. Imports Shipped by Majority-Owned Canadian Affiliates to U.S. Parents (2)	Intrafirm Trade Total Between Canadian Affiliates and Their U.S. Parents		Balance of Intrafirm Trade (5)
			Amount (3) = (1)+(2)	As a % of U.S.-Canada Merchandise Trade (4)	
1982	15,474	16,551	32,025	36.5	-1,077
1983	18,641	20,191	38,832	40.0	-1,550
1984	22,271	23,609	45,880	37.4	-1,338
1985	25,610	25,494	51,104	40.9	116
1986	25,946	24,450	50,396	39.6	1,496
1987	27,676	24,802	52,478	39.0	2,874
1988	31,188	30,204	61,382	39.1	984
1989	32,060	32,461	64,521	38.1	-401
1990	30,753	33,126	63,879	36.2	-2,373
1991	32,842	33,943	66,785	37.5	-1,101
1992	33,878	36,613	70,491	36.7	-2,735
1993	34,078	41,231	75,309	35.1	-7,153

Sources: U.S. Department of Commerce, Economics and Statistics Administration, Bureau of Economic Analysis, *U.S. Direct Investment Abroad* (various issues).

from 1985 to 1995. The significant increases in bilateral trade in recent years can be attributed to the implementation of the U.S.-Canada FTA and the NAFTA. Column (4) of Table 6.2 also indicates that Canada has enjoyed a substantial trade surplus with the United States from 1980 to 1985. During the 15-year period, the cumulative surplus of Canada from bilateral trade with the United States was about $177.7 billion.

Intrafirm trade statistics between related companies in the United States and Canada are provided in Tables 6.3, 6.4, and 6.5. Table 6.3 presents the information on intrafirm trade between U.S. MNCs and their majority-owned nonbank Canadian affiliates. According to U.S. Department of Commerce definition, a majority-owned foreign affiliate (MOFA) is a foreign affiliate in which the combined direct and indirect ownership interest of all U.S. parents exceeds 50 percent. The statistics in Table 6.3 cover only nonbank business entities. Column (1) of Table 6.3 shows the amount of U.S. exports shipped to MOFAs in Canada by U.S. parents, and column (2) provides the statistics on U.S. imports shipped

Table 6.4
Intrafirm Trade between Canadian MNCs and Their U.S. Affiliates, 1982–1993
(Millions of U.S. Dollars)

Year	U.S. Exports Shipped by U.S. Affiliates to Canadian Parent Group (1)	U.S. Imports Shipped to U.S. Affiliates by Canadian Parent Group (2)	Intrafirm Trade Total Between U.S. Affiliates and Their Canadian Parents		Balance of Intrafirm Trade (5)
			Amount (3) = (1)+(2)	As a % of U.S.-Canada Merchandise Trade (4)	
1982	740	4,218	4,958	5.7	-3,478
1983	811	4,357	5,168	5.3	-3,546
1984	881	4,847	5,728	4.7	-3,966
1985	867	4,764	5,631	4.5	-3,897
1986	833	5,032	5,865	4.6	-4,199
1987	878	5,717	6,595	4.9	-4,839
1988	1,028	6,737	7,765	4.9	-5,709
1989	1,502	7,162	8,664	5.1	-5659
1990	1,154	7,343	8,497	4.8	-6,189
1991	1,223	6,534	7,757	4.4	-5,311
1992	1,529	7,053	8,582	4.5	-5,524
1993	1,574	7,597	9,171	4.3	-6,023

Sources: U.S. Department of Commerce, Economics and Statistics Administration, Bureau of Economic Analysis, *Foreign Investment in the United States* (various issues).

by MOFAs in Canada to U.S. parents. The intrafirm trade totals between U.S. parents and their MOFAs in Canada are shown in column (3). We can see that the intrafirm trade total increased from $32.0 billion in 1982 to $75.3 billion in 1993. This represents a 135 percent increase over the 11-year period. Column (4) shows that intrafirm trade of U.S. MNCs accounted for 35 to 40 percent of U.S.-Canada merchandise trade. In 1993, this type of intrafirm trade accounted for 35.1 percent of U.S.-Canada merchandise trade. The balances of intrafirm trade for those years are shown in column (5). In recent years, U.S. MNCs have experienced significant trade deficits in intrafirm trade with their MOFAs in Canada.

Figure 6.1 provides the 1993 intrafirm trade statistics by industries. We can observe that 52 percent of U.S. exports shipped to MOFAs in Canada originated from MNCs in the transportation equipment (mainly automobile) industry. Other important industries involved in intrafirm exports to Canada include wholesale

Table 6.5
Intrafirm Trade between Related Companies in the United States and Canada,
1982–1993 (Millions of U.S. Dollars)

Year	Trade Total Between Majority-owned Canadian Affiliates and U.S. Parents (1)	Trade Total Between U.S. Affiliates and Canadian Parents (2)	Intrafirm Trade Total Between Related Companies in the U.S. and Canada (3) = (1) + (2)	Intrafirm Trade as % of U.S.-Canada Merchandise Trade (4)
1982	32,025	4,958	36,983	42.2
1983	38,832	5,168	44,000	44.8
1984	45,880	5,728	51,608	42.1
1985	51,104	5,631	56,735	45.4
1986	50,396	5,865	56,261	44.2
1987	52,478	6,595	59,073	43.8
1988	61,382	7,765	69,147	43.8
1989	64,521	8,664	73,185	43.2
1990	63,879	8,497	72,376	41.0
1991	66,785	7,757	74,542	41.8
1992	70,491	8,582	79,073	41.2
1993	75,309	9,171	84,480	39.4

Sources: Tables 7.3 and 7.4; U.S. Department of Commerce, *U.S. Direct Investment Abroad* (various years); and *Foreign Investment in the United States* (various years).

trade (17%), machinery except electrical (9.7%), and chemicals and allied products (6.4%).

The bottom half of Figure 6.1 presents the statistics of U.S. imports shipped by Canadian affiliates to U.S. parents by industries in 1993. We can observe that about two-thirds of intrafirm imports from Canada occurred in the transportation equipment (mainly automobile) industry. As a matter of fact, in 1993, the two-way intrafirm trade between Canada and the United States in transportation equipment amounted to $45 billion. Other industries that played important roles in U.S. intrafirm imports are the petroleum industry ($3.4 billion, or 8.1%) and chemicals and allied products ($1.6 billion, or 4.0%).

As Rugman (1986) noted, Canadian MNCs also played a significant role in intrafirm trade between Canada and the United States. The statistics on intrafirm trade between Canadian MNCs and their U.S. affiliates from 1982 to 1993 are shown in Table 6.4. Column (1) of that table presents the statistics on U.S. exports shipped by U.S. affiliates to Canadian parent group, and column (2) presents U.S. imports shipped to U.S. affiliates by Canadian parent group. Intrafirm trade totals between U.S. affiliates and their Canadian parents are shown

Figure 6.1
**Intrafirm Trade between U.S. MNCs and Their Canadian Majority-Owned
Affiliates by Industries, 1993**

U.S. Exports shipped to Canadian Affiliates by U.S. Parents
($34.1 billion)

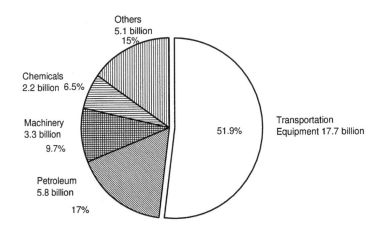

U.S. Imports Shipped by Canadian Affiliates to U.S. Parents
(41.2 billions)

Source: U.S. Department of Commerce (1995).

in column (3). We can observe that intrafirm trade between Canadian MNCs and their U.S. affiliates increased significantly from 1982 to 1993. In 1993, the intrafirm trade totals of Canadian MNCs was $9.1 billion, accounting for about 4.3 percent of U.S.-Canadian merchandise trade. Column (5) shows that Canadian MNCs enjoyed a substantial trade surplus on their intrafirm trade with the United States. Statistics by industries indicate that some Canadian manufacturing industries are playing dominant roles in intrafirm trade with the United States. These include the primary metal and electric and electronics industries.

Table 6.5 summarizes the information in Tables 6.3 and 6.4. Column (1) of Table 6.5 shows the intrafirm trade total between U.S. parents and their MOFAs in Canada, and column (2) provides the trade statistics between U.S. affiliates and their Canadian parents. Intrafirm trade totals between related companies in the United States and Canada are shown in column (3). In 1993, the bilateral intrafirm trade total between Canada and the United States was $84.5 billion. Because this amount is so large, a small change in the transfer prices of intrafirm trade may have a significant impact on the balances of payment and tax revenues of the two countries. The situation is more critical to Canada because Canadian income tax rates are higher than those in the United States (Bird, Perry, and Wilson, 1995).

Transfer Pricing Regulations in Canada

The Canadian legislation on transfer pricing and treatment of non–arm's-length transactions can be found in subsections 69(1), 69(2), and 69(3) of the Canadian Income Tax Act (see Appendix B).

Subsection 69(1) applies to the acquisition and disposition of goods and services. It requires that "fair market value" be used in non–arm's-length transactions. The subsection was enacted "to prevent related domestic organizations from artificially shifting income, deductions or both between entities" (Hogg, 1983, p. 57).

Subsections 69(2) and 69(3) apply to a wide range of domestic and international transactions that are not dealing at arm's-length. The criterion used by these two subsections is what is "reasonable in the circumstances." One objective is "to protect Canada against the loss of tax revenue resulting from income shifting on an international scale" (Hogg, 1983, p. 57).

There are no formal regulations explaining the criteria and standards under subsections 69(1), 69(2), and 69(3). However, Revenue Canada did issue Information Circular 87–2, *International Transfer Pricing and Other International Transactions*, in February 1987. (This Information Circular can be found in Tang, (1993). Paragraph 1 of the circular explains the purpose for its issuance:

This circular is for the guidance of any Canadian taxpayer related to entities in one or more foreign jurisdictions. It applies to international non–arm's-length transactions involving a Canadian taxpayer, and it describes the Department's [Revenue Canada's] approach to the tax treatment of international transfer pricing and other issues that have an effect on the income reported in Canada.

Paragraph 6 of the circular confirms that subsections 69(2) and 69(3) override subsection 69(1) and apply if the transaction involves a Canadian taxpayer and a nonresident with whom the taxpayer was not dealing at arm's length. The term ''reasonable arm's-length price'' was defined in paragraph 7 as the amount ''that would have been reasonable in the circumstances if the parties to the transaction had been dealing at arm's length, and may mean fair market value or another amount depending on the circumstances in a particular case.''

In paragraph 9, Revenue Canada states that it endorses and follows the methods set out in the 1979 OECD *Report on Transfer Pricing and Multinational Enterprises*. The transfer pricing methods acceptable by the 1979 OECD report are:

—the comparable uncontrolled price (CUP) method;

—the resale price method (RPM);

—cost plus method (CPLM); and

—other reasonable methods.

Information Circular 87–2 also provides transfer pricing guidelines applicable to intra-group services, research and development and the use of intangibles. However, the OECD 1979 report has been superseded by new guidelines (OECD, 1995), published on July 13, 1995. The final OECD guidelines accept three traditional transaction methods (CUP, RPM, and CPLM), the profit split method (PSM), and the transactional net margin method (TNMM). (Details of the new OECD guidelines are discussed in Chapter 5. After the OECD guidelines were released, in 1995, Revenue Canada and the Department of Finance issued a statement that Canada's transfer pricing rules will fully conform with the revised OECD guidelines. Revenue Canada is in the process of revising Information Circular 87–2.

On a Department of Finance Release No. 93–003 dated January 7, 1994, Canadian Finance Minister Paul Martin and National Revenue Minister David Anderson also clarified the application of the Canadian rules and guidelines for determining transfer prices for multinational intrafirm trade. Both ministers noted that difficulties may arise when a foreign jurisdiction requires the use of comparable profits method (CPM), which may generate transfer prices that do not conform to the arm's-length principle and would not be acceptable for Canadian tax purposes. To minimize such difficulties, both ministers recommended the following to Canadian taxpayers:

—use a pricing method that provides the best indication of the price unrelated parties would negotiate, such as the CUP, RPM or the CPLM method that are internationally recognized as appropriate transfer pricing methods;

—encourage U.S. affiliates to use transfer pricing methods that are acceptable under both Canadian and U.S. law;

—avoid establishing a price using the CPM method without ensuring that the price so established represents an arm's-length price; and

—consider using the advance-pricing agreement process announced by Revenue Canada.

Both ministers also pledged to work with major trading partners to develop common approaches to transfer pricing problems in order to minimize conflicts between tax administrations and provide greater certainty for taxpayers.

Other sections of the Canadian Income Tax Act may also have an impact on the transfer pricing practices of multinational companies. For example, Section 67 restricts deductions of expenses and outlays to those "reasonable in the circumstances." Section 245(1) disallows deductions that would unduly or artificially reduce the income:

245(1) In computing income for the purposes of this Act, no deduction may be made in respect of a disbursement or expense made or incurred in respect of a transaction or operation that, if allowed, would unduly or artificially reduce the income.

David Anderson, national revenue minister, stated in 1995 that Revenue Canada will meet with large businesses to develop a three- to five-year audit strategy. The main objectives of these meetings include the following:

—to outline the conditions of the audit;

—to identify any contentious issues that might impede the audit's progress;

—to increase opportunities for more preaudit and ongoing exchanges; and

—to describe trends and other financial and economic analyses that would be used during the period of the agreement.

In 1995, Revenue Canada also announced that real-time audits would be available to large corporations. This approach involves auditing taxpayers' records at the same time taxpayers are preparing their current-year returns. The approach has been successfully tested in several large businesses, including Northern Telecom and DuPont Canada. Revenue Canada will also accommodate any company requesting that audits for income tax, the goods and service tax (GST), payroll, and customs be conducted simultaneously.

The Canadian Advance-Pricing Agreement (APA) Program

In June 1993, Revenue Canada circulated a draft titled, "Information Circular on Advance Pricing Agreement [APA]," and dated May 21, 1993. In July 1993, Revenue Canada announced that it would introduce APA services for determining transfer prices in selected cases (Ward and Armstrong, 1994).

By the end of 1993, Revenue Canada had completed several test cases. The final draft, Information Circular 94–4, *International Transfer Pricing: Advance Pricing Agreements*, was released on December 30, 1994, and is reproduced in Appendix C. The objective of the circular is to provide an overview of the Canadian APA program. Detailed guidelines and procedures are available on request.

Revenue Canada (the department) considers an APA a binding agreement between a taxpayer and the department. As stated in paragraph 3 of the circular, "When the terms of the agreement are complied with, the Department will consider the results of applying the agreed transfer pricing methodology (TPM) to have satisfied the arm's-length principle of section 69 of the [Canadian Income Tax] Act." The normal term of an APA is three years, but it may vary depending upon the facts and circumstances of individual taxpayers. The Canadian APA process is similar to its counterpart in the United States (as explained in Chapter 4).

To be acceptable, a proposed TPM must meet the following two requirements:

1. It must comply with the provisions of section 69 of the Canadian Income Tax Act and adhere to the principles set out in Information Circular 87–2, *International Transfer Pricing and Other International Transactions*, and in the OECD guidelines on transfer pricing, as amended from time to time.
2. It must be consistent with the arm's-length principle and must be supported by reliable data.

Information Circular 94–4 also has the following requirements for an APA submission:

—The taxpayer must provide a detailed explanation and analysis of each proposed TPM, as well as the facts and circumstances on which it is based, and set out the reasons why the proposed TPM is appropriate to the situation. The taxpayer should also discuss the three transactional TPMs (the CUP, RPM, and CPLM) described in Information Circular 87–2 and provide reasons why they are or are not suitable to the situation (paragraph 20).

—To assist the department in reviewing and evaluating the proposed TPM, the taxpayer has to illustrate the effect of the proposed TPM by applying it to the operations of the previous three years and to the projected operations of the periods the APA will cover (paragraph 21).

—The APA submission must include detailed information about the taxpayer and the related parties involved in the APA (e.g., history, organizational structure, nature and scope of operations, transaction flows, and relevant financial and tax data) (paragraph 23).

—The taxpayer must put forward a set of critical assumptions under which the proposed TPM would operate. Critical assumptions are objective business and economic criteria that are fundamental to the application of the taxpayer's proposed TPM (paragraph 25).

Revenue Canada will levy a user charge for each APA request or renewal to cover out-of-pocket costs, including travel and accommodation. A taxpayer is also responsible for the cost of hiring an independent expert if the department considers it necessary to obtain the opinion from that expert. There is no charge for using the time of the APA program staff.

After an APA is implemented, the taxpayer must submit an annual report according to the terms of the APA. At a minimum, the annual report should include the following items (paragraph 28):

—a description of the actual operations of the taxpayer for the year;

—a discussion and explanation of any significant variance between expected results (as forecasted in the APA submission) and actual results;

—an accounting of any compensating adjustments, if permitted under the APA; and

—a demonstration of the extent of the taxpayer's compliance with the terms and conditions of the TPM and the information and explanations provided in the annual reports.

Revenue Canada also stated that it can revise an APA with the consent of the taxpayer and the competent authority of the other countries involved, when there is a change in any critical assumption, tax law, or treaty provision or if justified by changed circumstances. Revenue Canada may renew APAs upon request by the taxpayer. The Canadian APA program is administered by the International Tax Programs Directorate of Revenue Canada. Its address and telephone number can be found in paragraph 6 of Appendix C.

As of March 15, 1996, there were 35 Canadian APAs pending, while another half dozen APAs had be finalized. All the completed APAs were bilateral agreements with the United States. Revenue Canada is using a small-team approach to handle each APA request. The team generally includes the chief of the transfer pricing section of Revenue Canada's International Tax Programs Directorate, an analyst, an economist, a legal advisor, and an auditor. According to S. Claude Lemenlin, former chief of the transfer pricing section, the chief monitors the process, negotiates the agreement, and ensures consistency in the program. The analyst is officially in charge of a particular APA. The economist's involvement depends on the nature of the request. The legal adviser is the person who drafts the APA at the end of the process. The auditor brings his or her knowledge of the taxpayer and its operations to the negotiations and shares it with other members of the Revenue Canada team. Team members participate in all facets of the APA process, while the chief and the analyst make the final decision (Tax Management Inc., 1996).

TRANSFER PRICING IN MEXICO

In recent years, transfer pricing has become an important issue to Mexico as multinational companies expand their investment and intrafirm trade with that nation. The Mexican tax authority has also issued new regulations requiring the use of arm's-length prices for intrafirm trade. In the following sections, we will examine three related topics that have an impact on the transfer pricing environment in Mexico:

—U.S. Investment in Mexico and the maquiladoras;

—bilateral and intrafirm trade between Mexico and the United States; and

—new transfer pricing regulations in Mexico.

U.S. Investment in Mexico and the Maquiladoras

Table 6.6 provides statistics on bilateral direct investment positions between Mexico and the United States from 1982 to 1993. From column (1), we can observe that U.S. direct investment in Mexico did not change much between 1982 and 1987. During that period, the U.S. direct investment position (DIP) in Mexico fluctuated between $4.3 billion and $5.1 billion. However, U.S. investment began to take off in 1988 and increased continuously through 1993. At the end of 1993, U.S. DIP in Mexico amounted to $15.4 billion.

Column (2) shows the Mexican DIP in the United States from 1982 to 1993. Mexican direct investment in the United states is still relatively small compared with those of Canada and other countries. At the end of 1993, Mexican direct investment in the United States totaled $1.2 billion. The net U.S. investment position in Mexico for 1993 was $14.2 billion.

A large portion of U.S. investment in Mexico is invested in maquiladoras. These are in-bond or twin plants located in Mexico that process imported materials or commodities for reexport to the United States. The maquiladora program was created in 1996 as part of Mexico's border industrialization program (Groff and McCray, 1991; Hein and VanZante, 1991; Cohen, 1994). The main purposes of the program were to create jobs and generate foreign currency income. Most of the maquiladora operations take place in so-called twin border cities including El Paso (Texas) and Ciudad Juarez (Mexico), and San Diego (California) and Tijuana (Mexico). Most maquiladoras are subsidiaries of U.S. companies and other foreign MNCs. A maquiladora can import materials free of customs duties and value-added tax (VAT), process or assemble the goods, and export the finished goods. A maquiladora can also import machinery and equipment used in production free of import duties and VAT. When the finished goods are reexported to the United States, the U.S. Customs Service will collect duties on the value added to the goods.

The expansion of the maquiladora industry has been quite impressive over the past 15 years. For example, between January 1980 and January 1990, the total number of maquiladoras grew from 539 to 1,834 and the number of employees grew from 113,897 to 441,126 (Cohen, 1994). In 1994, there were more

Table 6.6
Bilateral Direct Investment Positions between Mexico and the United States,
1982–1993 (Millions of U.S. Dollars)

Year	U.S. Direct Investment Position in Mexico (1)	Mexican Direct Investment in the United States (2)	Net U.S. Investment Position (3)=(1)=(2)
1982	5,019	259	4,760
1983	4,381	244	4,137
1984	4,568	308	4,260
1985	5,087	533	4,554
1986	4,623	841	3,782
1987	4,913	180	4,733
1988	5,694	218	5,476
1989	7,079	350	6,729
1990	10,313	550	9,763
1991	12,257	747	11,510
1992	13,723	1,289	12,434
1993	15,413	1,214	14,199

Sources: U.S. Department of Commerce, Bureau of Economic Analysis, *Survey of Current Business* (various issues).

than 2,822 maquiladoras located near the U.S. border (Houde, 1994). There are many advantages of the maquiladoras for U.S. firms. These include low labor costs; special tariff treatment; reduced utility cost; easy access to U.S. transportation and communications facilities; and technical, managerial, and support services (Groff and McCray, 1991). Because of the maquiladora program and the implementation of NAFTA, bilateral trade between Mexico and the United States is booming. We will discuss more details about the bilateral trade relations between the two countries in the following section.

Bilateral and Intrafirm Trade between Mexico and the United States

Table 6.7 presents statistics on U.S. merchandise trade with Mexico from 1980 to 1995. Column (1) of the table covers U.S. exports to Mexico, and column (2) shows U.S. imports from Mexico for the 15-year period. The bilateral trade totals for those years are shown in column (3). We can observe that bilateral trade between the two countries fluctuated between $25 billion and $35

Table 6.7
U.S. Merchandise Trade with Mexico, 1984–1995 (Millions of U.S. Dollars)

Year	Exports to Mexico (1)	Imports from Mexico (2)	Trade Total (3)=(1)+(2)	Balance of Trade (4)=(1)-(2)
1980	15,145	12,580	27,725	2,565
1981	17,789	13,765	31,554	4,024
1982	11,817	15,566	27,383	-3,749
1983	9,082	16,776	25,858	-7,694
1984	11,992	18,020	30,012	-6,028
1985	13,635	19,132	32,767	-5,497
1986	12,392	17,302	29,694	-4,910
1987	14,582	20,271	34,853	-5,689
1988	20,643	23,277	43,920	-2,634
1989	24,982	27,162	52,144	-2,180
1990	28,279	30,157	58,436	-1,878
1991	33,277	31,130	64,407	2,147
1992	40,494	35,609	76,103	4,885
1993	41,478	40,428	81,906	1,050
1994	50,741	50,053	100,794	688
1995	46,195	62,362	108,557	-16,167

Sources: U.S. Department of Commerce, Economics and Statistics Administration, Bureau of the Census, *Statistical Abstract of the United States* (various issues); U.S. Department of Commerce, Economics and Statistics Administration, Bureau of Economic Analysis, *Survey of Current Business* (various issues).

billion from 1980 to 1987. However, the expansion in bilateral trade accelerated in 1988, and the trend continued into the mid-1990s with the implementation of NAFTA. From 1988 to 1995, bilateral trade between Mexico and the United States expanded by close to 150 percent.

The balances of U.S.-Mexican bilateral trade are shown in column (4) of Table 6.7. The statistics show that the United States was enjoying a trade surplus on its trade with Mexico from 1991 to 1994. However, in 1995 Mexico had a huge trade surplus ($16.1 billion) with the United States. This drastic change in trade balance may be the result of the significant devaluation of the Mexican peso that began in late 1994. On December 19, 1994, the peso's exchange rate was about 3.5 to the dollar. By July 1995, the value of the peso had dropped to 6.1 to the dollar, a 43 percent decline in six months.

The intrafirm trade statistics between Mexico and the United States are shown

Table 6.8
Intrafirm Trade between U.S. MNCs and Their Majority-Owned Nonbank
Mexican Affiliates, 1982–1993 (Millions of U.S. Dollars)

Year	U.S. Exports Shipped to Majority-Owned Mexican Affiliates by U.S. Parents (1)	U.S. Imports Shipped by Majority-Owned Mexican Affiliates to U.S. Parents (2)	Intrafirm Trade Total Between Mexican Affiliates and Their U.S. Parents		Balance of Intrafirm Trade (5)
			Amount (3) = (1)+(2)	As a % of U.S.-Mexican Merchandise Trade (4)	
1982	2,095	1,560	3,655	13.3	535
1983	2,018	1,869	3,887	15.0	149
1984	2,523	2,887	5,410	18.0	-364
1985	3,212	3,326	6,538	20.0	-114
1986	3,480	3,830	7,310	22.3	-350
1987	3,980	4,353	8,333	23.9	-373
1988	4,732	5,185	9,917	22.6	-453
1989	5,996	6,410	12,406	23.8	-414
1990	7,097	7,161	14,258	24.4	-64
1991	8,892	8,601	17,493	27.2	291
1992	10,096	10,739	20,835	27.4	-643
1993	10,761	11,807	22,568	27.6	-1,046

Sources: U.S. Department of Commerce, *U.S. Direct Investment Abroad* (various years).

in Tables 6.8, 6.9, and 6.10. Table 6.8 provides the statistics on intrafirm trade between U.S. MNCs and their MOFAs in Mexico from 1982 to 1993. Columns (1), (2), and (3) of Table 6.8 show that intrafirm trade between U.S. MNCs and their Mexican MOFAs expanded continuously over the 11-year period. In 1993, the intrafirm trade total between U.S. MNCs and their Mexican affiliates was $22.6 billion, six times more than the amount recorded in 1982. From column (4) of Table 6.8, we can observe that the intrafirm trade between U.S. parents and their Mexican affiliates accounted for 13.3 percent of U.S.-Mexican trade in 1982. This percentage has increased continuously since then, and by 1993, had climbed to 27.6 percent. The expansion of intrafirm trade with Mexico is the key reason why the Mexican tax authority has monitored multinational transfer pricing practices in recent years.

Table 6.9 shows the intrafirm trade statistics between Mexican MNCs and their U.S. affiliates from 1982 to 1993. Column (3) of the table indicates that this type of intrafirm trade expanded in the 1980s and early 1990s. However,

Table 6.9
Intrafirm Trade between Mexican MNCs and Their U.S. Affiliates, 1982–1993
(Millions of U.S. Dollars)

Year	U.S. Exports Shipped by U.S. Affiliates to Mexican Parent Group (1)	U.S. Imports Shipped to U.S. Affiliates by Mexican Parents Group (2)	Intrafirm Trade Total Between U.S. Affiliates and Their Mexican Parents		Balance of Intrafirm Trade (5)
			Amount (3) = (1)+(2)	As a % of U.S.-Mexican Merchandise Trade (4)	
1982	29	(D)	(D)	N.A.	N.A.
1983	23	125	148	0.6	-102
1984	24	97	121	0.4	-73
1985	25	100	125	0.4	-75
1986	22	345	367	1.1	-323
1987	20	448	468	1.3	-428
1988	42	498	540	1.2	-456
1989	58	521	579	1.1	-463
1990	69	624	693	1.2	-555
1991	53	607	660	1.0	-554
1992	183	498	681	0.9	-315
1993	232	575	807	1.0	-343

Notes: (D) = The data have been suppressed to avoid disclosure of data of individual companies.
N.A. = Not available.
Sources: U.S. Department of Commerce, *Foreign Investment in the United States* (various years).

the amount of intrafirm trade of Mexican MNCs was still quite small and accounted for only 1 percent of U.S.-Mexican merchandise trade in 1993.

Table 6.10 summarizes the intrafirm trade data in Tables 6.8 and 6.9. Column (3) of the table shows that the intrafirm trade total between Mexico and the United States was about $23.4 billion in 1993, accounting for 28.5 percent of U.S.-Mexican merchandise trade. Because of NAFTA and the expanding trade U.S. investment in Mexico, we can expect the intrafirm trade between the two countries to increase further in the future.

Transfer Pricing Regulations in Mexico

Before 1992, Mexican tax law gave its tax authority the power to make transfer pricing adjustments. Guidelines were not provided to taxpayers to determine proper transfer prices (Silva, 1995). In 1992, the tax law was amended to allow

Table 6.10
Intrafirm Trade between Related Companies in the United States and Mexico,
1982–1993 (Millions of U.S. Dollars)

Year	Trade Total Between Majority-owned Mexican Affiliates and U.S. Parents (1)	Trade Total Between U.S. Affiliates and Mexican Parents (2)	Intrafirm Trade Total Between Related Companies in the U.S. and Mexico (3) = (1) + (2)	Intrafirm Trade as % of U.S.-Mexican Merchandise Trade (4)
1982	3,655	(D)	N.A.	N.A.
1983	3,887	148	4,035	15.6
1984	5,410	121	5,531	18.4
1985	6,538	125	6,663	20.3
1986	7,310	367	7,677	25.9
1987	8,333	468	8,801	25.3
1988	9,917	540	10,457	23.8
1989	12,406	579	12,985	24.9
1990	14,258	693	14,951	25.6
1991	17,493	660	18,153	28.2
1992	20,835	681	21,516	28.3
1993	22,568	807	23,375	28.5

Notes: (D) = The data have been suppressed to avoid disclosure of data of individual companies.
N.A. = Not available.
Sources: Tables 7.2 and 7.3; U.S. Department of Commerce, *U.S. Direct Investment Abroad* (various years); and *Foreign Investment in the United States* (various years).

the use of comparable uncontrolled price (CUP), resale price method (RPM) or the cost plus method (CPLM). At that time, the management of most maquiladoras assumed that they were in compliance with the law because they were using CPLM. Maquiladoras normally sell their finished products for cost plus a small profit (between 1 to 5% of total costs).

In 1994, the U.S.-Mexican tax treaty entered into force. Article 5(5) of the treaty provides that a maquiladora may be treated as a permanent establishment (PE) of its U.S. parent and subject to Mexican income tax on the profit generated from its operations in Mexico. However, this treatment can be avoided if the U.S. parent can demonstrate that it conducts its transactions with the maquiladora at arm's length. In other words, maquiladoras in Mexico should receive arm's-length price for the work that they perform for U.S. parents in 1995 and future years.

In mid-1994, the maquiladora industry association formed a transfer pricing committee and retained Coopers & Lybrand to examine transfer pricing issues for maquiladoras (Matthews, 1995; McLees, Wilkins, and Valdes, 1995a). The committee's objectives are twofold: (1) to assist maquiladoras participating in the work of the committee in determining arm's-length prices and (2) to work with the industry leadership in promoting sound government policies for the industry on transfer pricing and the assets tax. Based on its analysis, the committee concluded that:

Both the U.S. transfer pricing rules and the OECD standards require a maquiladora that operates in the typical manner as a manufacturing service provided to receive a transfer price in a round-trip transaction that is sufficient to allow it to earn an appropriate arm's-length return on its own assets. Under this standard, different maquiladoras will earn different mark-ups on their cost, depending on the value of the assets owned by the maquiladora. (McLees, Wilkins, and Valdes, 1995a, p. 1622)

In 1995, the Mexican government amended the regulations it had released in 1994. Under the new regulations, the Mexican tax authority will not audit a maquiladora's compliance with the normal Mexican arm's-length pricing standards for 1995 if its taxable income for 1995 is equal to or greater than 5 percent of the combined inflation–adjusted book value of the maquiladora's assets and the foreign-owned assets used in its operations (the 5% of asset value test) (McLees, Wilkins, and Valdes, 1995b).

Due to the close coordination between the maquiladora industry and the Mexican tax authorities, most maquiladoras now accept the need to employ arm's-length prices for their intrafirm trade with foreign parents and other affiliates. The Mexican government is also prepared to accept internationally recognized principles, such as the OECD guidelines, to determine arm's-length prices. In other words, U.S. parents can no longer treat their maquiladoras as cost centers in the future. Each maquiladora also has to determine its arm's-length transfer price under Mexican law and acceptable international standards.

In late 1995, the Mexican tax authority issued the first transfer pricing ruling (equivalent to an APA in the United States) for a maquiladora (Fernández, 1995). An international tax partner at Deloitte & Touche, Washington, D.C., helped a maquiladora and its U.S. parent negotiate the advance ruling. Mexican tax authority stated that all ruling requests will be reviewed on a case-by-case basis in the future. The tax authority also expects to receive about 250 ruling requests in 1996 (Fernández, 1995). The expansion of the advance-ruling program should reduce the uncertainties for intrafirm trade and transfer pricing in Mexico.

SUMMARY AND CONCLUSIONS

In this chapter, we examined the bilateral investment and trade relationships between Canada and the United States and those between the United States and Mexico. Transfer pricing regulations in Canada and Mexico were also reviewed.

Statistics show that both U.S.-Canadian and U.S.-Mexican bilateral trade have expanded rapidly over the past 15 years. The same trend can be observed for U.S.-Canadian and U.S.-Mexican intrafirm trade.

Transfer pricing has always been an important issue to Canada because many Canadian businesses are invested by companies from the United States, Japan, the United Kingdom and other countries. Intrafirm trade also accounts for about 40 percent of the bilateral trade between Canada and the United States. Canadian transfer pricing regulations are brief and less formal than their counterparts of the United States. However, in recent years, Revenue Canada has implemented some innovative approaches such as the APA program and real-time auditing of taxpayers' returns. These programs should reduce uncertainties and tax payers' compliance costs in the long run.

Transfer pricing is becoming a big issue in Mexico because of expanding intrafirm trade and international investment. With the maquiladora program and the implementation of NAFTA, intrafirm trade and transfer pricing issues will be more important to the Mexican economy in the future than they had been in the past. Transfer pricing regulations in Mexico now require the use of arm's-length prices for intrafirm trade with foreign parents and other affiliates. Advance transfer pricing ruling is also available if requested by a taxpayer. Because Canada and Mexico are among the largest trading partners of the United States, we should monitor changes in their transfer pricing regulations from time to time to ensure that corporate transfer pricing policies are in compliance with regulations in the three NAFTA countries.

REFERENCES

Bach, Christopher L. 1996. U.S. International Transactions, Fourth Quarter and Year 1995. *Survey of Current Business* (April): 45–71.

Barraccia, Salvador M., and Mary C. Bennett. 1994. Canadian Release Increases Fears of U.S.-Canadian Transfer Pricing Disputes. *Tax Executive* (March–April): 95–100.

Baxter, George C., and Raymond A. Konopka. 1985. Transfer Pricing across the Canada-U.S. Border. *CA Magazine* (June): 50–55.

Bird, Richard M., David B. Perry, and Thomas A. Wilson. 1995. Tax System of Canada. *Tax Notes International* (January 9): 152–180.

Boidman, Nathan. 1987. Canada's Administrative Guidelines for Multinational Transactions: Information Circular No. 87–2. *Tax Executive* (Fall): 35–56.

———. 1995. Can an Efficient Transfer Pricing Strategy Be Developed under Canadian Law? *Tax Executive* (July–August): 290–296.

Boidman, Nathan, and Gary J. Gartner. 1993. Revenue Canada Issues Draft Transfer Pricing Agreement Circular for Intercompany Transactions. *Tax Management International Journal* (December): 664–666.

Canadian Business, 1995. The *Canadian Business* Directory of the Largest 500 Companies in Canada. *Canadian Business* (June): 104–127.

Chambers, Winston G. 1976. *Transfer Pricing, the Multinational Enterprise and Economic Development*. Ottawa: Engery, Mines and Resources Canada.

Cohen, Joshua A. 1994. The Rise of the Maquiladoras. *Business Mexico* (special edition): 52–55.

Cornell, David W., and Nancy D. Weatherholt. 1995. Making the Most of NAFTA. *Journal of Accountancy* (January): 53–58.

Dombey, Daniel. 1995. Mexico: Land of the Brave. *International Business* (August): 34–37.

Fernández, Albertina M. 1995. Mexico Issues First Maquiladora APA. *Tax Notes International* (November 13): 1276–1277.

Groff, James E., and John P. McCray. 1991. Maquiladoras: The Mexico Option Can Reduce Your Manufacturing Cost. *Management Accounting* (January): 43–46.

Harris, Edwin C. 1985. Intercompany Cross-Border Transactions: A Growing Concern for Revenue Canada. *CA Magazine* (June): 22–33.

Hein, Cheryl D., and Neal R. VanZante. 1991. Maquiladoras: Should U.S. Companies Run for the Border? *CPA Journal* (October): 14–22.

Hogg, Roy D. 1983. A Canadian Tax Overview of Transfer Pricing. *CA Magazine* (December): 54–62.

Houde, Marie-France. 1994. Mexico and Foreign Investment. *OECD Observer* (October/November): 10–13.

Humphreys, Brenda. 1994. International Transfer Pricing More Important Than Ever Before. *CMA Magazine* (May): 24–26.

———. 1995. Transfer Reactions. *CA Magazine* (September): 32–34.

Levey, Marc M., Patrick R. Gordon, and Gary D. Sanders. 1994. Planning for New and Existing Operations under the U.S.-Mexico Income Tax Treaty. *Journal of Taxation* (June): 368–371.

Matthews, Kathleen. 1995. Update on Transfer Pricing for Mexican Maquiladoras; Peso Devaluation. *Tax Notes International* (February 20): 607–610.

McLees, John A., John G. Wilkins, and Ignacio Valdes V. 1995a. Extension of Mexican Assets Tax Complicates Transfer Pricing for Maquiladoras. *Tax Notes International* (May 8): 1619–1630.

———. 1995b. Mexico Moves toward Resolution of Maquiladora Transfer Pricing Issues. *Tax Notes International* (July 24): 183–187.

Milburn, J. Alex. 1976. International Transfer Transactions: What Price? *CA Magazine* (December): 22–27.

Organization for Economic Cooperation and Development (OECD). 1979. *Transfer Pricing and Multinational Enterprises*. Paris: OECD.

———. 1995. *Transfer Pricing Guidelines for Multinational Enterprises and Tax Administration*. Paris: OECD.

Revenue Canada. 1987. *Information Circular No. 87–2*. International Transfer Pricing and Other International Transastions. February 27.

———. 1994. *Information Circular No. 94–4*. International Transfer Pricing: Advance Pricing Agreements. December 30.

Reynolds, Alan. 1994. Canada Is Being Taxed to Death. *Wall Street Journal* (October 14): A13.

Rugman, Alan M. 1986. The Role of Multinational Enterprises in U.S.-Canadian Economic Relations. In David L. McKee, ed., *Canadian-American Economic Relations*. New York: Praeger.

Silva, Hector. 1995. Mexico Takes Harder Line on Maquiladora Transfer Pricing. *International Tax Review* (March/April): 10–11.

Szalkowski, Todd G., and Laura Y. Fiske. 1995. Mexican Tax Authorities Examining Maquiladora Transfer Pricing Practices. *Tax Adviser* (January): 30.

Tamaki, George T., and Richard W. Pound. 1974. Intercompany Pricing: In Search of Guidelines. *Canadian Tax Journal* (September–October): 460–471.

Tang, Roger Y. W. 1980. Canadian Transfer Pricing Practices. *CA Magazine* (March): 32–45.

———. 1981. *Multinational Transfer Pricing: Canadian and British Perspectives*. Toronto: Butterworths.

———. 1993. *Transfer Pricing in the 1990s*. Westport, Conn.: Quorum.

Tax Management Inc. 1996. Canada Working on APA to Involve up to Five Nations, Lemelin Says. *BNA Transfer Pricing Review* (May 8): 12–16.

U.S. Department of Commerce. Economics and Statistics Administration. Bureau of Economic Analysis. 1995. *U.S. Direct Investment Abroad: Preliminary 1993 Estimates*. Washington, D.C.: U.S. Government Printing Office.

Ward, David A., and Neal Armstrong. 1994. Eliminating Transfer Pricing Uncertainties in Canada. *International Tax Review Supplement* (February): 3–8.

7

Intrafirm Trade and Transfer Pricing Regulations of Selected Countries in the European Union

The past decade has witnessed tremendous changes in the political and economic landscapes in Europe. These changes included the formation of the European Union (EU) and the enlargement of EU membership; the fall of the Berlin Wall and subsequent German unification; the collapse of the Warsaw Pact; the breakup of the former Soviet Union; and the end of the Cold War. These changes have enormous political and economic implications for Europe and the rest of the world.

Of course, it is beyond the scope of this book to study all the political and economic changes in Europe. In this chapter, we will review some segments of the legal and economic environments in Europe: intrafirm trade and transfer pricing regulations of five EU countries. These selected countries are major trading nations of Europe: France, Germany, Italy, Netherlands, and the United Kingdom. They are major players of the EU and important trading partners of the United States.

Transfer pricing and intrafirm trade are closely tied to multinational investment and international trade. Before we examine the transfer pricing regulations of these five countries, we will review their international investment activities and trade performances in recent years. Information on intrafirm trade related to the five EU countries and the United States will also be provided.

INTERNATIONAL INVESTMENT ACTIVITIES OF FIVE SELECTED EU COUNTRIES

The five EU countries selected have been active players in international investment for the past 25 years. Table 7.1 shows the direct investment abroad (investment outflows) from those five countries, Japan, Canada, and the United

Table 7.1
Direct Investment Abroad from Five EU Countries, Japan, Canada, and the United States: Outflows, Selected Years, 1971–1993 (Millions of U.S. Dollars)

Country	Cumulative Flows		Flows of Direct Investment Abroad		
	1971-1980	1981-1990	1991	1992	1993
France	13,940	85,618	20,501	19,097	12,167
Germany	24,846	86,573	22,879	17,745	11,673
Italy	3,597	28,707	7,326	5,948	7,231
Netherlands	27,829	52,940	12,270	14,096	10,079
United Kingdom	55,112	185,674	15,597	19,444	25,697
Japan	18,052	185,826	30,726	17,222	13,714
Canada	11,335	41,847	5,856	3,688	7,176
United States	134,354	170,041	31,294	41,004	57,871
Total	289,065	837,226	146,449	138,244	145,608

Source: Organization for Economic Cooperation and Development (1995a).

States. The data for the United States, Canada, and Japan are provided for comparative purposes. All these countries are members of the G-7 industrial nations with the exception of the Netherlands.

In Table 7.1, cumulative flows data are provided for 1971 to 1980 and 1981 to 1990, and data for individual years are shown for 1991 to 1993. From the cumulative flows data for the 1970s and 1980s, we can observe that the direct investment abroad total (from these eight countries) increased from $289 billion in the 1970s to $837 billion in the 1980s. Japan had the most impressive investment record during the 1980s. It increased its direct investment abroad by more than ten times from the 1970s to 1980s.

The top five capital exporting countries in the 1980s were Japan ($185.8 billion), the United Kingdom ($185.7 billion), the United States ($170.0 billion), Germany ($86.6 billion), and France ($85.6 billion). Also in the 1980s, the total direct investment abroad from the five EU Countries amounted to about $440 billion.

In the early 1990s, total direct investment abroad from the eight industrial countries fluctuated between $138 billion and $146 billion. While the U.S. and British investment abroad increased steadily from 1991 to 1993, direct investment from Japan, France, and Germany declined during the same period. In 1993, U.S. MNCs invested $57.9 billion and British MNCs invested $25.7 billion in other countries.

Table 7.2 shows the inflows of foreign direct investment into the five EU countries, Japan, Canada and the United States. Similar to Table 7.1, cumulative flows data for 1971–1980 and 1981–1990 and individual year data for 1991 to 1993 are provided in Table 7.2. As a whole, foreign direct investment in these eight countries increased from $151 billion in the 1970s to $641 billion in the 1980s. The three largest recipients of foreign direct investment in the 1980s were the United States ($359.7 billion), the United Kingdom ($130.4 billion), and France ($43.2 billion). Together, the five EU countries received a total of $244.8 billion of foreign investment in the 1980s. Interestingly, Japan received only $3.3 billion of foreign direct investment in the 1980s even though it provided $185.8 billion of direct investment to other countries (see Table 8.1). During the 1980s, the net investment received by the United States was about $190 billion (U.S. direct investment abroad less foreign direct investment in the United States).

In the early 1990s, the inflows of foreign direct investment leveled off due partly to the economic recessions experienced in Western Europe and the United States. Germany even recorded a negative inflow (divestment) of foreign investment in 1993. The total inflows of direct investment into the eight industrial countries was only $63.2 billion in 1993.

Now we can examine the bilateral investment relationship between the United States and other industrial countries. Table 7.3 shows the U.S. direct investment position (DIP) in the five EU countries, Japan, Canada, and Mexico at the end of 1994. Data for Japan, Canada, and Mexico are provided for comparative purposes. Also included in Table 7.3 are the direct investment positions (DIP) of those eight countries in the United States. Net U.S. DIP in each of these eight countries is shown in the last column of Table 7.3.

Column (1) of Table 7.3 shows that total U.S. DIP abroad at the end of 1994 was $612.1 billion, whereas foreign DIP in the United States at the same year end was $504.4 billion. Therefore, the net U.S. DIP abroad for 1994 was $107.7 billion. Table 7.3 indicates that the United States maintained very close investment relationships with the five EU countries, Japan, and Canada in 1994. At the end of 1994, the U.S. DIP in the five EU countries was $209.2 billion and those five countries' DIP in the United States was $259.6 billion. U.S. invest-

Table 7.2
Foreign Direct Investment in Five EU Countries, Japan, Canada, and the United States: Inflows, Selected Years, 1971–1993 (Millions of U.S. Dollars)

Country	Cumulative Flows		Flows of Foreign Direct Investment		
	1971-1980	1981-1990	1991	1992	1993
France	16,908	43,194	11,073	15,928	12,142
Germany	13,969	18,029	4,263	2,422	-286
Italy	5,698	24,888	2,481	3,210	3,751
Netherlands	10,822	28,203	5,002	6,994	5,651
United Kingdom	40,503	130,469	15,826	16,448	14,536
Japan	1,424	3,281	1,368	2,728	86
Canada	5,534	33,699	2,913	4,576	5,930
United States	56,276	359,650	26,086	9,888	21,366
Total	151,134	641,413	69,012	62,194	63,176

Source: Organization for Economic Cooperation and Development (1995a).

ment relationship with the United Kingdom was the strongest among all countries. About 16.7 percent ($102.2 billion) of U.S. DIP abroad was in the United Kingdom and British DIP in the United States accounted for 22.5 percent ($113.5 billion) of all foreign DIP in the United States at the end of 1994.

Japan's DIP ($103.1 billion) in the United States was the second highest among all countries. Because U.S. DIP ($37.0 billion) in Japan was relatively small, Japanese MNCs provided the United States with a net direct investment position of $66 billion at the end of 1994.

Table 7.3 also indicates that the United States invested heavily in Canada,

Table 7.3
U.S. Direct Investment Position (DIP) Abroad and Foreign Direct Investment
Position in the United States, 1994 (Millions of U.S. Dollars)

Countries	U.S. DIP Abroad (1)	Foreign DIP in the U.S. (2)	Net U.S. DIP (3)=(1)-(2)
All Countries	612,109	504,401	107,708
France	27,894	33,496	-5,602
Germany	39,886	39,550	336
Italy	14,998	2,437	12,561
Netherlands	24,150	70,645	-46,495
United Kingdom	102,244	113,504	-11,260
Japan	37,027	103,120	-66,093
Canada	72,808	43,223	29,585
Mexico	16,375	2,187	14,188
Other Countries	276,727	96,239	180,488

Note: Calculated on a historical-cost basis.
Source: U.S. Department of Commerce, Bureau of Economic Analysis, *Survey of Current Business* (various issues).

Mexico, and other countries. Interestingly, the United States had a net investment position of $180.5 billion in other countries not listed in Table 7.3. U.S.
Department of Commerce statistics show that the United States also had large
DIPs in four other countries: Switzerland ($34.5 billion); Bermuda ($29.2 billion); Brazil ($19.0 billion); and Panama ($13.8 billion).

Table 7.4
International Trade of the G-7 Countries and the Netherlands, 1995 (Billions of U.S. Dollars)

Country	Exports (1)	Imports (2)	Trade Balance (3)= (1)-(2)
France	286.0	273.6	12.4
Germany	509.4	445.7	63.7
Italy	189.8*	167.7*	22.1*
Netherlands	194.5	174.9	19.6
United Kingdom	204.9*	227.0*	-22.1*
Japan	443.1	336.0	107.1
Canada	192.2	168.4	23.8
United States	574.9	749.3	-174.4

*1994 figures.
Source: International Monetary Fund, *International Financial Statistics* (May 1996); Bach (1996).

INTERNATIONAL TRADE OF FIVE EU COUNTRIES AND THEIR BILATERAL TRADE WITH THE UNITED STATES

As we mentioned earlier, all the selected five EU countries are major trading nations of the world. Their recent trade statistics are shown in Table 7.4. Statistics for Japan, Canada and the United States are also provided. Together, the G-7 nations and the Netherlands accounted for about 52 percent of world trade. Most of the largest MNCs originated in these eight countries.

From Table 7.4, we can observe that the United States was the largest trading nation of the world in 1995, with exports of $754.9 billion and imports of $749.3 billion. On the other hand, the United States was also the country that had the largest trade deficit: $174.4 billion. Germany had the second largest trade volume in 1995, closely followed by Japan. However, Japan had the largest trade surplus ($107.1 billion) among all industrial nations. The international trade volume of the other four EU countries (France, Italy, the Netherlands, and the United Kingdom) and Canada are also substantial. All these countries, except the United Kingdom, had trade surpluses in recent years.

Table 7.5 provides an overview of the U.S. merchandise trade with Europe and the rest of the world. In 1995, most of the U.S. trade with Europe was trade with the European Union. U.S. exports to the EU amounted to about $121.3 billion in 1995, and U.S. imports from the EU in 1995 were $134.3 billion. U.S. merchandise trade with the EU accounted for about 19 percent of all U.S. merchandise trade.

The United States is currently trading heavily with its two NAFTA partners (Canada and Mexico) and the Asian Pacific region. For example, in 1995 the United States exported $173.8 billion of merchandise to Canada and Mexico and imported $210.2 billion of merchandise from the two NAFTA partners. As a result, U.S. merchandise trade with Canada and Mexico now accounts for about 29 percent of all U.S. merchandise trade.

U.S. trade with the Asian Pacific region is expanding rapidly. In 1995, U.S. merchandise exports to Japan, China, and the four Asian Dragons (Hong Kong, South Korea, Singapore, and Taiwan) amounted to $146.4 billion. U.S. imports from these countries totaled $251.0 billion. U.S. merchandise trade with these countries now accounts for 30 percent of U.S. trade. The United States also had a $105 billion trade deficit with these Asian Pacific countries.

INTRAFIRM TRADE RELATED TO FIVE EU COUNTRIES AND THE UNITED STATES

After reviewing the international trade statistics of the five EU countries, we can now examine the intrafirm trade data between these five EU countries and the United States. Table 7.6 shows the statistics of intrafirm trade between MNCs from the five EU countries and their subsidiaries in the United States for 1993. Again, the data for Japan and Canada are presented for comparative purposes.

We can observe that exports shipped by U.S. affiliates to all foreign parent groups in 1993 amounted to $47.2 billion, and imports shipped to U.S. affiliates by all foreign parent groups were $148.5 billion. As a result, the United States trade deficits from intrafirm trade of foreign MNCs for 1993 were $101.4 billion. About half of this deficit was generated by intrafirm trade between Japanese MNCs and their U.S. affiliates.

French MNCs imported about $4.6 billion of goods from their U.S. affiliates and exported $4.5 billion of merchandise to those affiliates. German MNCs imported only $2.5 billion of goods from their U.S. affiliates but exported $16.1 billion worth of merchandise to those affiliates. German exports to their U.S.

Table 7.5
U.S. Merchandise Trade with Europe and the Rest of the World, 1995 (Millions of U.S. Dollars)

Country & Region	U.S. Exports	U.S. Imports	Balance of Trade
Total, all countries	574,879	749,348	-174,469
Western Europe	132,205	147,786	-15,581
European Union	121,316	134,321	-13,005
Belgium and Luxembourg	12,755	8,751	4,004
France	14,246	17,217	-2,971
Germany	21,852	36,761	-14,909
Italy	8,690	16,485	-7,795
Netherlands	16,222	6,365	9,857
United Kingdom	27,994	26,716	1,278
Others	19,557	22,026	-2,469
Western Europe, excluding EU	10,889	13,465	-2,576
Eastern Europe	5,741	7,017	-1,276
Canada	127,589	147,870	-20,281
Mexico	46,195	62,362	-16,167
Japan	62,894	123,494	-60,600
China	11,684	45,549	-33,865
The Four Asian Dragons (Hong Kong, South Korea, Singapore and Taiwan)	71,809	81,966	-10,157
Other Countries	116,762	133,304	-16,542

Source: Bach (1996).

subsidiaries in 1993 included motor vehicles and equipment ($6.8 billion), industrial chemicals ($2.5 billion), and machinery ($2.3 billion).

The volume of intrafirm trade between Italian MNCs and their U.S. affiliates was quite small (about $2.6 billion) in 1993. The intrafirm trade total between Dutch MNCs and their U.S. affiliates was about $5.7 billion during 1993. British

Table 7.6
Intrafirm Trade between MNCs from Five EU Countries and Their Subsidiaries in the United States, 1993 (Millions of U.S. Dollars)

Country	Exports Shipped by U.S. Affiliates to the Foreign Parent Groups (1)	Imports Shipped to U.S. Affiliates by the Foreign Parent Groups (2)	U.S. Intrafirm Trade Balance (3)=(1)-(2)
All countries	47,166	148,540	-101,374
France	4,608	4,525	83
Germany	2,485	16,055	-13,570
Italy	791	1,807	-1,016
Netherlands	1,382	4,274	-2,892
United Kingdom	1,930	6,859	-4,929
Japan	28,062	78,426	-50,364
Canada	1,574	7,597	-6,023
The Rest of the World	6,334	28,997	-22,663

Source: U.S. Department of Commerce (1995a).

MNCs imported about $1.9 billion of merchandise from U.S. affiliates and exported $6.9 billion of goods to those affiliates in 1993.

As a whole, MNCs in the five EU countries imported about $11.2 billion of merchandise from their U.S. subsidiaries and exported $33.5 billion of goods to those subsidiaries in 1993. Although these intrafirm trade volumes are substantial, they are well below the intrafirm trade volume achieved by Japanese MNCs. In 1993, Japanese MNCs imported about $28.1 billion of goods from their U.S.

Table 7.7
Intrafirm Trade between U.S. MNCs and Their Affiliates in Five EU Countries, 1993 (Millions of U.S. Dollars)

Country	U.S. Exports Shipped to Foreign Affiliates by U.S. Parents (1)	U.S. Imports Shipped by Foreign Affiliates to U.S. Parents (2)	U.S. Intrafirm Trade Balance (3)=(1)-(2)
All countries	104,987	95,906	9,081
France	3,689	1,905	1,784
Germany	6,955	2,605	4,350
Italy	1,403	697	706
Netherlands	4,611	1,017	3,594
United Kingdom	7,927	4,502	3,425
Japan	8,125	2,671	5,454
Canada	34,078	41,231	-7,153
Mexico	10,761	11,807	-1,046
Other Countries	27,438	29,471	-2,033

Source: U.S. Department of Commerce (1995b).

affiliates and exported $78.4 billion of merchandise to those affiliates. We will discuss more details about Japanese intrafirm trade in Chapter 8.

Table 7.7 provides intrafirm trade statistics between U.S. MNCs and their affiliates in the five EU countries in 1993. Similar data for Japan, Canada, and Mexico are also presented. Relatively speaking, the intrafirm trade between U.S. MNCs and their affiliates in France, Italy, and Netherlands was quite small. The intrafirm trade between U.S. parents and their German affiliates amounted to about $9.6 billion in 1993, with the United States enjoying an intrafirm trade surplus of about $4.4 billion.

In 1993, U.S. MNCs exported about $7.9 billion of goods to their affiliates in Britain. These included $4.6 billion of manufacturing goods and $2.5 billion merchandise for wholesale trade. During the same year, U.S. MNCs imported $2.7 billion of goods from their affiliates in the United Kingdom.

As a whole, U.S. MNCs exported $24.6 billion of goods to their affiliates in the five EU countries and imported $10.7 billion of merchandise from their affiliates in 1993. This intrafirm trade volume was substantially lower than the intrafirm trade between U.S. MNCs and their affiliates in the two NAFTA countries (Canada and Mexico). Intrafirm trade between U.S. MNCs and their Canadian affiliates amounted to $75.3 billion. Intrafirm trade volume between the U.S. firms and their Mexican subsidiaries was about $22.6 billion in 1993.

TRANSFER PRICING REGULATIONS OF SELECTED EU COUNTRIES

France

The key provisions of transfer pricing regulations in France can be found in Article 57 and Article 238A of the French tax code. Article 57 authorizes the French tax administration to adjust the income or deductions reported by a French company that is controlled by a foreign party. However, the provisions of Article 57 also apply to an unrelated foreign party if that party is a resident of a tax haven. An English translation of Article 57 (Lowell, Burge, and Briger, 1994) follows:

To assess the income tax due by French businesses which are controlled by or which control businesses established outside France, the income which is indirectly transferred to the latter, either by increasing or decreasing purchase or sale prices, or by any other means, shall be added back to the net income shown in the accounts. The same applies to businesses which are controlled by a business or a group of businesses which are also controlling the businesses located outside France and involved in the transaction.

The condition of control or dependence is not required when the beneficiary of the transfer of the profits is located in a country or a territory with a privileged tax status.

If no precise data are available to allow a fair computation of the adjustments of the transfer prices, the taxable income is determined by comparison with the income of similar businesses managed under normal conditions. (pp. 16–22)

Article 238A is related to Article 57 and directed at selected transactions with individuals and companies located in tax haven jurisdictions. The following is an English translation of Article 238A (Lowell, Burge, and Briger, 1994):

Interest, arrears and other proceeds of bonds, claims, deposits and guarantees, royalties in consideration of the sale or license of patents, trade marks, know-how or manufacturing formulas and other similar rights, or the compensation for services, paid or owned by an individual or an entity domiciled or established in a foreign state or territory, where it benefits from a favorable tax regime, are not tax deductible unless the French debtor proves that the expenses correspond to real transactions and are not abnormal or magnified.

For the purpose of this article, an individual or company is deemed to be subject to a favorable tax regime in a foreign country or territory if, under that regime, it pays no tax or is liable to corporate tax or income tax at a substantially lower rate than in France. (pp. 16–22)

According to French regulations, a "tax haven" is defined as a jurisdiction that levies an income tax less than two-thirds of the French corporate income tax under the same circumstances. To carry out the authority provided by Article 57, the French tax administration must establish the following:

—the French company is controlled by or controls the foreign party or that both parties are controlled by another holding company or corporate group unless the foreign party is a resident of a tax haven jurisdiction; and

—profits were transferred out of France by granting abnormal advantages to the foreign party.

Article 238A shifts the burden of proof to the taxpayer. In cases involving Article 238A, the taxpayer must prove that the transaction was carried out for sound business reasons and the price charged was an arm's-length price. Both the French tax authorities and taxpayers can use the current OECD guidelines as a reference to determine arm's-length prices.

Transfer pricing cases in France are handled by the National and International Audit Service. However, the French tax authorities have a dismal record in prosecuting transfer pricing cases. In 80 percent of the cases between 1988 and 1991, the courts ruled in favor of taxpayers (BlanLuet, 1992). One reason is that the French tax administration does not have the general manpower, the economists, or enough evidence to defend those cases effectively. The courts often sided with taxpayers if transfer prices were established for business or market reasons (O'Haver, Levey, and Clancy, 1993).

To enhance its power to investigate transfer pricing practices, the French tax administration introduced new rules in the tax bill presented to the French Parliament on February 11, 1995. These provisions, if adopted, would amend several articles of the French tax code concerning transfer pricing (Delatte and Mouthon, 1996). Article 18 of the proposed legislation requires the taxpayer to provide the following documentation if the tax authorities establish that a taxpayer has transferred profits abroad under Article 57 of the tax code (Delatte and Mouthon, 1996):

—the nature of the intrafirm transactions;

—a description and rationale for the methods used in determining transfer prices; and

—the functions and activities performed by the related parties.

If the taxpayer fails to provide these documents, taxes may be imposed based on information available to the tax authorities and the taxpayer may be subject to severe penalties. The proposed regulations also extended the statute of limitations from three to five years for tax audit involving transfer pricing cases.

Germany

The main source of German regulations on transfer pricing can be found in the General Administrative Principles (GAP) released by the Federal Ministry of Finance on February 23, 1983. According to the interpretation of German tax authorities, the GAP is a "representation of law in force giving regard to present international practice" (Lowell, Burge, and Briger, 1994, pp. 16–35). The GAP applies to both German multinational companies (MNCs) and German subsidiaries of foreign multinationals.

The general rule is that related-party transactions will be examined in comparison with independent-party transactions in a situation of free competition. The underlying principle is "the normal degree of commercial prudence shown by a sound and conscientious business manager" (Radler and Jacob 1984; EIU/ E&Y, 1994), or "the theory of the sound and prudent business person" (Lowell, Burge, and Briger, 1994, pp. 16–34). A sound and prudent business manager will derive the transfer price, with all necessary care, from data available or that are accessible to the manager.

The GAP provides the following guidelines for the calculation of arm's-length prices:

—quoted market prices;

—prices charged between the taxpayer and an unrelated third party; and

—profit markups, methods of costing, or other business principles that influence pricing in a free market.

When reviewing the transfer price for a particular case, the German tax authorities will examine the following circumstances of that case:

—the uniqueness and quality of goods and merchandise transferred;

—the conditions of the market in which the goods or merchandise are used, consumed, processed or sold to unrelated parties;

—the functions performed by each party involved;

—contractual terms including payment methods, the bearing of risk and warranty, and so forth;

—in the case of long-term transfer relationships, the associated advantages and risks; and

—other special circumstances of competition.

Since the German Tax Authority endorses the latest OECD guidelines (OECD 1995b), we can use the following methods recommended by the OECD for the transfers of tangible or intangible property:

—comparable uncontrolled price method (CUP);
—resale price method (RPM);
—cost plus method (CPLM);
—profit split method (PSM); or
—transactional net margin method (TNMM).

Details of these methods are discussed in Chapter 5.

On cost-sharing arrangements (CSAs), German tax authorities may require subsidiaries of foreign multinationals to make available the books and records of their parent company and of other affiliates to support the deductibility of payments made by the taxpayers (Vögele, 1994). Specifically, German subsidiaries of foreign MNCs must submit the following documents:

—the contracts, side agreements, and records relating to the administrative or R&D services supplied by foreign parents and other affiliates; and
—all internal documents regarding the recording and allocation of the costs and similar items.

It is possible to negotiate an advance pricing agreement through the German tax authorities. Three types of arrangements are now available (Vögele, 1994):

1. bilateral rulings with the United States;
2. unilateral rulings binding the German authorities and the taxpayers; and
3. Unilateral binding opinions relating to major transfer pricing issues for which taxpayers may want to obtain approval in advance.

In recent years, German tax authority has expanded its investigations of transfer pricing practices. Its tax auditing scheme is very efficient. Price adjustments imposed by the tax authority may lead to an extremely high tax burden (Lowell, Burge, and Briger, 1994).

In a small survey concerning German transfer pricing audits, Dehnen (1995) discovered that 11 of the 15 companies surveyed had been subject to one or more German tax audits. Of these 11 audited companies, 4 indicated that transfer pricing was the main issue. Three firms also reported that the transfer pricing investigations were based on the tax auditors' claim that these companies had experienced losses over an excessive number of years. After the investigations were completed, three companies paid additional taxes to the German tax authorities based on negotiated settlements.

Italy

The statutory basis of Italian transfer pricing regulations can be traced to article 76(5) of the Testo Unico Imposte Dirette. Transfer prices for goods and services are governed by the concept of "normal value" as defined in article 9(3) of the code as follows (Levey, Oster, and Greco, 1993):

The average price or consideration paid for goods and services of the same or similar type, in free-market conditions and at the same level of commerce, at the time and place in which the goods and services were purchased or performed or, if there be none, at the time and place nearest thereto. In determining normal value, reference shall be made to the extent possible to price lists or tariffs of the party which has supplied the goods and services and, if there be none, to the indices and price lists of the Chambers of Commerce and to professional tariffs, taking normal discounts into account. For goods and services subject to price control, reference shall be made to the regulations in force.

The Italian Ministry of Finance also issued two circulars, on September 22, 1980, and December 12, 1981, to provide some criteria for applying the rules in the code concerning transfer pricing. The 1980 circular stated that transfer price is to be applied on a transaction-by-transaction approach. The same circular treated the comparable uncontrolled price (CUP) as the primary transfer pricing method, while the resale price method (RPM) and cost plus method (CPLM) are considered as secondary methods. The 1981 circular clarified that RPM and CPLM are of equal priority, while being secondary to the CUP method (Levey, Oster, and Greco, 1993).

Before the 1995 OECD guidelines were issued, Italy endorsed the principles and standards stated in the 1979 OECD report. Because Italy is a member of the OECD and participated in the development of the 1995 Guidelines, we can assume that the pricing methods recommended by the OECD (1995b) are acceptable to the Italian tax authorities.

In Italy, tax authorities may carry out a transfer pricing audit of a business when its rate of return is substantially lower than the average rate of the same industry. However, the number of transfer pricing investigations in Italy is still rather limited compared with other EU countries.

The Netherlands

There are no specific transfer pricing regulations in the Netherlands. However, associated companies are required to account for intracompany transactions based on arm's-length principles. The basic guideline in the Netherlands is that intrafirm transactions must represent "sound business practice" (Pape, 1996). Government authority for reallocation of income and deductions derived from the definition of profits is provided in article 7 of the Income Tax Act (Lowell, Burge, and Briger, 1994).

Article 7 defines business profits to include all profits and gains from the operations of a business. Profits and losses created by special relationships between related companies are excluded from taxable income. For example, if intrafirm transactions are not priced at arm's length and the reported profit of a Dutch subsidiary is less than the arm's-length profit, then the difference between the two profit figures will be treated as constructive dividends to its parent. On the other hand, if the reported profit of the Dutch subsidiary is substantially higher than the arm's length profit due to special treatment by the parent, an informal capital contribution from the parent company is recognized. Such special treatments may include interest-free loans and contribution of valuable intangibles without payment of royalties.

The Dutch government endorses current transfer pricing guidelines issued by the OECD (1995b). The transfer pricing methods recommended by the OECD are acceptable to Dutch tax authorities. Details of these methods are discussed in Chapter 5.

To avoid lengthy disputes with the Dutch tax authorities, taxpayers can apply for advance rulings in some areas of operations as follows (Lowell, Burge, and Briger, 1994; Boidman, 1992):

—financing activities that include allocation of financial profits to foreign branches;

—licensing activities; and

—supporting, preparatory and auxiliary activities.

An advance ruling on transfer prices for these activities may be given for three to four years and may be renewed for another four-year period if such ruling is consistent with current tax law and official policy.

On October 19, 1994, the Netherlands formalized procedures for taxpayers to apply for bilateral advance pricing agreements (Turro, 1994). The new procedures explain the paperwork flow and stipulate that the tax authorities are willing to enter into joint discussions with their counterparts in other countries. The Department of International Tax Affairs of the Ministry of Finance will represent the government to negotiate all bilateral APAs. The Dutch tax authorities will be bound by all APAs reached with the taxpayer and foreign governments.

The United Kingdom

The main source of British transfer pricing regulations can be found in sections 770 to 773 of the Income and Corporation Taxes Act of 1988. These sections are reproduced in Appendix D. According to section 770(1), when property is sold at an undervalue or bought at an overvalue and the parties involved are bodies of persons that control each other or that are under common control, the Inland Revenue may replace the price with an arm's-length price. However, this rule in section 770(1) does not apply to the following situations:

—in any case where the actual price is less than the arm's-length price, and the buyer is a U.K. resident and is carrying on a trade there, and the price of the property fails to be taken into account as a deduction in computing the profits or losses for tax purposes;

—in any case where the actual price is greater than the arm's-length price, and the seller is a U.K. resident, and the price of the property fails to be taken into account as a receipt in computing the profits or losses for tax purposes;

—in relation to any transaction to which section 493(1) or (3) applies; or

—in relation to any other sale, unless the Board [of Inland Revenue] so directs.

Section 771 contains special rules for transactions or activities of petroleum companies. Section 772 provides Inland Revenue the authority to obtain information and documentation from taxpayers for the purposes of section 770. Section 773 contains additional interpretations for sections 770, 771, and 772. For example, section 773 defines "body of persons" to include a partnership. It also states that "control" has the meaning given by section 840 of the act.

The Inland Revenue does not provide any additional regulations or rules to interpret the transfer pricing law in section 770 to section 773. However in "Guidance Notes" on "The Transfer Pricing of Multinational Enterprises," released on January 26, 1981, the Inland Revenue stated that it will be guided by the principles and standards set out in the 1979 OECD report. Before that report was superseded by the 1995 OECD guidelines, both the Inland Revenue and British taxpayers referred extensively to the OECD 1979 and 1984 reports for guidance on many transfer pricing issues (Lowell, Borge, and Briger, 1994). Now that these OECD reports have been superseded by the 1995 OECD guidelines, we can assume that the principles and pricing methods recommended by OECD (1995) are acceptable to the Inland Revenue.

In recent years, the Inland Revenue has intensified its investigations of corporate transfer pricing practices. For example, in 1992, the Inland Revenue issued a demand for £237 million in unpaid taxes against Nissan UK, the former distributor of Nissan Japan's automobiles in the United Kingdom (Pass, 1994). The Inland Revenue claimed that "falsely inflated" shipping invoices had been used to understate Nissan UK pretax profits from 1975 to 1992. The full story of the case of Inland Revenue versus Nissan UK can be found in Figure 7.1.

In 1994, the British government introduced a self-assessment system for corporation tax that fundamentally changed the way corporate tax is assessed. Before this system was introduced, companies submitted audited financial statements and other required information to the local tax inspector, and the district inspector then assessed the corporation tax. Effective since 1988, corporations are expected to submit formal tax returns and determine their own tax liability through a self-assessment system. On November 28, 1995, the Budget Day press release revealed that the chancellor had asked the Inland Revenue to consult interested parties over the coming months about any procedural changes

Figure 7.1
The Case of *Inland Revenue v. Nissan UK*

The Inland Revenue's litigation against Nissan UK, while not strictly a case of "pure" internal transfer pricing, provides useful insight into some of the general features of clandestine transfer pricing and its detection. In 1992 the Inland Revenue issued a demand for £237m in unpaid taxes against Nissan UK, the former distributor of Nissan Japan's motor cars in the UK. Nissan UK is a private company controlled by Octav Botnar, whose parent company is the Panama-incorporated European Motor Vehicles Corporation. The substance of the Inland Revenue's charge was that executives of Nissan UK, in collusion with a Norwegian freight transport company, had conspired to defraud the UK authorities of corporation tax. Transfer pricing, using "falsely inflated" shipping invoices, had been employed to under-record Nissan UK's pre-tax profits over the period 1975–92. In 1971 Nissan UK obtained an exclusive franchise to import cars from Nissan Japan. Until 1975 it paid for the cars with a single "cost, insurance and freight" payment to Nissan Japan's transport division NMCC. From 1975 onwards it employed, first, the services of a Dutch freight forwarder and then, from 1982, Scansivis, a Norwegian shipping firm. Over this period freight charges for imported cars were overstated by 40 to 60 percent by Scansivis, which arranged for moneys paid over to be "laundered" into a Swiss bank account.

In 1991, acting on a "tip-off," the Inland Revenue mounted a dawn raid against Nissan UK, searching 13 locations, including the company's headquarters, the offices of several of its legal and financial advisers, and the homes of a number of current and former executives of the company. Two directors of Nissan UK were subsequently found guilty at the Old Bailey of fraud, but the prime mover of the operation, Botnar, had already evaded arrest by moving to Switzerland.

Source: Pass (1994).

to the transfer pricing legislation that might be necessary as a result of the new self-assessment system (White and Atkinson, 1996; Symons and Thomas, 1996). Many businesses have expressed the following concerns for including transfer pricing regime within the self-assessment framework (White and Atkinson, 1996):

—it may lead to a prescriptive regulatory system that contains detailed regulations, administrative principles, and other instructions on how to arrive at arm's-length prices;

—taxpayers may be required to verify the arm's-length nature of their transfer prices and to confirm compliance with the arm's-length standard;

—it may require more transfer pricing investigations by the Inland Revenue and increase the degree of uncertainty for corporate transfer pricing practices; and

—it may increase the costs of compliance with legislation.

Two of the Big Six international accounting firms took the opportunity to make the following recommendations to the British tax authorities (White and Atkinson, 1996; Symons and Thomas, 1996):

—There is no need for the Inland Revenue to draft comprehensive new regulations for transfer pricing. A statement by the Inland Revenue that taxpayers may apply the principles and standards in the 1995 OECD *Transfer Pricing Guidelines* will clarify the status of the OECD guidelines in British law and practices.

—It will be useful if the Board of Inland Revenue would issue guidance on the nature of the particulars and documents that tax inspectors might ask a taxpayer to submit in the course of a transfer pricing enquiry.

—If transfer pricing is to be included in the self-assessment framework, the arm's-length test in the legislation should recognize that the transfer price on any one intrafirm transaction should not be considered in isolation from other intrafirm transactions.

—Taxpayers should be given the right to resubmit claims and elections following transfer pricing enquiries and be permitted "offsets" where undercharges compensate overcharges in other areas.

—In order to minimize the uncertainty concerning transfer pricing, advance clearance in the form of pretransaction rulings should be offered to all taxpayers.

Having held preliminary discussions with professional associations and industry/taxpayer groups, the Inland Revenue was expected to issue a consultative document in late 1996 or early 1997 (Pape, 1996). The new document may introduce penalties as part of a broader move to a self-assessment corporate tax system.

In Britain, taxpayers can also negotiate bilateral advance pricing agreements with the Inland Revenue in cases when the setting of transfer prices involves significant "doubt or difficulty" (White and Atkinson, 1996). The negotiation can be conducted through the mutual agreement procedure article in British double taxation conventions with treaty partners. For example, in 1992, Barclays and Sumitomo concluded their bilateral APAs with the IRS and the Inland Revenue under the authority of the U.S.-U.K. competent authority procedure (Boidman, 1992).

Other Recent Developments in the European Union

In July 1990, before the European Community (EC) became the European Union (EU), it adopted the following directives and convention:

—"Directive on Parent Companies and Subsidiaries";
—"Directive on Mergers, Divisions, Transfer of Assets, and Exchanges of Shares"; and
—"Draft Convention of Transfer Pricing Arbitration."

The purpose for adopting these were twofold: to harmonize tax legislation among member countries and to minimize the risk of double taxation. The "Directive on Parent Companies" and Subsidiaries prescribes that dividends paid by a subsidiary in one member state to a parent company in another member country will be paid without withholding tax. In addition, the dividends received by the parent should not be taxed by the recipient country (cited in Fox, 1991). One objective of this directive is to promote the free movement of capital among the member states.

The "Directive on Mergers, Divisions, Transfers of Assets, and Exchanges of Shares" will defer taxation of capital gains on a variety of noncash, cross-border transactions in shares or corporate assets. One objective is to remove tax disincentives for the above transactions involving only the EC (now, EU) countries. These two directives took effect on January 1, 1992.

The "Convention on Transfer Pricing Arbitration" provides a mechanism for binding arbitration when the competent authorities of the member states involved cannot agree on a transfer price that eliminates double taxation. An advisory commission was to be established to arbitrate the case if mutual consultation between competent authorities cannot resolve their differences. The commission was to consist of two representatives from each competent authority (or one by agreement), augmented by another member drawn from a list comprising five nominees from each member state (Fox, 1991).

The commission has the power to request information and summon parties before it. The taxpayers involved or their representatives may appear before the commission. Within six months of the advisory commission's ruling, the tax authorities involved must implement the commission's recommendations or argue for an alternative solution.

The Arbitration Convention became effective on January 1, 1995, after being ratified by the 12 member states of the European Union in 1994. The convention will not apply to the three new member states (Austria, Sweden, and Denmark) until after they ratify it. The Committee on Fiscal Affairs of the OECD is conducting a study on transfer pricing arbitration and will supplement the 1995 OECD guidelines with the conclusions of the study when it is completed.

In early 1996, Belgian tax authorities concluded its first bilateral advance pricing agreement (APA) with the IRS in the United States under article 25 of the U.S.-Belgium tax treaty (Kelly, 1996). This APA was requested by a U.S. MNC with wide-ranging operations in Belgium and other European countries. During the APA negotiation, the Belgian tax authorities formally accepted the principles and standards of the new OECD guidelines.

SUMMARY AND CONCLUSIONS

This chapter reviewed the international investment and trade activities of five selected EU countries (France, Germany, Italy, the Netherlands, and the United Kingdom). We also examined the key transfer pricing legislation and regulations of these countries.

Statistics show that these five EU countries are among the ten largest trading nations of the world. They are also the key players in international investment activities. For example, in the 1980s, the total direct investment abroad from the five EU countries amounted to about $440 billion. During the same period, these five countries also received a total of $245 billion of foreign investment.

The United States maintains very close investment and trade relationships with the five EU countries. At the end of 1994, the U.S. DIP in these five countries was $209 billion and these five countries' DIP in the U.S. amounted to about $260 billion. In 1995, the two-way trade between the United States and the five EU countries was about $193 billion. The volume of intrafirm trade between the United States and these EU countries was also quite substantial.

After reviewing the transfer pricing regulations of these five EU countries, we found that their regulations require the use of arm's-length principles for intrafirm trade. However, very few of them have detailed rules or guidelines for transfer pricing. Most tax authorities in these countries endorse the new OECD guidelines and use them to negotiate bilateral APAs with the Internal Revenue Service of the United States.

All five EU countries have intensified their investigations of multinational transfer pricing practices in recent years. Their tax auditing schemes are becoming more efficient and effective. These developments have significant tax planning implications for multinational businesses. To avoid substantial tax adjustments and penalties, multinational companies conducting business in Europe should review their transfer pricing policies to make sure that those policies are in compliance with the new OECD Guidelines and transfer pricing regulations of major European countries.

REFERENCES

Airs, Graham. 1994. UK Adheres to Arm's Length Approach. *International Tax Review Supplement* (February): 27–32.

Bach, Christopher L. 1996. U.S. International Transactions, Fourth Quarter and Year 1995. *Survey of Current Business* (April): 45–71.

Baldwin, Richard E. 1994. *Towards an Integrated Europe*. London: Centre for Economic Policy Research.

BlanLuet, Gauthier. 1992. France—Transfer Pricing: Theory and Practice. *European Taxation* (January): 21–24.

Boidman, Nathan. 1992. The Effect of the APA and Other U.S. Transfer Pricing Initiatives in Canada and Other Countries. *Tax Executive* (July–August): 254–261.

Bourgeois, Jacques H. J. 1995. EC or EU: More Than a Question of Semantics? *EC Tax Review* (1995/4): 188–189.

Cuadrado, Jean-Luc. 1994. France: Is the Arm's Length Method the Best Approach? *International Tax Review Supplement* (February): 9–19.

Dehnen, Peter H. 1995. Survey Results of German Transfer Pricing Audits. *Tax Executive* (May–June): 192–193.

Delatte, Oliver, and Etienne Mouthon. 1996. France Proposes New Transfer Pricing Rules. *Tax Notes International* (March 18): 867–868.

Deloitte & Touche. 1993. Netherlands Anti–Tax Haven Legislation. *Deloitte & Touche Review* (August 9): 5–6.

Donald, David C. 1991. Taxation for a Single Market: European Community Legislation on Mergers, Distributed Profits, and Intracompany Sales. *Law and Policy in International Business* (Vol. 22, No. 1): 37–73.

Douvier, Pierre-Jean. 1993. France: Transfer Pricing. *European Taxation* (December): 416–417.

Economic Intelligence Unit (EIU) and Ernst & Young (E&Y). 1994. *International Transfer Pricing 1994.* New York: EIU.

Eggert, Rolf. 1994. The German Transfer Pricing Approach. *KPMG Transfer Pricing News* (August): 10–11.

Fernández, Albertina M., and Susan M. Lyons. 1996. The Transatlantic Tax Outlook: European and U.S. Tax Relations. *Tax Notes International* (June 17): 1923–1925.

Fischer, Thomas C. 1995. *The Europeanization of America.* Durham, N.C.: Carolina Academic Press.

Fox, Jonathan. 1991. European Community Tax Directives. *International Tax Journal* (Spring): 45–50.

Gelin, Stephen, and Francois Rontani. 1996. Draft Tax Bill Announced by the French Government. *Tax Notes International* (February 26): 638–639.

Groenen, Alfred, and Spieros Spierendonk. 1994. Flexible Approach for Dutch Regime. *International Tax Review Supplement* (February): 21–26.

Hitzegrad, Hans-Jörg. 1994. Hidden Transfer of Profits from Germany to Abroad? *European Taxation* (January): 29–32.

Hornsby, Brian J., and Nicolaas T. Van der Klott. 1990. European Community Initiatives on Corporate Income Taxes: European and U.S. Perspectives. *Tax Management International Journal* (Vol. 19, No. 12): 515–526.

Kelly, Patrick L. 1996. Recent Developments in Advance Pricing Agreement in Belgium. *Tax Notes International* (May 27): 1681–1685.

Kourvetaris, George A., and Andreas Moschonas, eds. 1996. *The Impact of European Integration.* Westport, Conn.: Praeger.

Levey, Marc M., Lee A. Oster, and Fabio Greco. 1993. Section 482 Regs. and Italian Transfer Pricing Rules Are Often at Odds. *Journal of International Taxation* (October).

Lowell, Cym H., Marianne Burge, and Peter L. Briger. 1994. *U.S. International Transfer Pricing.* Boston: Warren, Gorham and Lamont.

Millington, A., I. F. Bowen, and B. T. Bayliss. 1996. Corporate Integration in the EU: Recent Developments. *Intereconomics* (March/April): 68–72.

O'Haver, Russ, Marc Levey, and Jim Clancy. 1993. When the Price Isn't Right. *Journal of European Business* (July/August): 57–63.

Organization for Economic Co-operation and Development (OECD). 1979. *Transfer Pricing and Multinational Enterprises.* Paris: OECD.

———. 1995a. *OECD Reviews of Foreign Direct Investment, United States.* Paris: OECD.

———. 1995b. *Transfer Pricing Guidelines for Multinational Enterprises and Tax Administrations.* Paris: OECD.

Pape, Sarah. 1996. Recent European Tax Developments—Coopers & Lybrand European Tax Forum. *Tax Notes International* (June 24): 2006–2011.

Pass, Christopher. 1994. Transfer Pricing in Multinational Companies. *Management Accounting* (U.K.) (September): 44, 46, 50.

Picciotto, Sol. 1992. International Taxation and Intrafirm Pricing in Transnational Corporate Groups. *Accounting, Organization and Society* (Vol. 7, No. 8): 759–792.

Radler, Albert J., and Jacob Friedheim. 1984. *German Transfer Pricing.* Boston: Kluwer.

Russell-Walling, Edward. 1995. The Fading Dream of the European Union. *International Business* (October): 30–38.

Stitt, Jain. 1991. Direct Taxation and the Single European Market. *European Management Journal* (September): 235–245.

Strobl, Jacob. 1980. German Tax Audits of Foreign Subsidiaries: Practice and Experience. *European Taxation* (Vol. 20, No. 9): 273–292.

Symons, Terry, and Hazel Thomas. 1996. PW Consultative Group of 24 MNCs Comments on Transfer Pricing and Self Assessment. *International Tax Review* (March/April): 10–11.

Turro, John. 1994. Netherlands Formalizes APA Procedures. *Tax Notes International* (November 14): 1531–1532.

U.S. Department of Commerce, Economics and Statistics Administration. Bureau of Economic Analysis. 1995a. *Foreign Direct Investment in the United States: Preliminary 1993 Estimates.* Washington, D.C.: U.S. Government Printing Office.

———. 1995b. *U.S. Direct Investment Abroad: Preliminary 1993 Estimates.* Washington, D.C.: U.S. Government Printing Office.

Vögele, Alexander. German Tax Authorities (1) Accept Audit Report in Lieu of Foreign Books and Records and (2) Encourage APAs. *International Tax Review* (May/June): 14–15.

Wacker, Raymond. 1993. Anti-Treaty Shopping Restrictions in the New U.S.-Netherlands Tax Treaty. *Tax Executive* (September–October): 383–390.

White, Robert A., and Mark Atkinson. 1996. Transfer Pricing and Self-Assessment: Comments in Response to an Inland Revenue Press Release on U.K. Transfer Pricing Procedures. *Tax Notes International* (April 8): 1175–1182.

8

Intrafirm Trade and Transfer Pricing Regulations: The Asian Pacific Regional Perspective

The Asian Pacific is the fastest growing region in the world. Many countries in the region, including Australia, China, and Singapore, have attracted substantial sums of foreign investment. Some including Japan, Hong Kong, South Korea, and Taiwan, have invested heavily in other countries. International trade and intrafirm trade are also booming for many countries in the region.

In Chapter 8, we will examine many issues related to intrafirm trade and transfer pricing from the Asian Pacific regional perspective. Specifically, we will cover the following topics:

—bilateral investment relationships between the United States and selected Asian Pacific countries (APCs);

—international trade of the APCs and their bilateral trade with the United States;

—interfirm trade between the United States and the APCs in recent years; and

—transfer pricing regulations of four major trading partners of the United States: Australia, China, Japan, and South Korea.

BILATERAL INVESTMENT BETWEEN THE UNITED STATES AND THE ASIAN PACIFIC COUNTRIES (APCs)

Table 8.1 shows the U.S. direct investment positions (DIPs) in Asian Pacific countries (APCs) and DIPs of the APCs in the United States. At the end of 1994, U.S. DIP in APCs was $108.4 billion, equivalent to about 17.7 percent of all U.S. DIP abroad. On the other hand, the APCs' DIP in the United States was $117.8 billion, accounting for 23.4 percent of all foreign direct investment

Table 8.1
U.S. Direct Investment Positions in Asian Pacific Countries (APCs) and APCs in the United States, 1994 (Millions of U.S. Dollars)

Country	U.S. DIPs in the APCs (1)	APCs DIPs in the U.S. (2)	Net U.S. DIPs in the APCs (3) = (1) - (2)
APC Total	108,402	117,835	-9,433
Australia	20,504	7,884	12,620
New Zealand	3,577	158	3,419
Japan	37,027	103,120	-66,093
South Korea	3,612	1,158	2,454
China	1,699	N.A.	N.A.
Hong Kong	11,986	1,723	10,263
Taiwan	3,882	1,438	2,444
Indonesia	5,015	N.A.	N.A.
Malaysia	2,382	451	1,931
Philippines	2,374	86	2,288
Singapore	10,972	1,135	9,837
Thailand	3,762	N.A.	N.A.
Other	1,610	N.A.	N.A.

Note: Calculated on a historical-cost basis.
N.A. = Not available.
Sources: U.S. Department of Commerce, Bureau of Economic Analysis, *Survey of Current Business* (various issues).

in that nation. As a result, the United States had a negative net DIP of $9.4 billion in the APCs.

U.S. DIP in Japan ($37.0 billion) at the end of 1994 was the largest among U.S. DIP in all APCs. U.S. Department of Commerce data reveal that U.S. direct investment in Japan was mainly in the following industries: petroleum ($6.1 billion, or 16.5 percent); manufacturing ($15.8 billion, or 42.8 percent); wholesale trade (6.8 billion, or 18.5 percent); and finance, insurance and real estate

($6.4 billion, or 17.3 percent). Besides Japan, U.S. MNCs also had significant investments in Australia ($20.5 billion), Hong Kong ($12.0 billion), Singapore ($11.0 billion), and Indonesia ($5.0 billion).

At the end of 1994, Japan's DIP in the United States was $103.1 billion, accounting for 87 percent of all APCs' DIP in the United States. Because Japan's DIP in the United States was substantially larger than the U.S. DIP in Japan, Japan had a net investment position of $66.1 billion in the U.S. at the end of 1994. One other Asian Pacific country that had significant investment position in the United Sates was Australia, which had a $7.9 billion DIP in the United States.

INTERNATIONAL TRADE OF THE APCs AND THEIR BILATERAL TRADE WITH THE UNITED STATES

Table 8.2 presents the international trade statistics of selected APCs for 1995 (1994 for some countries). We can observe that most of these countries are heavily involved in international trade. For example, Japan exported $443.1 billion of goods and imported $336 billion of merchandise in 1995. It is the third largest trading nation in the world (after the United States and Germany), with an annual trade surplus of about $107 billion. Hong Kong had a total trade volume of $365.9 billion and a trade surplus of $18.9 billion in 1995. Other countries that had international trade volume of more than $200 billion each are South Korea, China, Taiwan, and Singapore. Australia and Malaysia each had a trade volume of more than $100 billion.

Many of these countries have close bilateral trade relationships with the United States. Their trade statistics with the United States are shown in Table 8.3. Japan is the largest trading partner of the United States among all the APCs. Its annual trade volume with the United States was about $186.4 billion in 1995, accounting for about one-quarter of its foreign trade. Japan's trade surplus with the United States was $60.6 billion in 1995.

China is the United States' second largest trading partner in the Asian Pacific region. Its trade volume with the United States has expanded rapidly in recent years. In 1995, two-way U.S.-China trade was $57.2 billion, with China enjoying a trade surplus of $33.8 billion. Other countries that had substantial trade volumes with the United States include Taiwan, South Korea, Hong Kong, Singapore, and Malaysia.

INTRAFIRM TRADE BETWEEN THE APCs AND THE UNITED STATES

Intrafirm trade between the APCs and the United States can be divided into two categories: (1) those between U.S. MNCs and their affiliates in the APCs, and (2) those between U.S. affiliates and their foreign parent groups in the APCs. Intrafirm trade in the first category is summarized in Table 8.4. In 1993, U.S.

Table 8.2
International Trade of Selected Asian Pacific Countries, 1995 (Billions of U.S. Dollars)

Country	Exports (1)	Imports (2)	Trade Balance (3) = (1) - (2)
Australia	53.1	61.3	-8.2
New Zealand	13.7	14.0	-0.3
Japan	443.1	336.0	107.1
South Korea	125.1	135.1	-10.0
China	148.8	129.1	19.7
Hong Kong	173.5	192.4	18.9
Taiwan	111.6	103.7	7.9
ASEAN Countries*:			
Indonesia	40.1	32.0*	8.1
Malaysia	58.8*	59.6*	-0.8
Philippines	13.3*	22.5*	-9.2
Singapore	118.3	124.5	-6.2
Thailand	45.3*	54.5*	-9.2

*1994 figures.
Source: International Monetary Fund, *International Financial Statistics* (May 1996).
Note: ASEAN = Association of South East Asian Nations.

exports shipped to foreign affiliates by U.S. parents totaled $22.2 billion while U.S. imports shipped by foreign affiliates to U.S. parents amounted to $20.8 billion.

From Table 8.4, we can observe that U.S. MNCs had substantial intrafirm trade with their subsidiaries in Singapore, Japan, and Hong Kong. U.S. MNCs exported $3.1 billion of goods to affiliates in Singapore but imported $8.1 billion from those affiliates. A foreign affiliate is defined by the U.S. Department of Commerce as a foreign business enterprise in which a U.S. person owns or controls 10 percent of the voting securities or the equivalent. The intrafirm trade

Table 8.3
Bilateral Trade between the United States and Selected Asian Pacific Countries, 1995 (Billions of U.S. Dollars)

Country	U.S. Experts to the Asian Pacific Countries (1)	U.S. Imports from the Asian Pacific Countries (2)	U.S. Trade Balance (3)
Australia	10.5	3.4	7.1
New Zealand	1.5*	1.4*	0.1*
Japan	62.9	123.5	-60.6
South Korea	24.2	24.2	0.0
China	11.7	45.5	-33.8
Hong Kong	14.2	10.3	-3.9
Taiwan	18.5	29.0	-10.5
ASEAN Countries*:			
Indonesia	2.8*	6.5*	3.7*
Malaysia	7.0*	14.0*	-7.0*
Philippines	3.9*	5.7*	-1.8*
Singapore	14.9	18.6	-3.7
Thailand	4.9*	10.3*	-5.4*

*1994 figures.
Note: ASEAN = Association of South East Asian Nations.
Sources: Bach (1996); U.S. Department of Commerce, Economics and Statistics Administration, Bureau of the Census (1996).

between U.S. MNCs and their Japanese affiliates totaled $10.8 billion, with the United States enjoying a surplus of $5.5 billion. The intrafirm trade volume between U.S. MNCs and their affiliates in Hong Kong was about $7.1 billion in 1993.

Intrafirm trade statistics between U.S. affiliates and their foreign parent groups in the APCs are provided in Table 8.5. The table shows that U.S. exports shipped by U.S. affiliates to foreign parent groups amounted to $30.3 billion, whereas

Table 8.4
Intrafirm Trade between U.S. MNCs and Their Affiliates in Asian Pacific Countries, 1993 (Millions of U.S. Dollars)

Countries	U.S. Exports Shipped to Affiliates by U.S. Parents (1)	U.S. Imports Shipped by Affiliates to U.S. Parents (2)	U.S. Intrafirms Trade Balance (3)
All Asian Pacific Countries	22,174	20,770	1,394
Australia	2,958	592	2,366
New Zealand	166	26	140
Japan	8,125	2,671	5,454
South Korea	846	359	487
China	309	(D)	N.A.
Hong Kong	3,352	3,701	-349
Taiwan	1,190	1,025	165
Indonesia	280	(D)	N.A.
Malaysia	926	2,173	-1,247
Philippines	146	429	-283
Singapore	3,136	8,117	-4,981
Thailand	701	902	-201
Other	38	13	25

Notes: (D) = Data suppressed to avoid disclosure of data of individual company.
N.A. = Not available.
Source: U.S. Department of Commerce, Economics and Statistics Administration, Bureau of Economic Analysis (1995b).

U.S. imports shipped to U.S. affiliates by foreign parent groups totaled $86.7 billion in 1993. As a result, the United States experienced a large intrafirm trade deficit of $56.4 billion. Most of the intrafirm trade (about 91 percent) in this category was trade between Japanese MNCs and their affiliates in the United States. Intrafirm trade between Japanese MNCs and their U.S. affiliates also accounted for 57 percent of all U.S.-Japan merchandise trade in 1993. This is one reason why Japanese MNCs are important targets of transfer pricing investigations by the U.S. Congress and the Internal Revenue Service (IRS). Korean

Table 8.5
Intrafirm Trade between U.S. Affiliates and Their Foreign Parent Groups in
Asian Pacific Countries, 1993 (Millions of U.S. Dollars)

Country	U.S. Exports Shipped by Affiliates to Foreign Parent Groups (1)	U.S. Imports Shipped to Affiliates by Foreign Parent Groups (2)	U.S. Intrafirm Trade Balance (3)=(1)-(2)
All Asian Pacific Countries	30,335	86,715	-56,380
Australia	105	430	-325
New Zealand	2	492	-490
Japan	28,062	78,426	-50,364
South Korea	1,408	5,370	-3,962
China	426	(D)	N.A.
Hong Kong	37	541	-504
Taiwan	174	744	-570
Indonesia	19	14	5
Malaysia	2	13	-11
Philippines	2	(D)	N.A.
Singapore	21	58	-37
Thailand	N.A.	N.A.	N.A.
Other	78	254	-176

Notes: (D) = Data suppressed to avoid disclosure of data of individual companies.
N.A. = Not available.
Source: U.S. Department of Commerce, Economics and Statistics Administration, Bureau of Economic Analysis (1995a).

MNCs and their U.S. affiliates also had a large volume of intrafirm trade ($6.8 billion) in 1993.

TRANSFER PRICING REGULATIONS IN AUSTRALIA

In Australia, the commissioner of taxation has the authority to assess certain taxpayers involved in international transactions on the basis that arm's-length prices were used according to section 136 of the Income Tax Assessment Act (ITAA) of 1936 (Wallschutzky, 1995). Section 136 is a part of Division 13, Part III, and is designed to counter international profit shifting through transfer pricing manipulations. Before 1994, however, no regulation was provided as to how arm's-length prices should be determined.

On May 31, 1994, The Australian Taxation Office (ATO) released taxation ruling TR 94/14, which contains guidelines for the treatment of consideration paid with regard to the supply and acquisition of all forms of property, including services and intangible property. The ATO requires that the consideration paid by one party to a related party be consistent with the price that would have been reached through bargaining between independent parties. The ATO also stresses that appropriate arm's length price should reflect commercial and market realities, as well as the state of competition and the nature of business (Sabapathy, 1994).

On August 12, 1994, the Australian Taxation Office (ATO) issued Pre-Ruling Consultative Document (PCD) No. 6 on transfer pricing. The document offers guidelines on establishing transfer prices and outlines what documentation taxpayers should maintain.

PCD No. 6 explains the pricing methods that are acceptable to the ATO. These methods are the ones recommended by the OECD Guidelines:

—transaction-based methods, which include comparable uncontrolled price method (CUP), resale price method (RPM) and cost plus method (CPLM);

—profit-based methods, which include profit split method (PSM) and profit comparison method.

The document emphasizes that the profit comparison method is different from the comparable profits method (CPM) acceptable to the IRS in the United States. However, the differences between the two are "relatively minor and relate to the way in which the method is applied rather than to the kind of information that is required to apply the method" (Anderson, 1994a. p. 29). In reality, the profit comparison method is quite similar to the transactional net margin method (TNMM) recommended by the OECD. In paragraph 199, the ATO provides the following criteria for selecting the most appropriate pricing methods(s):

Preference should be given to the method or combination of methods which most closely reflects the operation of market conditions, is supported by available, verifiable and reliable data, and which requires few adjustments. This will usually be the method where the data provides the closest comparability. Generally, with more adjustments the result becomes more subjective and has lesser comparability.

On the types of documentation that taxpayers should keep, PCD No. 6 provides the following examples in paragraph 386:

—documents evidencing real bargaining and arm's length outcomes in relation to the taxpayer's related party dealings;

—pricing policies, documents relating to product profitability, relevant market information and profit contributions of each party;

—documents establishing the economic justification for entering into the relevant international dealings;

—documents establishing the reasons for the taxpayer's selection of a particular pricing methodology or methodologies;

—where other methodologies have been considered and rejected, details of these other methodologies, including reasons for their rejection (ideally, these documents should be created contemporaneously with the decision making);

—documentation establishing the structure and nature of the company and the group to which it belongs;

—documentation establishing the taxpayer's sales and operating results and the nature of its dealings with related parties; and

—documentation setting out the taxpayer's marketing and pricing strategies, including market penetration strategies.

Many taxpayers welcomed the detailed guidelines provided by PCD No. 6, but some tax practitioners criticized that it would force more taxpayers into using profit-based methods because they do not have sufficient information to make the required comparisons for transaction-based methods (Anderson, 1994a; Wallschutzky, 1995).

On April 20, 1995, the ATO issued Draft Taxation Rulings TR 95/D11 on the application of Division 13 of Part III of ITAA to international dealings between an entity and a permanent establishment of that entity (Anderson, 1995b). The draft ruling is based on ''the single entity approach'' of Australian tax law, which does not recognize a permanent establishment as a separate legal entity. The permanent establishment is considered as the head office. Therefore, transactions between parts of the same entity cannot be recognized for tax purposes in Australia. The objective of the draft ruling is to ensure that income and expenses are properly allocated to Australian operations and international dealings are done according to the arm's-length principle. This ruling is very relevant to financial institutions such as banks and investment service companies that use branch operations extensively.

On September 29, 1995, the ATO released another three draft rulings on transfer pricing as follows:

—Draft Taxation Ruling TR 95/D22: The use of arm's-length transfer pricing methodologies in international dealings between associate enterprises;

—Draft Taxation Ruling TR95/D23: Documentation and other practical issues associated with transfer pricing; and

—Draft Taxation Ruling TR95/D24: Guidelines on the application of penalty tax for international transfer pricing adjustments.

In TR95/D22, the ATO discussed the transaction-based methods and profit-based methods again. However, unlike PCD No. 6, TR95/D22 gives clear priority to transaction-based methods and states that profit-based methods should be used only in extreme circumstances. TR95/D22 also requires taxpayers to "select the method that is the most appropriate or best suited to the facts and circumstances of the particular case." (Anderson 1994a, p. 26).

In TR95/D23, the ATO defines five broad categories of documentation that taxpayers should maintain (Anderson, 1995a):

—documentation created in the ordinary course of business;

—the analysis of the functions, assets, risk strategies, and so forth, of the business;

—the process supporting the selection and rejection of the methodologies;

—the application of the methodologies and a reasonable sample checking of results; and

—the ongoing review and monitoring process.

The TR95/D24 provides detailed guidelines on the application of audit penalties for international transfer pricing adjustments.

Besides providing specific guidelines for international transfer pricing, the ATO is at the forefront in negotiating bilateral or multilateral advance pricing agreements (APAs). As we mentioned in Chapter 4, the ATO concluded the first bilateral APA with the IRS in the United States involving sales of Apple Computer products to an Australian affiliate in 1991. On July 14, 1994, the ATO released draft ruling TR94/D32, which provides guidelines and procedures for obtaining an APA. The ATO reaffirmed its commitment to the APA process and is prepared to consider bilateral or unilateral APAs (Cox, 1994). The Australian APA process includes the following steps: (1) request for a prelodgment meeting; (2) prelodgment meeting; (3) formal application; (4) statement of proposal; and (5) issue of the APA. Taxpayers obtaining APAs are required to submit annual reports to the ATO.

FOREIGN INVESTMENT AND TRANSFER PRICING REGULATIONS IN CHINA

Foreign Investment in China

Since China opened its door to foreign investors in 1979, business investment in China has been expanding rapidly. Table 8.6 provides three types of foreign direct investment statistics from 1979 to 1994: (1) number of contracts; (2) amount contracted; and (3) amount utilized. Record numbers of contracts (83,437) were reported for 1993, and the amount contracted reached a record

Table 8.6
Foreign Direct Investment in China, 1979–1994 (Millions of U.S. Dollars)

Year	Number of contracts (1)	Amount contracted (2)	Amount utilized (3)
1979-1982	922	4,608	1,771
1983	470	1,731	916
1984	1,856	2,650	1,419
1985	3,073	5,931	1,956
1986	1,498	2,834	2,245
1987	2,233	3,709	2,647
1988	5,945	5,297	3,740
1989	5,779	5,600	3,774
1990	7,273	6,596	3,410
1991	12,978	15,410	4,366
1992	48,764	58,052	11,008
1993	83,437	111,436	27,515
1994	47,490	75,611	33,787

Source: Duiwai Jingji Maoyi Nianjian (Foreign economic relations and trade yearly) (various issues).

of $111.4 billion in 1993. The amount utilized (column 3) provides the best indication of foreign investment implemented in China. Between 1979 and 1994, the amount of investment utilized in China was about $100 billion. In 1994 alone, the amount utilized was $33.8 billion.

The expansion of foreign direct investment in China continued in 1995. According to statistics published by the World Bank and the China State Statistical Bureau, China topped the world's importers of foreign private capital in 1995 by attracting about $35 billion of foreign direct investment (cited in Lococo, 1996). In the first quarter of 1996, many foreign investors were also rushing to

Table 8.7
Foreign Direct Investment (Amount Contracted) in China by Country or Region,
1990–1994 (Millions of U.S. Dollars)

Country/Region	1990	1991	1992	1993	1994
All Countries/Regions	6,596	15,410	58,052	111,436	75,611
Hong Kong & Macao	3,943	7,507	41,531	76,753	47,969
Taiwan	1,000	3,430	5,543	9,965	4,878
United States	358	548	3,121	6,813	4,675
Japan	457	812	2,173	2,960	3,529
Germany	456	558	1,229	2,493	745
Others	382	2,555	4,455	12,452	13,815

Source: Duiwai Jingji Maoyi Nianjian (Foreign economic relations and trade yearly) (various issues).

beat the April 1996 deadline for duty-free concessions for imports of capital
equipment.

Table 8.7 explains the sources of foreign investment for amounts contracted
from 1990 to 1994. We can observe that more than 60 percent of foreign investment in recent years came from Hong Kong and Macao. About 10 percent
of the investment was from Taiwan. U.S. investors provided roughly 6 percent
of foreign investment in China. Other countries providing significant investment
capital to China included Japan and Germany.

Table 8.8 provides the details of U.S. direct investment in China from 1979
to 1994. Between 1979 and 1994, U.S. MNCs provided close to $7 billion of
investment (amount utilized) to China. As of 1994, however, U.S. direct investment in China was still small compared with amounts invested by other
countries and regions.

Foreign investment enterprises (FIEs) have created many job opportunities for
Chinese workers and have helped improve the competitiveness of China's exports. For example, in 1994, FIEs employed about 12.6 million workers and
produced RMB 400 billion (or about U.S. $50 billion) worth of products, ac-
counting for 12.8 percent of China's national industrial output (Li, 1995b). Exports by FIEs are playing vital roles in China's foreign trade. In 1991, exports
by FIEs were $12.1 billion, accounting for 16.7 percent of China's export total.
In 1992, exports by FIEs went up to $17.4 billion, accounting for 20.4 of
China's exports (Li, 1995).

Table 8.8
U.S. Direct Investment in China, 1979–1994 (Millions of U.S. Dollars)

Year	Number of contracts	Amount contracted	Amount utilized
1979-1982	21	281	13
1983	25	470	5
1984	62	165	256
1985	100	1,152	357
1986	102	527	315
1987	104	342	263
1988	269	370	236
1989	276	641	284
1990	357	358	456
1991	694	548	323
1992	3,265	3,121	511
1993	6,750	6,813	2,063
1994	4,017	4,675	1,889

Source: Duiwai Jingji Maoyi Nianjian (Foreign economic relations and trade yearly) (various issues).

In the past, most of the FIEs also traded heavily with their associated companies in foreign countries. There are several reasons (or incentives) for many FIEs to shift their profits abroad (Li, 1995b):

—to recover investment in China as soon as possible to avoid political and currency exchange risks in China;

—to shift profits to parent companies before sharing them with joint venture partners in China;

—to inflate the costs of technology and equipment transferred to the FIE to obtain a greater share of equity investment and to increase the costs of fixed and intangible assets for tax purposes; and

—to realize tax savings by moving profits to low tax jurisdictions such as Hong Kong or other tax havens.

Chinese tax authorities are aware of these motives (or incentives) for transfer pricing manipulations. Transfer pricing regulations in China have also been revised in recent years.

Transfer Pricing Regulations in China

The Chinese government enacted basic transfer pricing legislation in the following two statutes in 1991:

—Income Tax Law of the People's Republic of China for Foreign Investment Enterprises (FIEs) and Foreign Enterprises (FEs) (income tax law);

—Regulations for the Implementation of the Income Tax Law of the People's Republic of China for Foreign Investment Enterprises and Foreign Enterprises (implementation regulations).

Foreign investment enterprises (FIEs) include (1) equity joint ventures between a foreign entity and a Chinese entity, (2) cooperative (contractual) joint ventures between Chinese and foreign entities and (3) wholly foreign-owned enterprises (limited liability companies owned by one or more foreign entities). Equity joint ventures are governed by the Chinese Law on Joint Ventures Using Chinese and Foreign Investment, promulgated in 1979, while cooperative joint ventures are governed by the Law on Chinese-Foreign Contractual Cooperative Enterprises, passed in 1988. Foreign enterprises are operations of foreigners that do not constitute FIEs. These may include representative offices, foreign contractors and so forth (Chan and Wong, 1996). Representative offices are established to carry out liaison activities for the parent company in another country. Article 13 of the Income Tax Law stipulates that the prices charged or paid in intrafirm transactions between FIEs (or FEs) and their associated enterprises must be the same as the prices charged or paid in comparable uncontrolled transactions between independent companies (Chen, 1993). If arm's-length prices are not used for intrafirm transactions, the tax authorities have the right to adjust the income of related FIEs or FEs.

Chapter 5 of the Implementation Regulations is entitled, "Business Dealings between Associated Enterprises." Article 52 of the Implementation Regulations defines "associated enterprises" as those companies or economic units that have any of the following relationships with a FIE (Li, 1995b):

—direct or indirect ownership of, or control over, such matters as finances, business operations, or purchases and sales;

—direct or indirect ownership or control of both entities by a third party; or

—any other relationship arising from mutual interests.

Article 54 provides that the tax authorities may use one of the following four methods (in the order of preference) to establish arm's-length prices for intrafirm transactions between FIEs (or FEs) and associated enterprises:

—the comparable uncontrolled price method;

—the resale price method;

—the cost plus method; or

—any other reasonable method.

Article 54 is similar to requirements under the 1968 regulations for section 482 of the U.S. Internal Revenue Code. The 1968 regulations of section 482 are explained in Chapter 3.

Article 55 of the regulations states that if the interest charged or paid for intracompany financing is higher or lower than the arm's-length price, or if the interest rate is higher or lower than the normal interest rate for similar transactions, the tax authorities can make adjustments with reference to the normal interest rate.

Article 56 of the Implementation Regulations is concerned with fees for services between an FIE and its associated enterprises. If such fees are different from arm's-length prices, the tax authorities can make adjustments with reference to normal service fees for similar services. Article 57 stipulates arm's-length price requirements for the transfer and use of property between related companies. Article 58 states that an FIE (or FE) cannot deduct management fees paid to associated enterprises.

On October 29, 1992, the State Tax Administration released Tax Management Measures Concerning Business Associated Enterprises. These measures are reprinted in Appendix E. They provide additional rules for the implementation of article 13 of the Income Tax Law and articles 52 to 58 of the Implementation Regulations. The Tax Management Measures define "associated enterprises" as enterprises that have one of the following relationships with other enterprises:

1. holding, directly or indirectly, a minimum total of 25 percent of the shares of one or the other;

2. being owned, directly or indirectly, by the same third party, or at least 25 percent of the shares being controlled by the same third party;

3. loan funds from or to other enterprises making up at least 50 percent of the owned funds of enterprises, or 10 percent of the total loan funds of enterprises being guaranteed by other enterprises;

4. more than half of the senior managerial personnel such as board directors or directors, or one of the standing board directors of enterprises being assigned by other enterprises;

5. production and business operations of enterprises conducted only when other enter-

prises are providing them with royalties (including industrial property rights, proprietary technology, etc.);

6. raw materials, spare parts and fittings (including price and transaction terms, etc.)
   bought for production and business operations of enterprises being controlled or supplied by other enterprises;

7. marketing of products produced or commodities (including prices and transaction
   terms) being controlled by other enterprises; or

8. having, in the area of interests, other connections including family and kinsfolk relations, that have actual control over production/business operations and transactions
   of enterprises.

In 1993, Chinese tax authorities began requiring FIEs and FEs to submit with
their income tax returns, annual reports on business transactions between FIEs
and FEs and their associated enterprises. Separate reports must be prepared for
business transactions with each associated enterprise (Chan and Wong, 1996).
The information required includes the type, content, date, quantity, unit price,
and total amount of each transaction. Failure to comply with this requirement
may result in fines or prosecution in serious cases. From this report and taxpayers' profit-and-loss histories, Chinese tax authorities were able to develop a
profile of taxpayers' characteristics and scrutinize their intrafirm transactions.

Investigations of Corporate Transfer Pricing Practices in China

Chinese tax authorities have conducted many investigations of corporate
transfer pricing practices since the mid-1980s. In 1987, the Shenzhen municipal
government took the first initiative to issue the Provisional Measures on the Tax
Administration of the Transactions Between an FIE in Shenzhen Special Economic Zone and its Associated Enterprises (PMTA). Shenzhen, a city close to
Hong Kong, is home to thousands of FIEs invested by MNCs from Hong Kong,
Macao and Taiwan. The PMTA provided the Shenzhen Tax Bureau with legal
authority to conduct tax audits until national transfer pricing legislation and
regulations were enacted in the 1990s (Chan and Chow, 1995). Between 1988
and 1992, the Shenzhen Tax Bureau conducted 203 audits and made adjustments
totaling about U.S. $82 million.

In 1991, a comprehensive study was conducted to examine the 1990 prices
of 1,500 commodities produced by FIEs. The study discovered that, by importing materials at inflated prices and exporting goods at artificially low prices,
FIEs transferred U.S. $2.7 billion of funds abroad in 1990. This amounted to
27.1 percent of their total imports and exports (Chen, 1993).

Chinese tax authorities are becoming more experienced in transfer pricing
enforcement. Recently, the State Administration of Taxation established an elite
transfer pricing group to monitor corporate transfer pricing practices and tax
enforcement activities in China (Chan and Wong, 1996). Officials belonging to
this elite group have visited many other countries to study foreign transfer pric-

ing enforcement practices. This group does not deal directly with taxpayers; it mainly provides technical support to local tax officials.

INTRAFIRM TRADE AND TRANSFER PRICING REGULATIONS IN JAPAN

Japan's International Investment Activities

As mentioned in Chapter 7, Japan had the most impressive foreign direct investment record among all industrial nations in the 1980s, according to statistics published by the OECD. Japan increased its direct investment abroad by more than ten times from the 1970s to the 1980s. The total outflows of direct investment from Japan for the 1980s was $185.8 billion. This was slightly higher than the direct investment outflows of $185.7 billion from the United Kingdom. The U.S. direct investment outflows for the same period was $170.0 billion.

Table 8.9 presents the statistics of Japan's foreign direct investment by region and country for fiscal year 1993 and the cumulative amounts for fiscal years 1951 to 1993. These statistics were published by Japan's Ministry of Finance. We can observe that during fiscal year 1993, Japan's MNCs invested a total of $36.0 billion in other countries. About 40.9 percent (or $15.3 billion) was invested in the United States. Other countries receiving large sums of Japanese investment included the United Kingdom ($2.5 billion), the Netherlands ($2.2 billion), Australia ($1.9 billion), and China ($1.7 billion).

The cumulative data for fiscal years 1951 to 1993 also show that the bulk of Japan's investment during that period went to North America or Europe. The United States was the largest recipient of Japanese direct investment during fiscal years 1951 to 1993. About 43.8 percent, or $184.9 billion, of Japan's direct investment came to America during that period. The United Kingdom was the second largest recipient and obtained a total of $31.7 billion of Japan's direct investment. Other countries receiving large sums of Japanese direct investment during the same period include Australia ($22.7 billion), Indonesia ($15.2 billion), Singapore ($8.5 billion), Canada ($7.8 billion), Brazil ($7.6 billion), and Germany ($7.3 billion).

The surge of foreign direct investment in the United States in the 1980s can be attributed to the following (OECD, 1995):

—favorable macroeconomic conditions that included strong U.S. economic growth rates in the 1980s, combined with the size of the U.S. market and an open investment climate;

—the depreciation of the U.S. dollar, which lowered the value of U.S. assets in foreign currencies;

—deregulation of financial markets and many industries;

Table 8.9

**Japan's Foreign Direct Investment by Region and Country, Fiscal Years 1951–1993
(Millions of U.S. Dollars)**

Country and Region	Fiscal Year 1993		Fiscal Year 1951-1993	
	Amount	% of Total	Amount	% of Total
Total, all countries	36,025	100%	422,555	100%
North America	15,287	42.4%	184,868	43.8%
United States	14,725	40.9%	177,098	41.9%
Canada	562	1.6%	7,769	1.8%
Europe	7,940	22.0%	83,637	19.8%
United Kingdom	2,527	7.0%	31,667	7.5%
Netherlands	2,175	6.0%	18,397	4.4%
Germany	760	2.1%	7,334	1.7%
France	545	1.5%	5,974	0.7%
Switzerland	426	1.2%	3,128	0.7%
Other	1,507	4.2%	17,137	4.1%
Asia	6,637	18.4%	66,517	15.7%
China	1,691	4.7%	6,163	1.5%
Hong Kong	1,238	3.4%	12,748	3.0%
South Korea	245	0.7%	4,868	1.2%
Taiwan	292	0.8%	3,719	0.9%
Singapore	644	1.8%	8,481	2.0%
Malaysia	800	2.2%	5,615	1.3%
Thailand	578	1.6%	6,465	1.5%
Philippines	207	0.6%	2,150	0.5%
Indonesia	813	2.2%	15,222	3.6%
Other	129	0.4%	1,806	0.3%
Oceania	2,035	5.6%	25,817	6.1%
Australia	1,904	5.3%	22,667	5.4%
Other	131	0.4%	3,150	0.7%
Middle East	217	0.6%	4,447	1.1%
Latin America	3,370	9.4%	49,917	11.8%
Panama	1,390	3.9%	20,129	4.8%
Brazil	419	1.2%	7,614	1.8%
Mexico	53	0.1%	2,180	0.5%
Other	1,508	4.2%	19,994	4.7%
Africa	539	1.5%	7,351	1.7%

Source: Ministry of Finance, Japan.

Table 8.10
Japan's Foreign Direct Investment by Industry, Fiscal Years 1951–1993 (Millions of U.S. Dollars)

Industry	Cases		Amount Invested	
	No.	%	Amount	%
Total	75,029	100%	422,555	100.0%
Manufacturing	22,577	30.1%	115,112	27.2%
Food	2,089	2.8%	6,123	1.4%
Textile	2,723	3.6%	5,540	1.3%
Wood & pulp	997	1.3%	4,057	1.0%
Chemical	2,380	3.2%	16,300	3.9%
Metal	2,374	3.2%	12,794	3.0%
Machinery	2,714	3.6%	11,491	2.7%
Electrical goods	3,769	5.0%	27,235	6.4%
Transportation equipment	1,283	1.7%	15,007	3.6%
Miscellaneous	4,248	5.7%	16,465	3.9%
Nonmanufacturing	48,386	64.5%	300,293	71.1%
Agriculture	1,411	1.9%	1,846	0.5%
Fishery	879	1.2%	957	0.2%
Mining	1531	2.0%	19,758	4.7%
Construction	1,231	1.6%	3,627	0.9%
Trade	16,383	21.9%	45,364	10.7%
Finance	2,938	3.9%	81,271	19.2%
Service	7,388	9.9%	50,152	11.9%
Transportation	5,119	6.8%	23,809	5.6%
Real estate	8,357	11.1%	65,966	15.6%
Miscellaneous	3,149	4.2%	7,543	1.8%
Branches	1,528	2.0%	6,555	1.5%
Other	2,538	3.4%	695	0.2%

Source: Ministry of Finance, Japan.

—threats of entry barriers in the U.S. markets that played an important role in attracting Japanese investment in the automotive sector; and

—other factors including lower production costs in the United States, availability of a skilled labor force, and political stability.

Table 8.10 shows the statistics of Japan's foreign investment by industry for fiscal years 1951 to 1993. About 71.1 percent (or $300.3 billion) of Japan's direct investment was in nonmanufacturing industries. Surprisingly, only 3.9 percent of all cases of Japan's foreign direct investment were in finance (including banking), but the finance industry attracted $81.3 billion, or 19.2 percent, of Japanese foreign direct investment. Other industries receiving large sums of Japan's foreign direct investment included real estate ($66 billion), service ($50.2 billion), and trade ($45.4 billion). Three manufacturing industries also received substantial Japanese direct investment: electrical goods ($27.2 billion), chemical ($16.3 billion), and transportation equipment ($15.0 billion).

Intrafirm Trade of Japan's MNCs

Table 8.11 provides the data for Japan's intrafirm trade associated with U.S. affiliates of Japanese MNCs from 1980 to 1993. Two types of statistics are presented: (1) U.S. exports shipped by U.S. affiliates to Japanese parent groups; and (2) U.S. imports shipped to U.S. affiliates by Japanese parent groups. These statistics are available in various issues of *Foreign Direct Investment in the United States* and *U.S. Direct Investment Abroad*, prepared by the Bureau of Economic Analysis of U.S. Department of Commerce.

From Table 8.11 we can observe that in 1996, U.S. exports shipped by U.S. affiliates to Japanese parent groups were $28.1 billion, accounting for 65% of all exports shipped by U.S. affiliates of Japanese MNCs. U.S. imports shipped to U.S. affiliates by Japanese parent groups were $78.4 billion, accounting for 84 percent of all imports shipped to U.S. affiliates of Japanese MNCs. This means that total intrafirm trade between Japanese MNCs and their U.S. affiliates in 1993 was about $106.5 billion, which is equivalent to 69 percent of the U.S.-Japan merchandise trade in 1993.

Table 8.11 also shows that U.S. exports shipped by U.S. affiliates to Japanese parent groups increased from $14.2 billion in 1980 to $28.1 billion in 1993. On the other hand, imports shipped to U.S. affiliates by Japanese parent groups went up from $21.9 billion in 1980 to $78.4 billion in 1993. The table also indicates that the percentage of intrafirm imports shipped to U.S. affiliates was significantly higher than intrafirm exports shipped by those same affiliates. For example, in 1993, 84 percent of imports shipped to U.S. affiliates were intrafirm imports while only 65 percent of exports shipped by those affiliates were intrafirm exports.

Table 8.12 provides Japan's intrafirm trade statistics by industry for 1993. We can observe that the bulk of Japan's intrafirm trade in U.S. trade occurred in wholesale trade for industrial and consumer goods: motor vehicles and equipment, electrical goods, professional and commercial equipment, and machinery and equipment. Intrafirm trade for motor vehicle and equipment (for manufacturing and wholesale) totaled $32.1 billion in 1993, accounting for about 30 percent of all intrafirm trade between Japanese MNCs and their U.S. affiliates.

Table 8.12 also shows that the intrafirm trade ratios varied significantly among industries. For example, the intrafirm imports ratio for professional and com-

Table 8.11
Japan's Intrafirm Trade Associated with U.S. Affiliates of Japanese MNCs, 1980–1993 (Millions of U.S. Dollars)

| | Exports shipped by U.S. Affiliates | | | Imports shipped to U.S. Affiliates | | |
| | To Japanese Parent Groups | | | By Japanese Parent Groups | | |
Year	Total	Amount	% of Total	Total	Amount	% of Total
1980	19,136	14,167	74%	27,653	21,920	79%
1981	22,659	16,397	72%	33,285	26,085	78%
1982	21,514	13,737	64%	35,901	26,931	75%
1983	22,816	13,991	61%	36,568	28,323	77%
1984	23,764	15,775	66%	47,824	38,688	81%
1985	22,715	15,779	69%	58,102	47,863	82%
1986	21,260	12,332	58%	63,802	52,248	82%
1987	20,413	10,866	53%	72,564	57,356	79%
1988	26,400	14,463	55%	77,688	63,903	82%
1989	34,076	18,856	55%	84,511	70,904	84%
1990	39,293	22,420	57%	87,475	73,085	84%
1991	41,553	24,394	59%	87,835	70,699	80%
1992	31,856	25,207	79%	75,392	65,899	87%
1993	43,045	28,062	65%	93,437	78,426	84%

Source: U.S. Department of Commerce, *Foreign Direct Investment in the United States* (various years).

mercial equipment industry was 99 percent, while a similar ratio for the machinery and equipment industry was only 58 percent. In addition, there may be significant differences in intrafirm imports ratios and intrafirm exports ratio for the same industry. We can observe such significant differences between intrafirm imports and exports in the professional and commercial equipment industry (99% versus 30%) and machinery industry (79% versus 25%).

Transfer Pricing Regulations and Tax Investigations in Japan

In March 1986, Japan introduced its transfer pricing legislation in Article 66–5 of the Special Taxation Measures Law (STML). The acceptable pricing meth-

Table 8.12
Japan's Intrafirm Trade in U.S. Trade by Industry, 1993 (Millions of U.S. Dollars)

Industry	Exports shipped by U.S. affiliates			Imports shipped to U.S. affiliates		
		To Japanese parent groups			By Japanese parent groups	
	Total	Amount	% of Total	Total	Amount	% of Total
Total, all industries	43,045	28,062	65%	93,437	78,426	84%
Manufacturing	7,611	2,685	35%	15,556	12,889	83%
Machinery	3,408	855	25%	7,740	6,132	79%
Motor vehicle & equipment	451	335	74%	4,826	4,613	96%
Other manufacturing	3,752	1,495	40%	2,990	2,144	72%
Wholesale trade	35,117	25,225	72%	77,503	65,378	84%
Motor vehicle & equipment	7,087	5,525	78%	27,438	21,578	79%
Professional and commercial equipment	1,151	345	30%	10,859	10,762	99%
Metal & minerals	8,933	6,905	77%	5,615	3,945	70%
Electrical goods	1,917	1,414	74%	19,849	19,481	98%
Machinery & equipment	7,943	4,954	62%	7,116	4,147	58%
Other durable goods	2,345	1,594	68%	4,440	4,151	93%
Farm product raw materials	3,806	3,006	79%	475	350	74%
Others	1,935	1,482	77%	1,711	964	56%
Other industries	317	152	48%	378	159	42%

Source: U.S. Department of Commerce, Economics and Statistics Administration, Bureau of Economic Analysis (1995a).

ods in STML and accompanying regulations (STML Enforcement Order No. 81 and Enforcement Ordinance No. 11) are similar to those stated in the 1968 regulations of section 482 of the U.S. Internal Revenue Code and those in the 1979 OECD report. The rules provide four alternative methods to determine an arm's-length price for intrafirm transactions:

1. the comparable uncontrolled price method (CUP);
2. the resale price method (RPM);
3. the cost plus method (CPLM); and

4. other methods (a method similar to any of the three above or the method provided under the cabinet ordinance).

The law does not specify a priority in the use of the first three methods. Japanese authorities believe that a lack of priority allows more flexibility in establishing an appropriate arm's length price (Tomomatsu, 1989). For several years subsequent to 1986, the tax auditing activities of Japan's National Tax Administration (NTA) had been rather limited. In 1986, tax audits by NTA's examiners resulted in adjustments of about U.S. $80 million (Lanman, 1995).

In 1991, the Ministry of Finance introduced new legislation to strengthen the power of tax authorities to enforce transfer pricing regulations. The changes introduced include the following:

—extending the statute of limitations for transfer pricing audits from three years to six years;

—extending the record-keeping requirements from five years to six years; and

—authorizing tax auditors to obtain information from another company doing comparable business.

Since the early 1990s, the NTA has recruited more international examiners and intensified its investigations of corporate transfer pricing practices. Tax authorities disclosed that the NTA assessed transfer pricing adjustments totaling about U.S. $14 billion against 80 corporate cases during the nine years ending June 1995. The following are some prominent cases (Baik and Patton, 1995):

—Coca-Cola Japan was assessed a $145 million deficiency in March 1995. This assessment was related to royalties paid by Coca-Cola Japan to its U.S. parent between 1990 and 1992. The NTA stated that the royalties paid exceed an arm's length amount by over $346 million.

—In September 1994, the NTA assessed deficiencies and penalties of $405,000 against Commerzbank (a German bank) and several other Japanese branches of foreign banks. At issue are financial and global trading activities carried out by these banks.

—Assessments were made against Japanese subsidiaries of three large European pharmaceutical firms: Hoechst, Ciba-Geigy and Roche. The assessment against Hoechst was $24.9 million. The assessments against Ciba-Geigy and Nippon Roche were $55 million and $33 million, respectively.

—Recently, the NTA assessed a $9.5 million deficiency against Procter & Gamble's Japanese subsidiary.

Some writers suggested that these huge transfer pricing assessments by the NTA may be a "retaliatory taxation" against the new U.S. section 482 regulations and recent U.S. tax assessments against Japanese corporations (Akamatsu, 1993a; Lanman, 1995). However, the NAT asserted that its transfer pricing investigations and tax policies are designed to collect revenues for Japan's treasury and denied any intention to retaliate against the U.S. government.

Japan's Pre-Confirmation System (PCS)

Japan's Pre-Confirmation System (PCS) agreements are equivalent to the Advance Pricing Agreements (APA) available in Canada and the United States. The PCS was established in Japan shortly after its transfer pricing regulations were released in 1986. However, from 1986 to 1993, only a few taxpayers had concluded PCS agreements with the NTA. In November 1992, Matsushita Electric obtained an APA (from the IRS) that had been accepted by the NTA. J. P. Morgan also reached an APA with the IRS and the NTA concerning transactions between J. P. Morgan and its branches in Japan.

In 1993, the NTA revised its PCS procedure to conform with the APA procedure in the United States (Baik and Patton, 1995). (Details of the U.S. APA process are discussed in Chapter 4.) The new PCS procedure contains provisions for obtaining bilateral and multilateral PCS agreements. The NTA also encouraged both Japanese and foreign-affiliated taxpayers to apply for PCS agreements. In 1994, Apple Computer Japan Inc. successfully negotiated a PCS agreement with the NTA. In August 1995, Apple Computer (the U.S. parent company) also concluded a bilateral APA with the NTA and the IRS. The agreement covered some intrafirm transactions between Apple (U.S. parent) and Apple Japan Inc. Since early 1994, at least 50 other taxpayers have consulted the NTA about the U.S. APA process, the NTA's PCS and similar APA procedures in other countries (Baik and Patton, 1995).

In October 1994, at a meeting of the Pacific Association of Tax Administrators (PATA), tax administrators from the U.S., Canada, Japan and Australia agreed to set up a bilateral advanced pricing agreement (BAPA) system. It encourages PATA member nations to inform each other when one member receives APA applications from taxpayers.

TRANSFER PRICING REGULATIONS IN SOUTH KOREA

South Korea is one of a few newly industrialized developing countries that has established comprehensive rules and regulations on transfer pricing. The first set of transfer pricing legislation in South Korea can be found in Article 20 of the old Corporation Tax Law (CTL), which was amended by the Corporate Income Tax Law Enforcement Decree (CITL-ED) in 1988 and became effective for fiscal years starting on or after January 1, 1989. On January 24, 1990, Korea's Office of National Tax Administration (NTA) also issued detailed pricing guidelines (NTA Order No. 1062) to implement the rules introduced in 1988 (Kee and Jeong, 1990; Brooks, 1990). The old rules allowed the use of the following four methods for establishing an arm's-length price:

—the comparable uncontrolled price method (CUP);

—the resale price method (RPM);

—the cost plus method (CPM); and

—other reasonable methods.

These methods were consistent with those allowable under the 1968 regulations of section 482 of the U.S. Internal Revenue Code and those recommended by the 1979 OECD report.

On December 5, 1995, South Korea's National Assembly passed the International Tax Coordination Law, which revised the old law applicable to cross-border transactions. Later in 1995 the Ministry of Finance and Economy (MOFE) also promulgated the new law's enforcement decree. Both the law and the enforcement decree became effective on January 1, 1996, except the provisions relating to advance pricing agreements and thin capitalization rules, which take effect January 1, 1997 (Cook and Masaki, 1996; Lee, Lee, and Donaldson, 1996). The new law and enforcement decree provides new rules and procedures for the following areas:

—transfer pricing;

—tax haven rules;

—thin capitalization rules;

—advance pricing approval system; and

—intergovernmental tax cooperation procedures.

The new rules for transfer pricing change the definition of a related party. Under the old rules, any person (or party) owning a share in the company is a related party. Under the new regulations, parties will be deemed "related" if (1) one party directly or indirectly owns 50 percent or more of the voting shares of the other party; or (2) a party is effectively controlling another even without any equity relationship (Lee, Lee, and Donaldson, 1996).

To keep up with the new OECD 1995 guidelines, the new regulations now accept the three traditional transactional methods (CUP, RPM, and CPLM) and two profit-based methods: the profit-split method (PSM) and transactional net margin method (TNMM). The rules also state that the two profit-based methods can be applied when the three traditional transactional methods cannot be reliably applied for equitable results.

For tax years beginning on or after January 1, 1996, taxpayers have to select the most reasonable transfer pricing method and report the method and its selection basis together with the annual tax return. Upon request by the tax authorities, a taxpayer also has to submit the following documentation within 60 days: pertinent transaction contracts, price lists, manufacturing costs, organizational chart, group pricing policies, and other relevant information (Lee, Lee, and Donaldson, 1996). The deadline for submitting these documents may be extended for another 60 days. Taxpayers who fail to submit documents requested after the final deadline may have to pay a fine of up to about U.S. $38,000.

The new law also has a provision to counter profit shifting to a tax haven. Under the new regulations, if a South Korean company retains profits in its controlled foreign company located in a tax haven, the profits retained will be treated as constructive dividends paid to the Korean company and taxable in South Korea. A tax haven is defined as a jurisdiction having an effective tax rate of 15 percent or less.

The thin capitalization rules are designed to discourage the establishment of thinly capitalized foreign controlled companies in South Korea. The regulations establish a safe harbor debt-to-equity ratio of three to one for manufacturing companies (or six to one for certain financial institutions). If the debt-to-equity ratio of a foreign-controlled company is greater than that allowable, interest payments to controlling foreign stockholder(s) on the "excess debt" will be treated as constructive dividend distribution (Cook and Masaki, 1996). These thin capitalization rules will be effective on January 1, 1997.

The new law and enforcement decree also introduced an advance pricing approval system that is effective on January 1, 1997. The NTA will handle the evaluations and approval of all advance-pricing agreement (APA) requests. The enforcement decree also provides details on the application, screening procedures, notification procedures and reporting requirements for an APA. The term of an APA is normally three years and renewable for another three years. A taxpayer with an approved APA has to submit a report annually on the following matters (Kim, Moller, and Yeo, 1996):

—whether applicable critical assumptions are valid;
—the method used to establish the normal price;
—how the difference between the normal price and the transaction price was reconciled; and
—other matters to be disclosed for the APA.

On international cooperation procedures, the new law allows the tax authorities to exchange information with foreign tax authorities and to cooperate with them on tax collection and audits (Lee, Lee, and Donaldson, 1996).

The new law and enforcement decree also made significant changes in such areas as competent authority procedure, income tax, offshore gift tax, branch profit tax, and value-added tax (VAT). (Discussion of these changes can be found in Baik, 1995; Cook and Masaki, 1996; Kim, Moller, and Yeo, 1996; and Lee, Lee, and Donaldson, 1996).

SUMMARY AND CONCLUSIONS

This chapter provides an overview of the bilateral investment relationship and intrafirm trade between the United States and selected Asian Pacific countries

(APCs). We also reviewed the transfer pricing regulations of four major trading partners of the United States: Australia, China, Japan, and South Korea.

On bilateral investment relationship, we discovered that U.S. DIP in APCs at the end of 1994 was $108.4 billion, accounting for 17.7 percent of all U.S. DIP abroad. U.S. direct investment in the APCs was concentrated in Japan, Australia, Hong Kong and Singapore. The APCs' DIP in the United States was $117.8 billion, contributed mostly by Japanese investors.

Many countries in the Asian Pacific region are among the larger trading nations in the world, including Japan, Hong Kong, China, Singapore, and Taiwan. These countries (territory, in the case of Hong Kong) also have substantial bilateral trade relationships with the United States.

The intrafirm trade total between U.S. MNCs and their affiliates in the APCs was about $43 billion in 1993, with the United States enjoying a small surplus of $1.4 billion. The intrafirm trade between U.S. affiliates and their foreign parent groups in the APCs amounted to $111 billion in 1993. The United States had a huge trade deficit of $56.4 billion from intrafirm trade of MNCs from the APCs. About 96 percent of this type of intrafirm trade in 1993 was conducted by Japanese MNCs and their subsidiaries in the United States.

All four countries selected (Australia, China, Japan, and South Korea) have changed their transfer pricing regulations in recent years. They are ready to adopt most of the 1995 OECD guidelines to establish acceptable transfer pricing methods. Their tax authorities have also intensified their investigations of corporate transfer pricing practices and will continue to do so in the future.

Australia, Japan, and South Korea are prepared to expand their APA programs. These three countries have formal systems in place to handle taxpayers' requests for APAs. Tax administrators from member countries of PATA are coordinating their efforts to promote bilateral or multilateral APAs.

Because of space limitations, we only discussed the transfer pricing regulations of only four countries in the region. Multinational companies conducting businesses in the Asian Pacific region should also study the transfer pricing regulations of other countries and jurisdictions, including Taiwan, Singapore, Indonesia, Thailand, the Philippines, and Hong Kong. Many international accounting firms have up-to-date information and transfer pricing experts to serve their clients.

Companies should also review their transfer pricing policies and procedures to make sure that these elements are in compliance with the new rules and regulations of the APC. Documentation required by tax authorities must be maintained and studies should be done to determine whether APAs should be sought from host countries in the region.

REFERENCES

Adhikari, Ajay, and Shawn Z. Wang. 1995. Accounting for China. *Management Accounting* (April): 27–32.

Akamatsu, Akiya. 1993a. Japanese NTA Announces Stepped-Up Enforcement of Transfer Pricing Regulations. *Tax Notes International* (November 1): 1094.

———. 1993b. Japanese NTA Reports 50 Companies Penalized for Transfer Pricing Abuses over Six-Year Period. *Tax Notes International* (October 11): 902.

Anderson, Philip. 1994a. Pre Ruling Consultative Document No. 6: Help or Hindrance on Transfer Pricing? *CCH Journal of Australian Taxation* (November): 22–31.

———. 1994b. Transfer Pricing: The ATO Reaffirms Its Position while the OECD Reenters the Debate. *CCH Journal of Australian Taxation* (August/September): 38–40.

———. 1995. Transfer Pricing for Permanent Establishments: The ATO's Views in TR 95d11. *CCH Journal of Australian Taxation* (June/July): 32–35.

———. 1995–1996. Transfer Pricing Draft Rulings: Helpful Guidance or a Compliance Nightmare? *CCH Journal of Australian Taxation* (December/January): 30–38.

Azzi, John. 1996. Correlative Adjustments to Relieve Double Taxation Arising from an Adjustment by a Foreign Tax Administration. *Asia-Pacific Tax Bulletin* (April): 127–130.

Baik, Sunghak Andrew. 1995. Recent Tax Developments in Korea. *Tax Notes International* (December 4): 1475–1479.

Baik, Sunghak Andrew, and Michael Patton. 1995. Japan Steps Up Transfer Pricing Enforcement, Joins the APA Fray. *Tax Notes International* (November 13): 1271–1275.

Brooks, Janet. 1990. Transfer Pricing Regulations Introduced in Korea. *Tax Notes International* (August): 802–803.

Chan, Bill, and Ray Wong. 1996. Transfer Pricing in China: Caution and Patience Are Required! *International Tax Revenue* (January/February): 1–6.

Chan, K. Hung, and Lynne Chow. 1995. A Tax Perspective on International Transfer Pricing for Business Operations in China. *Hong Kong Accountant* (January/February): 48–55.

Chen, Xiaohong. 1993. The Development of China's Transfer Pricing System. *Tax Notes International* (October 11): 887–889.

Chernotsky, Harry I. 1987. The American Connection: Motives for Japanese Foreign Direct Investment. *Columbia Journal of World Business* (Winter): 47–54.

Cheung, Brossa, Daniel Ho, and Shirley Kann. 1996. Strategic Issues and Implications of PRC Tax Reform. *International Tax Journal* (Winter): 83–100.

Cook, Ken, and Yasuko Masaki. 1996. Korea's New International Tax Coordination Law. *Tax Notes International* (January 22): 243–245.

Cooper, Helene, and Joseph Kahn. 1995. China Plans to Cut Tariffs, End Quotas in Bid to Join Trade Group. *Wall Street Journal* (November 20): A10.

Cooper, Tony. 1995. A Comparison of the Profit-Based Pricing Methodologies under the Transfer Pricing Rules of Australia and the United States: Are They a Voluntary Compliance Option for the Taxpayer? *Australian Tax Forum* (Vol. 12, No. 1): 91–113.

Cox, Timothy W. 1994. Australian Tax Office Releases Draft Ruling on Advance Pricing Agreements. *Tax Notes International* (October 24): 1279–1280.

Deloitte Touche Tohmatsu International. 1993. *People's Republic of China: International Tax and Business Guide*. New York: Deloitte Touche Tohmatsu International.

Fony, John I., and John W. Darcy. 1990. Tax Planning for U.S. Investment in Japan. *East Asian Executive Reports* (January): 9, 12–16.

Hamlin, Kevin. 1995. Greater China's Business Future. *International Business* (May): 32–36.

Happell, Michael. 1994. Transfer Pricing: The Australian Tax Office's New Strategy. *International Tax Review* (September/October): 14–15.

Healy, Tim. 1996. China 2000. It's Inflation Stupid—And Tight Credit. *Asia Week* (March 22): 46–49.

Ho, Arthur, Bill Chan, and Joyce Peck. 1994. Investing in China—PW Partners Discuss Strategies and Techniques at London MNC Conference. *International Tax Review* (July/August): 1–10.

Jacob, Rahul. 1996. The Taxman Cometh. *Time* (March 11): 20.

Jo, Yong Ho. 1995. Republic of Korea—1994 Revisions to Tax Laws. *Asia-Pacific Tax Bulletin* (February/March): 85–86.

Kahn, Joseph. 1995. As China Prospers, Its Tax Man Fumbles. *Wall Street Journal* (July 26): A8.

Kee, Yoong Neung, and Young-Cheol Jeong. 1990. Korea's Transfer Pricing Rules: A Comprehensive Analysis. *East Asian Executive Reports* (May): 9, 19–24.

———. 1991. South Korea—Transfer Pricing Rules: Update on Developments. *East Asian Executive Reports* (January): 8, 17–18.

Kim, Woo Taik, Steffan Moller, and Dong Jun Yeo. 1996. South Korea—Recent Changes to the Tax Law. *Asia-Pacific Tax Bulletin* (April): 119–122.

Kinneally, Darryl, and Kunihiko Ohkawa. 1994. *Japan. Tax Developments Yearbook.* Tokyo: Arthur Anderson.

Lanman, John E. 1995. Transfer Pricing Audits—Are They Adequate Procedures? *Asia-Pacific Tax Bulletin* (February/March): 60–64.

Lanman, John E., and Tom Anderson. 1989. Anti-Tax Avoidance: A Survey of Statutory and Nonstatutory Rules. *East Asian Executive Reports* (November): 12–14.

Lee, Kyung Geun, J. Y. Lee, and Robert M. Donaldson. 1996. Korea Announces New Law on Coordination of International Tax Matters. *Tax Notes International* (February 26): 628–631.

Leung, Alden. 1995. Recent and Future Development in PRC Accounting Practices. *Hong Kong Accountant* (March/April): 53–55.

Li, Jinyan. 1995a. Tax Implications of Doing Business in China. *Canadian Tax Journal* (Vol. 43, No. 1): 75–103.

———. 1995b. Transfer Pricing Law and Policy in China. *Tax Notes International* (October 2): 931–944.

Li, Yong. 1995. The Role of Joint Ventures and Foriegn-owned Enterprises in Foreign Trade. *People's Republic of China Yearbook 1994/1995.* Beijing: PRC Yearbook Ltd., pp. 127–128.

Lococo, Ed. 1996. Foreign Direct Investment Flood to Become a Trickle. *Hong Kong Standard* (May 13).

Mito, Toshihide. 1995. 1994 Tax Reforms and the Future. *JETRO China Newsletter* (May–June): 18–23.

Organization for Economic Cooperation and Development (OECD). 1992. *International Direct Investment Policies and Trends in the 1980s.* Paris: OECD.

———. 1995a. *OECD Reviews of Foreign Direct Investment: United States.* Paris: OECD.

———. 1995b. *Transfer Pricing Guidelines for Multinational Enterprises and Tax Administrations.* Paris: OECD.

Sabapathy, Saba. 1994. Australian Tax Office Issues First in Series of Transfer Pricing Rulings: Basic Concepts, ''Deemed'' Arm's Length Consideration Examined. *Tax Notes International* (August 22): 563–565.

Thomas, Gary M., and Akiya Akamatsu. 1994. Some Current Japanese Transfer Pricing Issues for Foreign-Affiliated Companies. *Tax Notes International* (July 18): 127–128.

Tomomatsu, Christine. 1989. Intercompany Pricing of Intangibles under Section 482: A Comparison with Japanese Tax Policy. *Hastings International and Comparative Law Review* (Vol. 13): 179–204.

Towers, Steve. 1995. Australia, Major Changes to International Tax Law during the Past Twelve Months. *Asia-Pacific Tax Bulletin* (February/March): 39–43.

Twist, Alan. 1993. More Taxing Time for Foreigners in Korea. *Business Asia* (November 8): 12.

U.S. Department of Commerce. Economics and Statistics Administration. Bureau of Economic Analysis. 1995a. *Foreign Direct Investment in the United States: Preliminary 1993 Estimates*. Washington, D.C.: U.S. Government Printing Office.

———. Bureau of Economic Analysis. 1995b. *U.S. Direct Investment Abroad: Preliminary 1993 Estimates*. Washington, D.C.: U.S. Government Printing Office.

———. Bureau of the Census. 1996. *Statistical Abstract of United States 1995*. Washington, D.C.: U.S. Government Printing Office.

Wallschutzky, I. G. 1995. Transfer Pricing: The Shape of Things to Come from the Australian Taxation Office. *Asia-Pacific Tax Bulletin* (February/March): 83–85.

Xin, Wei, and Graham Brown. 1995. Recent Legal Developments in China Affecting Tax and Investment. *Asia-Pacific Tax Bulletin* (February/March): 43–54.

9

Intrafirm Trade and Transfer Pricing Regulations: Reflections on the Past and a New Management Paradigm for the Future

In Chapter 1, we noted that the primary purposes of this book are to provide the latest information on intrafirm trade of MNCs and to explain the new transfer pricing regulations issued by the U.S. government and by its major trading partners around the world. The issues on intrafirm trade of U.S. MNCs are covered in Chapter 2, while intrafirm trade issues related to non-U.S. MNCs are discussed in Chapters 6 through 8. Chapters 3 and 4 explain U.S. regulations and government programs on transfer pricing. Chapter 5 describes the details of the 1995 OECD transfer pricing guidelines. New regulations and transfer pricing programs related to Canada, Mexico, and selected countries in the European Union (EU) and the Asian Pacific region are reviewed in Chapters 6 through 8.

When we reviewed issues on intrafirm trade and transfer pricing regulations in Chapters 2 through 8, we did it by country or by region one at a time. In this last chapter, we will take a global view to summarize major findings from the research on the following topics:

—the new international business and tax environment;

—literature and realities of intrafirm trade;

—major changes in transfer pricing regulations;

—investigations of corporate transfer pricing practices; and

—advance-pricing agreement programs.

In addition, we will propose a new paradigm for resolving transfer pricing problems and issues. Some general conclusions from the research will be provided in the last section of the chapter.

MAJOR FINDINGS FROM THE RESEARCH

The New Environment for Intrafirm Trade and Transfer Pricing

In Chapter 1, we noted that the past decade has witnessed enormous changes in social, political, economic, and technological environments in the United States and throughout the world. Most of these changes affect the environments within which MNCs operate and impact the volume and directions of intrafirm trade. The relationships between environmental changes and major issues of intrafirm trade and transfer pricing are highlighted in Figure 1.1 in Chapter 1. Major changes in the environments can be summarized as follows:

—Globalization and expansion of trade: the globalization of the world economy was well documented by Naisbitt (1982, 1994), Naisbitt and Aburdene (1990), Drucker (1989), Thurow (1996), and Vernon, Wells, and Raygan (1996). A truly globalized MNC "can produce its products anywhere, using resources from anywhere, by a subsidiary located anywhere, to a quality found anywhere, to be sold anywhere" (Naisbitt, 1994, p. 50). The world as we know it has become a global village, and the world economy has changed from international to transnational (Drucker, 1989). As shown in Table 1.1, between 1985 and 1994, the world trade volume more than doubled.

—Increase in international investment and the dominant role played by MNCs: according to OECD (1995a) statistics, the cumulative outflows of direct investment abroad from the OECD countries in the 1980s (about $1 trillion) was more than triple that of the 1970s ($302 billion). In the early 1990s, most of the G-7 nations were still increasing their direct investment in foreign countries. Also in the 1980s and early 1990s, the United States, the United Kingdom, and China were among the largest recipients of inward direct investment. The flows of direct investment from country to country in the past three decades were carried out largely by MNCs in industrial countries. As a result, many large MNCs depend heavily on foreign markets as sources of revenue and profits. They also own large portions of their assets overseas.

—The increases in mergers, acquisitions, and strategic alliances: statistics show that mergers, acquisitions, and strategic alliances were widely used investment alternatives in the 1980s and early 1990s. In 1995, there were 5,887 merger and acquisition deals completed with a total value of $388.2 billion. During the same year, there were 5,098 merger and acquisition deals completed in major overseas markets, with a total value of $257.8 billion. Strategic business alliances bring together the specific skills and resources of two or more organizations to achieve such objectives as penetrating new markets, improving research capabilities, and establishing distribution or service networks to better serve customers. Companies in many industries, including automobile, aircraft, computer and telecommunication, established strategic alliances in the 1980s and early 1990s.

—Restructuring, reengineering, and other organizational changes: surveys done by two of the Big Six accounting firms in 1994 discovered that between 75 percent and 80 percent of the largest U.S. companies had already begun reengineering and would be increasing their commitment to it over the next few years (Hammer and Stanton, 1995). The list of companies includes Chrysler, Ford, IBM, PepsiCo, GTE, Hewlett-Packard, Hallmark, Johnson & Johnson, and many others. Many small companies have also adopted the concept and reengineered their business processes. Reengineering often leads to restructuring and downsizing. A report by Byrne (1994) indicated that 25 large corporations in the United States laid off a total of 623,750 employees in 1993.

—Advances in information technologies: over the past four decades, drastic improvements in communication and computer technologies have changed the way we work and how we communicate with each other. According to Tesler (1995), we have gone through four different computing paradigms since the 1960s: batch processing (1960s); timesharing (1970s); desktop computing (1980s); and the network computing paradigm (1990s). A fully networked corporation can do business anywhere, anytime, and can share information and ideas with other colleagues through corporate networks or the Internet. Changes in information technologies and the expansion of Internet web sites and related technologies have altered business practices in many MNCs.

All these environmental changes affect each other. The cause-and-effect relationships between the environmental changes and their impact on intrafirm trade and transfer pricing are illustrated in Figure 1.2 of Chapter 1. Globalization and the expansion of trade usually lead to increases in international direct investment and more cross-border mergers, acquisitions, and strategic alliances. These activities, in turn, will lead to further expansion of trade, including intrafirm trade. Many mergers and acquisitions may lead to reengineering, restructuring, or other organizational changes. These changes may necessitate an overhaul of corporate transfer pricing systems. Advances in information technologies should facilitate the globalization process of MNCs and expansion of all forms of trade and investment. These changes may create new problems and opportunities for corporate transfer pricing systems.

The Literature and Realities of Intrafirm Trade

Because of the importance of intrafirm trade, many studies have been carried out to examine various aspects of intrafirm trade related to U.S. MNCs (e.g., Lall, 1978; Helleiner and Lavergne, 1979; Little, 1986, 1987; Cho, 1988, 1990; OECD, 1993; Hipple, 1990, 1995). These studies were reviewed separately in Chapter 2. All of them provided valuable insight into different issues of intrafirm trade related to U.S. foreign trade. Lall (1978) and Helleiner and Lavergne (1979) identified some variables that explained interindustry differences in U.S. intrafirm exports and imports. Little (1986, 1987) explained some interesting findings on the relationship between direct investment and intrafirm trade. Cho (1988) provided a useful framework of major determinants of intrafirm trade: product-specific factors; region-specific factors; government-specific factors; and firm-specific factors.

The OECD (1993) discovered that the greater the research and development (R&D) and skill intensities are and the higher the international orientation is, the more U.S. parent firms are engaged in intrafirm exports. Hipple (1990) noted that U.S. intrafirm trade comprised a significant share of U.S. foreign trade and contributed to deficit pressures on the U.S. trade balance.

All of these studies have broadened our understanding of intrafirm trade of MNCs from a U.S. perspective. Much remains to be learned, however, about intrafirm trade and multinational transfer pricing. We need to study changes in transfer pricing regulations in various countries and their impact on intrafirm trade and corporate transfer pricing practices.

In reality, U.S. international intrafirm trade can be divided into two categories: (1) trade between U.S. parents and their majority-owned foreign affiliates (MOFA); and (2) trade between U.S. affiliates and their foreign parent groups. Fortunately, comprehensive statistics of these two types of intrafirm trade are maintained and published regularly by the U.S. Department of Commerce through the two series, *U.S. Direct Investment Abroad* and *Foreign Direct Investment in the United States*.

U.S. Department of Commerce statistics indicate that international intrafirm trade between U.S. parents and their MOFAs increased steadily from 1982 to 1993. In 1993, U.S. exports shipped to MOFAs were $105.0 billion, while U.S. imports shipped by those affiliates to U.S. parents totaled $95.9 billion. The total intrafirm trade volume for U.S. MNCs and their MOFAs was $200.9 billion in 1993.

Detailed statistics about intrafirm trade between U.S. affiliates and their foreign parent groups from 1982 to 1992 were presented in Chapter 2. We noted that both the U.S. exports shipped by U.S. affiliates to foreign parent groups and U.S. imports shipped to U.S. affiliates by foreign parent groups increased gradually from 1982 to 1993. However, the rate of increase in imports shipped to U.S. affiliates by foreign parent groups was much higher than that of exports shipped by U.S. affiliates to foreign parent groups. In 1993, U.S. exports shipped by U.S. affiliates to foreign parent groups were $47.2 billion, while U.S. imports shipped to U.S. affiliates by foreign parent groups totaled $148.5 billion. The combined intrafirm trade total between U.S. affiliates and their foreign parent groups was $195.7 billion. During the same year, the United States experienced a significant trade deficit of $101.3 billion on intrafirm trade between non-U.S. MNCs and their affiliates in the United States.

If we combine the totals for the two types of international intrafirm trade related to the United States, we can obtain the U.S. intrafirm trade total. In 1993, that total was $396.6 billion, accounting for 37.9 percent of all U.S. merchandise trade. It is obvious that even a small change in the transfer prices of intrafirm trade can have a significant impact on the U.S. balance of payments and tax revenue collected by the Internal Revenue Service (IRS).

Table 9.1 summarizes all bilateral trade and intrafirm trade with the United States in 1993 by country. The data provided in each column can be described as follows:

Table 9.1
Bilateral Trade and Intrafirm Trade with the United States by Country, 1993
(Dollar Amount in Billions of U.S. Dollars)

Country	Bilateral Trade with the United States (1)	Intrafirm Trade between U.S. MNCs and their MOFAs (2)	Intrafirm Trade between U.S. Affiliates and their FPGs (3)	Intrafirm Trade Total Related to U.S. Trade (4) = (2) + (3)	Ratio of Intrafirm Trade to Bilateral Trade (5) = (4) ÷ (1)
All Countries	1,046,307	200,893	195,706	396,599	37.9%
NAFTA Partners:	296,410	97,877	9,978	107,855	36.4%
Canada	214,504	75,309	9,171	84,480	39.4%
Mexico	81,906	22,568	807	23,375	28.5%
European Union:	197,230	42,718	46,504	89,222	45.2%
Belgium & Luxembourg	16,408	3,200*	926	4,126	25.2%
France	28,442	5,594	9,133	14,727	51.8%
Germany	46,933	9,560	18,540	28,100	60.0%
Italy	19,501	2,100	2,598	4,698	24.1%
Netherlands	21,120	5,628	5,656	11,284	53.4%
United Kingdom	47,151	12,429	8,789	21,218	45.0%
Other	17,675	4,207	862	5,069	48.6%
Asia:	399,816	39,343	116,445	155,788	39.0%
China	40,272	800*	900*	1,700	4.2%
Hong Kong	19,397	7,053	578	7,631	39.3%
Japan	153,912	10,796	106,488	117,284	76.2%
South Korea	31,162	1,205	6,778	7,983	25.6%
Singapore	23,625	11,253	79	11,332	48.0%
Taiwan	40,432	2,240	918	3,158	7.8%
Other	91,016	5,996	704	6,700	7.4%
Other Countries	152,851	20,955	22,779	43,734	28.6%
Addendum OPEC	51,335	3,845	6,135	9,980	19.4%

MNC   = Multinational corporation.
MOFA   = Majority owned foreign affiliate.
FPG   = Foreign parent group.
NAFTA = North American Free Trade Agreement.
OPEC   = Organization of Petroleum Exporting Countries
*Estimates.
Source: U.S. Department of Commerce (1995a, 1995b).

—Column 1: bilateral trade total between the country and the United States;

—Column 2: intrafirm trade total between U.S. MNCs and their MOFAs abroad;

—Column 3: intrafirm trade total between U.S. affiliates and their foreign parent groups;

—Column 4: intrafirm trade total related to U.S. foreign trade; and

—Column 5: ratio of intrafirm trade to bilateral trade.

From Table 9.1, we can observe that the country having the largest volume of intrafirm trade with the United States in 1993 was Japan. Of the $117.3 billion intrafirm trade total between Japan and the United States, 91 percent (or $106.5 billion) was carried out by Japanese MNCs and their subsidiaries in the United States. About $32.0 billion of intrafirm trade between Japan and the United States involved the manufacturing and wholesale trade of motor vehicles and equipment. Another $21.0 billion involved wholesale trade of electrical goods.

The country that had the second largest intrafirm trade volume with the United States in 1993 was Canada ($84.5 billion). Interestingly, about 89 percent of intrafirm trade between Canada and the United States ($75.3 billion) was carried out by U.S. MNCs and their MOFAs in Canada. The largest item of intrafirm trade between Canada and the United States was motor vehicles and related equipment, which amounted to $60.2 billion in 1993. Intrafirm trade between U.S. MNCs and their Mexican MOFAs reached a total of $22 billion in 1993, most of which occurred in manufacturing industries. Intrafirm trade between U.S. MNCs and their MOFAs in the EU countries totaled $42.7 billion in 1993. U.S. firms had strong intrafirm trade relationships with their MOFAs in the United Kingdom, Germany, the Netherlands, and France.

Column (5) in Table 9.1 shows that the ratio of intrafirm trade to bilateral trade varied significantly from country to country in 1993. For example, Japan had the highest intrafirm trade ratio, 76.2 percent. This means that 76.2 percent of the U.S.-Japan bilateral trade in 1993 was intrafirm trade. The 60 percent intrafirm trade ratio for Germany was the second highest. The ratio for the United Kingdom was 45.0 percent, and that for Canada was 39.4 percent. China had the lowest intrafirm trade ratio, 4.2 percent. However, the low intrafirm trade ratio for China applied only to U.S.-China bilateral trade in 1993.

Several writers, including Little (1986) and Cho (1988), have suggested that intrafirm trade of U.S. MNCs may be related to the international direct investment made by those companies. After reviewing their international direct investment activities, we noted that at the end of 1994, the U.S. direct investment position (DIP) abroad was $612.1 billion, compared with $504.4 billion of foreign DIP in the United States. Most of U.S. DIP abroad in 1994 was invested in developed countries such as Canada, EU member countries, Japan, and Australia. Countries with large direct investment in the United States include the United Kingdom, Japan, the Netherlands, Canada, Germany, and France. In 1993, U.S. MNCs had 16,484 MOFAs abroad, most of which were located in

Canada, EU countries, and Japan. Together, these 16,484 had a combined total assets of $1.7 trillion and generated sales revenue of $1.3 trillion in 1993. This amount is larger than the U.S. merchandise trade total in 1993. Taken together, these MOFAs produced a net income of $67 billion in 1993, and the average net income to sales ratio was 5.3 percent. In contrast, the average net income ratio to sales of 12,207 U.S. affiliates of non-American MNCs for 1993 was a negative 0.8 percent. In the past, many non-American MNCs have given the perception that they have been reducing their tax liability by understating U.S.-derived income (Wartzman, 1993). This is one reason why the IRS has adopted a more aggressive approach in scrutinizing the transfer pricing practices of non-American MNCs.

Major Changes in Transfer Pricing Regulations

The past ten years have witnessed significant changes in U.S. transfer pricing regulations as well as the OECD *Transfer Pricing Guidelines* (OECD, 1995b). In the United States, Congress added the super-royalty provision to section 482 of the Internal Revenue Code through the Tax Reform Act of 1986. As part of the Act, Congress directed the Treasury Department and the IRS to study transfer pricing issues to determine whether or how existing regulations should be revised. In the process of revising the 1968 regulations, the Treasury Department and the IRS issued *A Study on Intercompany Pricing* (a white paper) in 1988, the 1992 proposed regulations, and the 1993 temporary regulations. On July 1, 1994, the IRS released the final regulations of section 482.

On January 30, 1992, the IRS also issued proposed cost sharing regulations. The final regulations (section 1.482–7) on cost sharing arrangements were released on December 20, 1995, and are effective for taxable years beginning on or after January 1, 1996. On February 9, 1996, the IRS also issued the final regulations under section 6662 relating to the imposition of accuracy-related penalties. Thus, it has taken about ten years for the U.S. Treasury Department and the IRS to revise all major transfer pricing regulations in the United States.

The OECD is taking a leadership role in developing international taxation principles and transfer pricing guidelines to fulfill its mission "to contribute to the expansion of world trade on a multilateral, non-discriminatory basis and to achieve the highest sustainable economic growth in member countries" (OECD, 1995b, p. ii). In the past, this role has been performed mainly by the Committee on Fiscal Affairs of the OECD. Over the past two decades, the Committee on Fiscal Affairs of the OECD has issued a number of reports or guidelines in the areas of transfer pricing and international taxation:

—The 1979 OECD report, *Transfer Pricing and Multinational Enterprises* (OECD, 1979).

—The 1984 OECD report, *Transfer Pricing and Multinational Enterprises: Three Taxation Issues* (OECD, 1984).

—The 1995 OECD *Transfer Pricing Guidelines for Multinational Enterprises and Tax Administrations* (OECD, 1995b), which supersedes the other two reports.

The OECD guidelines are widely accepted among member as well as non-member countries. In the following paragraphs, we will summarize the final section 482 regulations and the OECD guidelines in two areas: transfer pricing methods recommended for tangible and intangible property.

For sales and transfers of tangible property, section 482 regulations require the use of one of the following six methods, subject to the best-method rule:

1. the comparable uncontrolled price method (CUP);

2. the resale price method (RPM);

3. the cost plus method (CPLM);

4. the comparable profits method (CPM);

5. the profit split method (PSM); and

6. unspecified methods that might be applicable to the facts and circumstances of a particular transaction.

Details of these methods are discussed in Chapter 3. According to the best-method rule, the best transfer pricing method is one that provides the most reliable measure of an arm's-length result given the facts and circumstances of the business activity. Two primary factors should be considered in deciding which method provides the most reliable measure of an arm's length result:

—the degree of comparability between the controlled transaction (or taxpayer) and any uncontrolled comparables; and

—the quality of the data and assumptions used in the analysis.

For the transfers of intangible property, the final section 482 regulations require the use of any of the following four methods subject to the best-method rule:

1. the comparable uncontrolled transaction method (CUT);

2. the comparable profit method (CPM);

3. the profit split method (PSM); and

4. unspecified methods.

The concept of CUT is similar to that of CUP for tangible property. Both the RPM and CPLM allowable for sales and transfers of tangible property are not listed separately as transfer pricing methods acceptable for transfer of intangible property.

The 1995 OECD guidelines recommend two sets of five transfer pricing methods in establishing arm's-length prices for tangible and intangible property: (1) the three traditional transaction methods, which include comparable uncontrolled price method (CUP), resale price method (RPM), and cost plus method (CPLM); and (2) transactional profit methods, which include the profit split method (PSM) and transactional net margin method (TNMM). The TNMM examines the net profit margin (e.g., return on assets, return on sales, or other similar measures) that a taxpayer realizes from a controlled transaction to derive a transfer price for the controlled transaction. A TNMM operates in a manner similar to the cost plus and resale price methods. The OECD indicates its preference of traditional transaction methods (CUP, RPM, and CPLM) over all other methods.

The list of transfer pricing methods acceptable by the OECD Guidelines and the U.S. regulations for the transfer of tangible property are very similar. In the OECD final guidelines, the TNMM method was used (instead of the CPM method in the OECD draft Guidelines) because several OECD countries strongly opposed the use of CPM (Hamaekers, 1996; Taly, 1996).

As of August 1996, tax authorities of many countries were in the process of revising their tax regulations to conform with the 1995 OECD guidelines. These countries include Australia, Canada, Japan, and many EU countries.

Investigations of Corporate Transfer Pricing Practices

In Chapter 1, we mentioned that there are many stakeholders in corporate intrafirm trade and transfer pricing. These stakeholders include (1) stakeholders within the corporate family (e.g., the buying and selling divisions and top management); (2) domestic government agencies that include the IRS, Customs Service, Congress, and others; (3) foreign government agencies and tax authorities, (4) international organizations including the OECD, the United Nations, and the European Union; and (5) other stakeholders, including joint venture partners, suppliers, and final customers. Because of the conflicting interests of these stakeholders, many issues in intrafirm trade and transfer pricing are bound to be controversial. In this section, we will focus our discussion on the conflicts and adversary relationship between tax authorities and taxpayers.

One basic reason behind the adversary relationship between tax authorities and taxpayers is that there are substantial differences among the income tax rates of many countries, and corporate profits may be affected by differentials in tax rates and tax legislation among countries. Table 9.2 shows the corporate marginal tax rates and dividend withholding rates of 42 selected countries (or tax jurisdictions). We can observe substantial differences among the tax rates of several countries. In several tax havens (e.g., the Bahamas, Bermuda), there are no taxes on income, profit, earnings, or capital gains. Many MNCs can take

Table 9.2

Corporate Income Tax Rates and Dividend-Withholding Tax Rates in Selected Countries

Country	Corporate Income Tax Rate (%)[a]	Dividend Withholding Tax Rate(%)[b]	Country	Corporate Income Tax Rate (%)[a]	Dividend Withholding Tax Rate (%)[b]
North America			Latin America		
United States	35	30	Argentina	30	12
Canada	38	25	Brazil	37	15
			Chile	35	35
Europe			Colombia	30	7
Belgium	40.17	25.75	Mexico	34	34
Denmark	34	30	Panama	34	20
France	33.33	25	Peru	30	0
Germany			Venezuela	34	0
Domestic Corp. Distributed	30	25			
Domestic Corp. Undistributed	45		Asia		
Branches of Foreign Corp.	42		China	30	20
Ireland	40	0	Hong Kong	16.5	0
Italy	36	32.4	India	40	24.725
Netherlands	40	25	Indonesia	30	20
Norway	28	25	Japan	37.5	20
Spain	35	25	Malaysia	30	0
Sweden	28	30	Philippines	35	35
Switzerland	21.7 to 46.65	35	Singapore	27	0
United Kingdom	33	0	South Korea	30	25
			Taiwan	25	25
Australasia			Vietnam	25	10
Australia	33	30	Tax Haven (No Income Tax Imposed)		
New Zealand	38	30	Bahamas		
			Bermuda		
Africa			Cayman Islands		
Egypt	42	0			
Kenya	35	10			
Morocco	36	10			
South Africa	35	15			

Note: All corporate income and dividend withholding tax rates listed were in effect as of January 1, 1995.

[a]For those countries with graduated income tax structures, rates listed are the maximum rates that can be applied.

[b]Nontreaty rates.

Source: Price Waterhouse (1995).

advantage of these differences, as suggested by Shulman (1966) about 30 years ago:

Greater profits will result from shipping goods into low income tax countries at prices which are lowered in order to raise income in such countries. And if prices of goods shipped from such countries to the United States are set high, the rate differential may result in maximizing corporate profits in both countries. (p. 30)

However, tax authorities in most countries are aware of these kinds of tactics practiced by some MNCs. Over the past ten years, tax authorities in many countries, including Australia, Canada, Germany, Japan, and the United States, have strengthened their transfer pricing regulations and intensified their investigations of corporate transfer pricing practices. For example, in 1993, the U.S. Congress provided additional funding for the IRS to hire international examiners, increasing their numbers by more than 300 percent from 225 examiners and 14 economists in the early 1980s to the 1994 level of 692 examiners and 76 economists (Deloitte & Touche, 1994). The number of international tax examiners and economists is expected to increase during the next several years.

In other chapters of this book, we have provided examples of tax investigations (and adjustments) imposed by the IRS or foreign tax authorities. Some of these cases involved such well-known companies as Coca-Cola, the AIU Insurance, PepsiCo, and Nissan (Reed, Holyoke, and Harbrecht, 1994). Table 9.3 provides a summary of large proposed section 482 income adjustments of U.S. MNCs and non-American MNCs from fiscal years 1989 to 1994. The table covers only cases with $20 million or more of total proposed adjustments. From Table 9.3, we can observe that 64 large transfer pricing cases were closed in fiscal year 1994, with proposed adjustments amounting to $3.5 billion. Thirty-three of these cases involved U.S. MNCs, while 31 cases were related to non-American MNCs. The proposed section 482 income adjustments for non-American MNCs for 1994 increased more than three times from fiscal year 1994 to 1995. However, as explained by the General Accounting Office (GAO, 1995), ''Proposed adjustments to income may or may not result in increased tax collections, depending on such things as whether a company has offsetting adjustments, offsetting corporate net operating losses carried over from other years, or success in challenging the proposed adjustment'' (p. 19).

In 1993, the IRS began the planning and implementation of two related programs to improve tax enforcement in the United States: Tax Systems Modernization (TSM) and the Compliance 2000 program. The purpose of TSM is to reorganize the IRS to make it more cost efficient. In 1993, the IRS had seven regions and 63 districts. In addition, the IRS also had ten service centers replicating each other's activities (Richardson, 1994a). In the near future, the number of regions was expected to be reduced from seven to five. The IRS is also involved in reducing the size of the national office and redeploying between 800 and 1,000 positions from the national office and about 1,000 from the

Table 9.3

Proposed Section 482 Income Adjustments of U.S. MNCs and Non-American MNCs with $20 Million or More of Total Proposed Adjustment, Fiscal Years 1989–1993

Fiscal Year	U.S. MNCs		Non-American MNCs	
	No. of Firms	Adjustment Amount (Bil. U.S. $)	No. of Firms	Adjustment Amount (Bil. U.S. $)
1989	31	4.1	12	0.7
1990	26	4.4	11	1.6
1991	23	1.2	12	1.1
1992	37	3.1	13	1.0
1993	33	1.1	18	0.7
1994	33	1.5	31	2.0

Sources: U.S. General Accounting Office (1995), p. 19.

regional office. The main objective of the Compliance 2000 program is to promote voluntary compliance, as explained by IRS Commissioner Richardson (1994b):

Enhancing voluntary compliance is the thrust of the Service's Compliance 2000 strategy. Compliance 2000 combines traditional enforcement efforts with other initiatives, such as taxpayer outreach and education programs, Market Segment Understandings, Audit Technique Guides, Advanced Pricing Agreements, and our Nonfiler Program. These initiatives provide alternative ways to avoid and resolve controversies. The goal is to enable taxpayers to take an active role in the voluntary compliance process to ensure that issues are reported and resolved earlier, more cooperatively, and more efficiently. (p. 468)

Details of these programs are discussed in Richardson (1994a, 1994b, 1994c). In the following section, we will summarize the key components of the APA program.

Advance-Pricing Agreement Programs

The first formal advance-pricing agreement (APA) program was offered by the IRS on March 1, 1991, with the release of Revenue Procedure 91–22. The program was designed as a dispute resolution process, supplementing the traditional administrative, judicial, and treaty mechanisms for resolving transfer pricing issues. On May 25, 1995, the IRS issued Announcement 95–49 as a proposed update of Revenue Procedure 91–22. This proposed update is reproduced in Appendix B. The new revenue procedure, if approved, will restate the rules currently contained in Revenue Procedure 91-22 and makes some substantial changes (Patton and Wood, 1995).

An APA is a binding agreement between the IRS and a taxpayer on the prospective application of a TPM, consistent with the arm's-length standard, for the taxpayer's transfer pricing practices. An APA may or may not cover all of the taxpayer's pricing arrangements. Revenue Procedure 91–22 allows a taxpayer the flexibility to limit its APA to "specified prospective tax years," "specified affiliates," and "specified intercompany transactions." The APA may be applied to prior tax years with the consent of the IRS. Details of the APA process and documents required are described in Chapter 4.

The IRS has established an impressive record with the APA program. As of June 30, 1996, the IRS had issued 64 APAs since the program began. There were also 129 pending APAs at various stages of development. In addition, taxpayers had held preliminary talks with the IRS on 50 new APA matters. The APAs included so far cover operations in Puerto Rico and more than 20 foreign countries. The complete APAs also cover about 20 industries or product areas.

An APA is a renewable agreement that can be unilateral (agreed to by the IRS), bilateral (agreed to by the IRS and one foreign tax authority), or multilateral (including two or more foreign tax authorities). The APA reduces the burden on the taxpayer of dealing separately with the various functions of the IRS involved with transfer pricing issues. The agreement also simplifies the procedures for dealing with different tax authorities (in cases of bilateral and multilateral APAs). Many countries, including Australia, Canada, Japan, and the Netherlands, have enacted legislation and established organizations for their APA programs. For example, the Australian Taxation Office (ATO) issued a draft ruling related to APAs on July 14, 1994. The ATO is committed to the APA process and is prepared to consider either bilateral or unilateral APAs (Cox 1994). Revenue Canada issued its information Circular 94–4, *International Transfer Pricing: Advance Pricing Agreements*, on December 30, 1994. That information circular is reprinted as Appendix E. As of March 15, 1996, there were 35 Canadian APAs pending, while a half-dozen APAs had been completed. All the completed APAs were bilateral agreements with the United States.

In 1993, Japan's National Tax Administration (NTA) revised its Pre-Confirmation System (PCS) procedure to conform with the APA procedure in the United States (Baik and Patton, 1995). The new PCS procedure contains provisions for obtaining bilateral and multilateral PCS agreements. The NTA also encouraged both Japanese and foreign-affiliated taxpayers to apply for PCS agreements. In 1994, Apple Computer Japan Inc. successfully negotiated a PCS agreement with the NTA. In August 1995, Apple Computer (the U.S. parent company) also concluded a bilateral APA with the NTA and the IRS.

In October 1994 at a meeting of the Pacific Association of Tax Administrators (PATA) in Sydney, Australia, tax administrators from the United States, Canada, Japan, and Australia agreed to set up a bilateral advance-pricing agreement (BAPA) system. Common rules were also to be established for multilateral APAs involving the four countries.

A NEW PARADIGM FOR RESOLVING TRANSFER PRICING PROBLEMS AND ISSUES

In this book, we have discussed many problems and issues related to intrafirm trade and transfer pricing. These issues and problems are very complex, and the environment is constantly changing. As the change in global environment accelerates, we need a new paradigm to deal with the most important issues and problems in intrafirm trade and transfer pricing. The new paradigm should include the following three elements:

—a multidisciplinary approach aimed at resolving many of the current transfer pricing problems and issues;

—solutions that balance the interest of important stakeholders of intrafirm trade and transfer pricing; and

—a strategic management process to manage a corporate transfer pricing system.

The first two elements apply to both the taxpayers (i.e., multinational corporations) and tax administrations in dealing with issues concerning intrafirm trade and transfer pricing. The last element is concerned with corporate management only.

The Need for a Multidisciplinary Approach and Balancing of the Interests among Stakeholders

Many problems and issues in intrafirm trade and transfer pricing are related to theories and practices in such disciplines as marketing, behavioral science, business policy, international business, economics, and finance, law, taxation, and accounting (see also Tang, 1993). A report by Business International Corporation and Ernst & Young (1991) also noted that designing and managing a successful transfer pricing policy involves making decisions affecting many functional areas:

—capital investment budgeting;

—manufacturing the product internally or buying it from external sources;

—output level;

—product pricing for external customers of both intermediate and final products; and

—the overall corporate strategy.

In addition, transfer pricing decisions may have significant impact on salary increases, bonuses, promotions, and nonpecuniary rewards (Eccles, 1987). Therefore, it is important to take a multidisciplinary and collaborative approach in dealing with many transfer pricing problems and issues.

Figure 9.1 illustrates transfer pricing and its interfaces with related disciplines. Examples of the interfaces (from A to H) are shown below:

A. between transfer pricing (TP) and marketing: market and pricing research to establish comparable uncontrolled prices and resale prices for goods and services transferred between divisions;

B. between TP and behavioral science: behavioral implications of various transfer pricing methods on the divisions involved in intrafirm trade;

C. between TP and business policy: the use of transfer pricing as a means to achieve corporate goals and strategies;

D. between TP and international business: theories of multinational enterprises and international trade; and major determinants of intrafirm trade;

E. between TP and economics and finance: the use of various transfer pricing methods and their effects on divisional return on investment; and management of funds transferred between the parent company and foreign subsidiaries;

F. between TP and law: legal implications of the use of various transfer pricing methods; and legislation and regulations on restrictive business practices;

G. between TP and taxtion: arm's-length principles; transfer pricing regulations of various countries; the APA program and its effects on corporate transfer pricing practices;

H. between TP and accounting: transfer pricing and its effect on divisional performance measurement; and financial reporting for corporate segments and related party transactions.

A working knowledge of these disciplines is required to effectively resolve many problems and issues in intrafirm trade and transfer pricing. Figure 9.1 also implies that we can approach the same issue from many different perspectives. For example, the purchases of components and immediate goods from outside sources can be viewed as a purely economic issue or as an accounting issue related to responsibility accounting and performance evaluation. From a legal and tax point of view, the prices paid for immediate goods from outside sources may be used to establish arm's-length prices for internal sales. In a multinational context, the same issue may involve international trade practices and funds transfers involving two or more currencies. In other words, the resolution of this and many other issues requires the cooperation and expertise of many functional units, including accounting, finance, purchasing, law, and logistics.

Another key element of the new paradigm is to find solutions that will balance

Figure 9.1
Transfer Pricing and Its Interfaces with Selected Disciplines

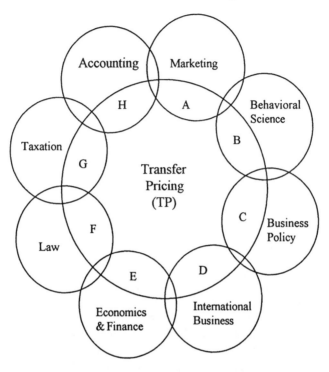

Source: Tang (1993).

the interests among many important stakeholders, which include taxpayers, domestic tax authorities, foreign tax authorities, joint venture partners, and corporate shareholders. All of these groups, plus other indirect stakeholders (e.g., the OECD and the EU), may have conflicting roles and different interests, as explained in Chapter 1. However, most of these stakeholders also wish to minimize tax compliance costs and help select transfer pricing method(s) that are consistent with the arm's-length principles. A new regulation should not be issued unless taxpayers and other stakeholders are given a chance to comment on the regulation and provide suggestions. If possible, a cooperative relationship should replace the old-style adversary relationship between taxpayers and tax authorities. Many innovative programs can be successful only if there is cooperation and trust between taxpayers and the tax authorities. The APA program and competent authority procedures are excellent examples.

From a company's (i.e., taxpayer's) point of view, the claims of all stakeholders cannot be satisfied at all times. The company must identify the most important stakeholders and give highest priority to pursuing transfer pricing policies that satisfy the interests and requirements of those stakeholders.

A Strategic Management Process for Managing a Corporate Transfer Pricing System

Besides using a multidisciplinary approach to deal with many problems and issues, corporate management must adopt a strategic management process in managing its transfer pricing system. In the past, many authors have provided various models of strategic management process (Hill and Jones, 1995; Wheelen and Hunger, 1995; Weihrich and Koontz, 1993; Robbins and Coultar, 1996). Basically, a strategic management process includes a series of steps to analyze the environment, formulate corporate transfer pricing policies and strategies, implement those policies and strategies, evaluate the results, and provide feedback to corporate management. Figure 9.2 illustrates the key steps of such a process for managing a transfer pricing system. These steps are explained briefly as follows:

Step 1: The first step is to identify the corporate mission, existing objectives, and important strategies. The corporate mission is the basic purpose or reason for the company's existence (Wheelen and Hunger, 1995). Objectives (or goals) are important ends toward which organizational and individual activities are directed (Weihrich and Koontz, 1993). One such objective may be to obtain a certain rate of return on investment or to capture a specific share of a particular market segment. A strategy is the pattern or plan stating how the organization will accomplish its mission and objectives. As explained by Mintzberg and Quinn (1996), strategies "normally exist at many different levels in any large organization" and "may be looked at as either a priori statement to guide action or a posteriori results of actual decision behavior."

Steps 2, 3, and 4: Environmental analysis is analyzing the external and internal environments to identify opportunities and threats confronting the firm and reviewing current financial strategies (including tax strategies) and transfer pricing policies to determine their strengths, weaknesses, and deficiencies in the transfer pricing system. Benchmarking should be done if information is available on the situation, policies, and strategies adopted by competing firms. Many books and articles are available on how to analyze the environment and conduct an analysis of strengths, weaknesses, opportunities, and threats (called a SWOT) for an organization (e.g., Robbins and Coultar, 1996; Mintzberg and Quinn, 1996). A study of all new transfer pricing regulations and relevant tax matters must be conducted for countries where the company has operations. Benchmarking is necessary to study how other firms analyzed the new environment and formulated their transfer pricing policies and strategies. Details of a benchmarking process can be found in such books as McNair and Leibfried (1992) and Chang and Kelly (1994).

Step 5: Reformulate new financial strategies and transfer pricing policies based on the results of environmental analysis. At a minimum, the statement of policies and procedures should cover the following (Tang, 1981):

Figure 9.2
A Strategic Management Process for Managing a Transfer Pricing System

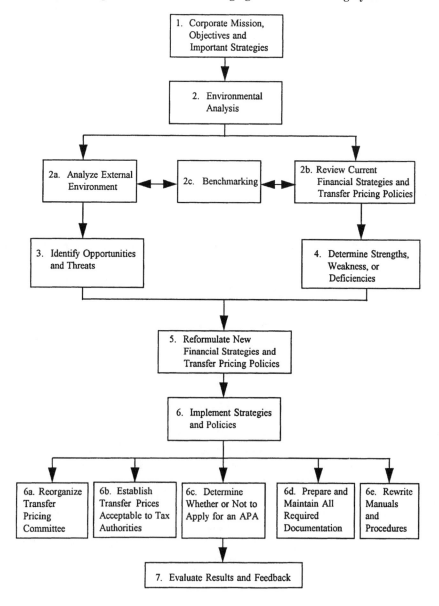

—objectives of the system;

—list of products covered;

—formulas for determining prices;

—sources of information for determining market prices;

—documentation requirements;

—policy regarding purchases from outside sources;

—procedures to be followed in the event of disputes;

—the role of an arbitration committee or a price arbitrator; and

—review of policy and procedures.

Step 6: Implement strategies and policies that may include, but not be limited to, the following:

—Reorganize corporate transfer pricing committee and transfer pricing department. The committee and department must include cross-functional staff to work as a team to deal with critical issues and maintain the day-to-day operations of the transfer pricing system;

—Establish transfer prices for tangible and intangible goods, services, and cost-sharing arrangements to meet all requirements of tax regulations and to achieve corporate objectives;

—Determine whether or not to apply for an APA. If the decision is positive, determine whether the company should pursue a unilateral, bilateral, or multilateral APA. Details of the APA program and processes are described in Chapter 4.

—Rewrite manuals and procedures and explain the changes in policies and strategies to corporate and divisional management.

Step 7: Evaluate the results and provide feedback to corporate management to revise transfer pricing policies and strategies in the future. Such policies and strategies should be reviewed periodically (e.g., once a year), or when there are important changes in the operating environment.

The implementation of this seven-step process should ensure that transfer pricing policies and strategies are linked to corporate strategic imperatives and company objectives. In this way, managers can also become more proactive and alert to changes and new opportunities in the environment.

GENERAL CONCLUSIONS

Nearly 20 years ago, the author (Tang, 1979) predicted that the magnitude and complexity of multinational transfer pricing will increase due to the following factors:

—large multinational enterprises are expanding their foreign investments;

—international trade, which consists of a large amount of transfers between related business entities, is increasing; and

—tax and customs authorities of many countries are intensifying their surveillance of multinational transfer pricing practices.

These factors are still operative today. In this book, we have provided many statistics and related cases. As the process of globalization continues, many MNCs will expand their overseas investment and integrate their operations across national borders. Intrafirm trade will grow further in the next decade. Over the past ten years, we have seen many changes in transfer pricing regulations in the United States and in many other countries. By 1996, most industrial nations and the OECD have revised their transfer pricing regulations and guidelines. Advance-pricing agreements are being offered by more than 15 countries. These new regulations and programs should reduce the uncertainties surrounding intrafirm trade and transfer pricing. However, the cost of tax compliance is still too high for an average multinational taxpayer. The documentation requirements for the APA process, cost-sharing arrangements, and other procedures are far too numerous. These requirements should be simplified as soon as possible to minimize the tax compliance costs and administrative burden for taxpayers and tax administrations. As of August 1996, the proposed update for advance-pricing agreement revenue procedure had not been finalized, meaning that time remains for taxpayers to submit their comments and suggestions.

As we gain more experience with APA programs in the United States, Canada, and many other countries, we should develop databases of the best APA practices by industry and by country in order to disseminate nonconfidential information among those taxpayers who plan to apply for APAs or wish to learn more about the programs. This task could be sponsored jointly by the IRS and such associations as the American Taxation Association, the Tax Executives Institute, the American Management Association, or the Institute of Management Accountants. These type of programs should promote a greater use of advance-pricing agreements among taxpayers in the future.

REFERENCES

Abdallah, Wagdy M. 1989. *International Transfer Pricing Policies*. Westport, Conn.: Quorum.

———. 1990. How MNCs Can Choose the Right Price for Intracompany Transfers. *Journal of European Business* (March/April): 33–37.

Al-Eryani, M., P. Alam, and S. Akhter. 1990. Transfer Pricing Determinants of U.S. Multinationals. *Journal of International Business Studies* (Third Quarter): 409–425.

Baik, Sunghak Andrew, and Michael Patton. 1995. Japan Steps Up Transfer Pricing Enforcement, Joins the APA Fray. *Tax Notes International* (November 13): 1271–1275.

Barber, Hoytl. 1993. *Tax Havens*. New York: McGraw-Hill.

Borkowski, Susan C. 1996. An Analysis (Meta-and Otherwise) of Multinational Transfer Pricing Research. *International Journal of Accounting* (Vol. 31, No. 1): 39–53.

Business International Corporation (BIC) and Ernst & Young (EY). 1991. *International Transfer Pricing*. New York: BIC/EY.

Byrne, John A. 1994. The Pain of Downsizing. *Business Week* (May 9): 60–63.

Chang, Richard Y., and P. Keith Kelly. 1994. *Improving through Benchmarking*. Irvine, Calif.: R. Chang Associates.

Cherecwich, Paul, Jr. 1996. The Fast Changing World of Corporation Taxation. *Tax Executive* (May–June): 178–186.

Cho, Kang Rae. 1988. Determinants of Intra-firm Trade: A Research for a Theoretical Framework. *International Trade Journal* (Winter): 167–185.

———. 1990. The Role of Product-Specific Factors in Intra-firm Trade of U.S. Manufacturing Multinational Corporations. *Journal of International Business Studies* (Second Quarter): 319–330.

Cox, Timothy W. 1994. Australian Tax Office Releases Draft Ruling on Advance Pricing Agreements. *Tax Notes International* (October 24): 1279–1280.

Davis, H. Thomas, Jr. 1994. Transfer Prices in the Real World—10 Steps Companies Should Take Before It's Too Late. *CPA Journal* (October): 82–83.

Deloitte & Touche. 1994. Studies Continue Pressure for Transfer Price Examination. *Deloitte & Touche Review* (July 25): 5.

Drucker, Peter F. 1989. *The New Realities*. New York: Harper & Row.

Eccles, Robert G. 1985. *The Transfer Pricing Problem: A Theory for Practice*. Lexington, Mass.: Lexington Books.

———. 1987. Analyzing Your Company's Transfer Pricing Practices. *Journal of Cost Management* (Summer): 21–33.

Ely, Mark H. 1996. International Controversies: The IRS and Compliance 2000. *Tax Notes International* (January 15): 223–227.

Fraedrich, John P., and Connie Rae Bateman. 1996. Transfer Pricing by Multinational Marketers: Risky Business. *Business Horizon* (January–February): 17–22.

Hamaekers, Hubert. 1996. The New OECD Transfer Pricing Guidelines for Multinational Enterprises and Tax Administrations. *Asia-Pacific Tax Bulletin* (January/February): 15–25.

Hammer, Michael, and James Champy. 1993. *Reengineering the Corporation*. New York: HarperCollins.

Hammer, Michael, and Steven A. Stanton, 1995. *The Reengineering Revolution*. New York: HarperCollins.

Hay, Diane, Frances Horner, and Jeffrey Owens. 1994. Past and Present Work in the OECD on Transfer Pricing and Selected Issues. *Tax Notes International* (July 25): 249–264.

Helleiner, Gerald K. 1981. *Intra-firm Trade and the Developing Countries*. New York: St. Martin's Press.

Helleiner, Gerald K., and Real Lavergne. 1979. Intra-firm Trade and Industrial Exports to the United States. *Oxford Bulletin of Economics and Statistics* (November): 209–222.

Hill, Charles W. L., and Gareth R. Jones. 1995. *Strategic Management: An Integrated Approach*. Boston: Houghton Mifflin.

Hipple, F. Steb. 1990. Multinational Companies and International Trade: The Impact of Intrafirm Shipments on U.S Foreign Trade 1977–1982. *Journal of International Business* Studies (Third Quarter): 495–504.

————. 1995. *Multinational Companies in United States International Trade*. Westport, Conn.: Quorum.

Horngren, Charles T., Gary L. Sundem, and William O. Stratton. 1996. *Introduction to Management Accounting*. Upper Saddle River, N.J.: Prentice-Hall.

Johnson, W., and R. Kirsch. 1992. International Transfer Pricing and Decision Making in the United States Multinationals. *International Journal of Management* 89(2): 554–561.

Lall, Sanjaya. 1973. Transfer Pricing by Multinational Manufacturing Firms. *Oxford Bulletin of Economics and Statistics* (August): 173–193.

————. 1978. The Pattern of Intra-firm Exports by U.S. Multinationals. *Oxford Bulletin of Economics and Statistics* (August): 209–223.

Little, Jan Sneddon. 1986. Intrafirm Trade and U.S Protectionism, Thoughts Based on a Small Survey. *New England Economic Review* (January/February): 42–51.

————. 1987. Intra-Firm Trade: An Update. *New England Economic Review* (May/June): 46–51.

Lowell, Cym H. 1996. Relationship of Section 482 to International Corporate Tax Planning. *Journal of Corporate Taxation* (January): 36–56.

Lowell, Cym H., Marianne Burge, and Peter L. Briger. 1994a. *U.S. International Transfer Pricing*. Boston: Warren, Gorham & Lamont.

McNair, C. J., and Kathleen H. J. Leibfried. 1992. *Benchmarking*. Essex Junction, Vt.: Oliver Wight Publications.

Mensser, Merle D. 1988. A Contract Price Policy For Multinationals. *Management Accounting* (October): 27–31.

Mintzberg, Henry, and James Brian Quinn. 1996. *The Strategy Process: Concepts, Contexts, Cases*. Upper Saddle River, N.J.: Prentice-Hall.

Naisbitt, John. 1982. *Megatrends*. New York: Warner Books.

————. 1994. *Global Paradox*. New York: William Morrow & Co.

Naisbitt, John, and Patricia Aburdene. 1990. *Megatrends 2000*. New York: Avon Books.

Organization for Economic Cooperation and Development (OECD). 1979. *Transfer Pricing and Multinational Enterprises*. Paris: OECD.

————. 1984. *Transfer Pricing and Multinational Enterprises: Three Taxation Issues*. Paris: OECD.

————. 1993. *Intra-Firm Trade*. Paris: OECD.

————. 1995a. *OECD Reviews of Foreign Direct Investment: United States*. Paris: OECD.

————. 1995b. *Transfer Pricing Guidelines for Multinational Enterprises and Tax Administrations*. Paris: OECD.

Patton, Michael F., and Kenneth W. Wood. 1995. The APA Program Lifecycle Moves from Start-Up to Growth State: Proposed Update of Rev. Proc. 91–22. *Tax Management International Journal* (August 11): 363–370.

Pice Waterhouse. 1995. *Corporate Taxes: A Worldwide Summary*. New York: Price Waterhouse.

Reed, Stanley, Larry Holyoke, and Douglas Harbrecht. 1994. Here Come the Great Global Tax War. *Business Week* (May 30): 55–56.

Revenue Canada, 1994. *Information Circular 94–4*. International Transfer Pricing: Advance Pricing Agreements. December 30.

Richardson, Margaret M. 1994a. IRS's Focus on Compliance Will Continue, Using Systems Modernization and New Tools Such as Advance Pricing Agreements. Interviewed by Lloyd L. Plaine. *Journal of Taxation* (February): 82–83.

———. 1994b. Remarks at the Tax Executive Institute's 49th Annual Conference. *Tax Executive* (November–December): 466–472.

———. 1994c. Remarks of Margaret Milner Richardson. *Taxes* (December): 717–721.

Robbins, Stephen P., and Mary Coultar. 1996. *Management*. Upper Saddle River, N.J.: Prentice-Hall.

Scholes, Myron S., and Mark A. Wolfson. 1992. *Taxes and Business Strategy: A Planning Approach*. Englewood Cliffs, N.J.: Prentice-Hall.

Shulman, James S. 1966. Transfer Pricing in Multinational Business. Ph.D. dissertation, Harvard University.

———. 1967. When the Price Is Wrong—By Design. *Columbia Journal of World Business* 2 (May–June): 69–76.

Sollenberger, Harold M., and Arnold Schneider. 1996. *Managerial Accounting*. Cincinnati, Ohio: South-Western College Publishing.

Taly, Michel. 1996. Comparison of CPM and TNMM Transfer Pricing Methods: A Point of View. *Tax Notes International* (January 29): 351–353.

Tang, Roger Y. W. 1979. *Transfer Pricing Practices in the United States and Japan*. New York: Praeger.

———. 1980. Canadian Transfer Pricing Practices. *CA Magazine* (March): 32–45.

———. 1981. *Multinational Transfer Pricing: Canadian and British Perspectives*. Toronto: Butterworths.

———. 1993. *Transfer Pricing in the 1990s*. Westport, Conn.: Quorum.

Tesler, Lawrence G. 1995. Networked Computing in the 1990s. *Scientific American*. The Computer in the 21st Century (Special Issue): 10–21.

Thurow, Lester C. 1996. *The Future of Capitalism*. New York: William Morrow & Co.

Turro, John. 1994. Pacific Association of Tax Administrators Reaches Consensus on Common APA Guidelines. *Tax Notes International* (November 7): 1431–1432.

U.S. Department of Commerce. Economics and Statistics Administration. Bureau of Economic Affairs. 1995a. *Foreign Direct Investment in the United States: Preliminary 1993 Estimates*. Washington, D.C.: U.S. Government Printing Office.

———. 1995b. *U.S. Direct Investment Abroad: Preliminary 1993 Estimates*. Washington, D.C.: U.S. Government Printing Office.

U.S. General Accounting Office (GAO). 1995. *International Taxation: Transfer Pricing and Information on Non-payment of Tax*. Washington, D.C.: GAO.

Vernon, Raymond, Louis T. Wells, Jr., and Subramanian Raygan. 1996. *The Manager in the International Economy*. Upper Saddle River, N.J.: Prentice-Hall.

Wartzman, Rick. 1993. Foreign Companies Formed to Understate U.S.-Derived Income. *Wall Street Journal* (June 4): A2.

Weihrich, Heinz, and Harold Koontz. 1993. *Management: A Global Perspective*. New York: McGraw-Hill.

Wheelen, Thomas L., and J. David Hunger. 1995. *Strategic Management and Business Policy*. Reading, Mass.: Addison-Wesley.

Yanker, P. 1982. *Transfer Pricing and Performance Evaluation in Multinational Corporations*. New York: Praeger.

Appendix A:
Section 482 of the U.S. Internal Revenue Code

In any case of two or more organizations, trades, or businesses (whether or not incorporated, whether or not organized in the United States, and whether or not affiliated) owned or controlled directly or indirectly by the same interests, the Secretary may distribute, apportion, or allocate gross income, deductions, credits, or allowances between or among such organizations, trades, or businesses, if he determines that such distribution, apportionment, or allocation is necessary in order to prevent evasion of taxes or clearly to reflect the income of any of such organizations, trades, or businesses. In the case of any transfer (or license) of intangible property (within the meaning of section 936(h)(3)(B)), the income with respect to such transfer or license shall be commensurate with the income attributable to the intangible.

Appendix B:
Sections 69(1), 69(2), and 69(3) of the Canadian Income Tax Act of 1972

69. (1) Except as expressly otherwise provided in this Act.

    (a) where a taxpayer has acquired anything from a person with whom he was not dealing at arm's length at an amount in excess of the fair market value thereof at the time he so acquired it, he shall be deemed to have acquired it at that fair market value;

    (b) where a taxpayer has disposed of anything

        (i) to a person with whom he was not dealing at arm's length for no proceeds or for proceeds less than the fair market value thereof at the time he so disposed of it, or

        (ii) to any person by way of gift *inter vivos*, he shall be deemed to have received proceeds of disposition therefore equal to that fair market value; and

    (c) where a taxpayer has acquired property by way of gift, bequest or inheritance, he shall be deemed to have acquired the property at its fair market value at the time he so acquired it.

(2) Where a taxpayer carrying on business in Canada has paid or agreed to pay, to a non-resident person with whom he was not dealing at arm's length as price, rental, royalty or other payment for or for the use of reproduction of any property, or as consideration for the carriage of goods or passengers or for other services, an amount greater than the amount (in this subsection referred to as "the reasonable amount") that would have been reasonable in the circumstances if the non-resident person and the taxpayer had been dealing at arm's length, the reasonable amount shall, for the purpose of computing the taxpayer's income from the business, be deemed to have been the amount that was paid or is payable therefor.

(3) Where a non-resident person has paid, or agreed to pay, to a taxpayer carrying on business in Canada with whom he was not dealing at arm's length as price,

rental, royalty or other payment for or for the use or reproduction of any property, or as consideration for the carriage of goods or passengers or for other services, an amount less than the amount (in this subsection referred to as ''the reasonable amount'') that would have been reasonable in the circumstances if the non-resident person and the taxpayer had been dealing at arm's length, the reasonable amount shall, for the purpose of computing the taxpayer's income from the business, be deemed to have been the amount that was paid or is payable therefor.

Appendix C:
Revenue Canada, Income Tax Information Circular 94–4, *International Transfer Pricing: Advance Pricing Agreements* (APA), December 30, 1994

INTRODUCTION

1. Revenue Canada (the Department) has put in place an Advance Pricing Agreement (APA) program to assist Canadian taxpayers in determining transfer prices acceptable for the purposes of the Canadian *Income Tax Act* (the Act) and, when applicable, the various international tax conventional Canada has with foreign governments.

2. This information circular is an overview of the APA program. It highlights the main features of the program and sets out the basic requirements. Detailed guidelines and procedures are available on request. The detailed guidelines do not address cost-sharing and licensing arrangements, which will be the subject of a separate release.

NATURE AND PURPOSE

3. An APA is considered to be a binding agreement between a taxpayer and the Department. When the terms of the agreement are complied with, the Department will consider the results of applying the agreed transfer pricing methodology (TPM) to have satisfied the arm's-length principle of section 69 of the Act. APA prospectively confirms an appropriate TPM, and its application, to specific crossborder non–arm's-length transactions for a specified term. The purpose of APAs is to promote voluntary compliance by assuring taxpayers that the TPMs they use to establish transfer prices are acceptable.

4. Usually, an APA applies to transactions completed from the beginning of the taxation year in which the Department accepted the request for an APA. However, the decision to apply an agreed-upon TPM retroactively (i.e., to non–statute-barred years) rests with the responsible district office and the taxpayer.

5. As noted in paragraph 3 above, APAs focus on and pertain to future taxation periods. The term of an APA is usually three years, but will vary depending on the particular facts and circumstances of individual taxpayers. However, terms of APAs covering cost-sharing or expense allocations could be longer.

6. The International Tax Programs Directorate at Headquarters administers the APA program. For more information about the program, contact:

Director General
International Tax Programs Directorate
Revenue Canada
Ottawa, ON K1A 0L8
Telephone: (613) 952–7470

THE APA PROCESS: AN OVERVIEW

7. The APA process is designed to produce an understanding among all interested parties of the TPM to be employed, the type of transactions to be covered, the expected results of applying the TPM, and the term of the APA.

8. The taxpayer proposes the TPM and provides supporting documentation and explanations to demonstrate that the proposed TPM produces arm's-length results. The Department evaluates each APA request by analysing and reviewing the data submitted, and by meeting with the taxpayer. If the proposal is acceptable, the taxpayer and the Department execute an APA.

9. When the related foreign parties involved in an APA request are residents of a country with which Canada has an income tax treaty, the Department will encourage the Canadian taxpayer to have the related parties simultaneously apply to their tax administration for a comparable agreement, or such similar arrangement, using the same transfer pricing methodology. If this is the case, the Canadian competent authority will try to arrange a competent authority agreement with that treaty partner for the APA (commonly called a bilateral APA). When the Canadian competent authority and the competent authority of the treaty country reach an agreement covering an APA, the taxpayer can be assured that the TPM to be used in determining the transfer prices of the transactions covered in the APA will be accepted by the tax administrations of both countries. In this way, the taxpayer can avoid potential double taxation.

10. The Department will accept applications for unilateral APAs (involving only the Canadian taxpayer and the Department). When an APA application involves related entities in several jurisdictions, the taxpayer can propose a multilateral APA (involving Canada and two or more treaty partners), or a combination of bilateral and unilateral APAs.

11. If, in the case of a unilateral APA, a treaty country adjusts the taxable income of a foreign-related entity involved in the APA and this gives rise to double taxation, and the adjustment affects the transactions covered in the unilateral APA, the Canadian taxpayer can request competent authority assistance. In resolving the double taxation issue, the Canadian competent authority can vary from the terms and conditions of the unilateral APA. All unilateral APAs will contain a clause to this effect.

12. The APA program is available to all Canadian taxpayers. Smaller organizations may experience less demanding requirements when applying for an APA.

PRINCIPLES OF THE APA PROCESS

13. A proposed TPM must comply with the provisions of section 69 of the Act, and adhere to the principles set out in Information Circular 87–2, *International Transfer Pricing and Other International Transactions*, and in the Organisation for Economic

Cooperation and Development guidelines on transfer pricing, as amended from time to time.

14. A proposed TPM must be consistent with the arm's-length principle and must be supported by reliable data, the extent and nature of which is outlined in paragraph 20 below and described more particularly in the detailed guidelines.

PREFILING MEETINGS

15. Taxpayers can request one or more prefiling meetings with departmental officials to informally explore the suitability of an APA, and to discuss the nature and extent of the documentation to be submitted, the possible need for expert opinions, and the time frame for the process. District office staff will usually participate in prefiling meetings.

ACCEPTING, DECLINING, OR WITHDRAWING AN APA REQUEST

16. The Department will first evaluate APA requests at, or following, the prefiling meetings. In circumstances when an APA is not appropriate, the Department may exercise its discretion and decline a request. The Department will advise the taxpayer of its reasons and will give the taxpayer the opportunity to make further representations.

17. Taxpayers may withdraw their APA request at any time. When this happens, neither the taxpayer nor the Department will have any obligations to each other, except for the commitments set out in any executed contract for user charges, as referred to in paragraphs 18 and 19 below.

USER CHARGES

18. The Department will levy a user charge for each APA request or renewal to cover anticipated ''out-of-pocket'' costs (e.g., travel and accommodation). There is no charge for staff time.

19. While the Department has its own specialists in several disciplines, in some circumstances the Department may consider it necessary to obtain the opinion of an independent expert. In such instances, the taxpayer and the Department will together select the independent expert. Usually, the taxpayer is responsible for the costs of the independent expert. However, all parties to the APA would have access to the independent expert's reports and opinions.

REQUIREMENTS OF AN APA SUBMISSION

20. The taxpayer must provide a detailed explanation and analysis of each proposed TPM, as well as the facts and circumstances on which it is based, and set out the reasons why the proposed TPM is appropriate to the situation. The taxpayer should also discuss the three transactional TPMs (the comparable, uncontrolled price, the resale price, and the cost-plus methods) described in Information Circular 87–2, and provide reasons why they are or are not suitable to the situation. The taxpayer is responsible for ensuring that the Department has all relevant information.

21. To assist the Department in reviewing and evaluating the proposed TPM, the taxpayer will usually illustrate the effect of the proposed TPM by applying it to the operations of the previous three years, and to the projected operations of the periods the APA will cover.

22. There may be instances where it is not possible or practicable to illustrate the effect of applying a proposed TPM to prior or future years (e.g., the business may not have been in operation for three years, or the proposed transactions relate to new products or processes). In such cases, the Department and the taxpayer will discuss and determine, during the prefiling meetings, necessary alternative data.

23. The APA submission must include detailed information about the taxpayer and the related parties involved in the APA (e.g., history, organizational structure, nature and scope of operations, transaction flows, and relevant financial and tax data). In addition, the taxpayer must provide information used to establish a proposed TPM. This information may include functional analyses, profitability measurements, economic studies, general industry trends, and available information on competitors and comparable or similar businesses. Because all APA requests will not usually require the same type or level of information, the taxpayer and the Department will discuss and agree on detailed and specific information requirements during prefiling meetings.

24. The taxpayer must put forward a set of critical assumptions under which the proposed TPM would operate. Critical assumptions are objective business and economic criteria that are fundamental to the application of the taxpayer's proposed TPM (i.e., any assumed criterion that if changed would significantly affect the substantive terms of the APA, whether or not the change is within the taxpayer's control).

25. Any change in critical assumptions during the term of an APA may result in the APA being revised, revoked, or canceled. The decision to revise, revoke, or cancel an APA would be made after all parties to the APA, including the relevant competent authorities of participating countries for bilateral or multilateral APAs, have examined and evaluated the impact of any changes in critical assumptions on the overall terms and conditions of the APA.

26. An APA may include a provision to permit the parties to make a compensating adjustment to bring actual operating results, as determined according to the TPM, within a range of expected operating results as set out in the APA.

ANNUAL APA REPORTS

27. Taxpayers have to file annual reports according to the terms of their APA. Failure to file an annual report as required may result in cancellation or revocation of the APA.

28. Each APA is unique, and the particular requirements of each annual report (e.g., content, scope, filing date) will be set out in the APA. Annual reports should, at a minimum, contain:

- a description of the actual operations of the taxpayer for the year;
- a discussion and explanation of any significant variance between expected results (as forecasted in the APA submission) and actual results;
- an accounting of any compensating adjustments, if permitted under the APA; and
- a demonstration of the extent of the taxpayer's compliance with the terms and condi-

tions of the APA, including the continuing relevance and soundness of critical assumptions.

29. Staff from Headquarters and the relevant district office will examine and evaluate the results of applying the TPM and the information and explanations provided in the annual reports. The Department will confer with the taxpayers and the competent authorities of the other countries, as necessary.

AUDIT

30. District offices will be responsible for auditing APAs as part of the regular audit cycle. They will not re-evaluate the TPM, but will focus on establishing that taxpayers have complied with the terms and conditions of the APA, and verifying the accuracy of the representations in the APA and annual reports. They will also test the accuracy and consistency of the application of the TPM, the related supporting data, and the continuing relevance and soundness of critical assumptions.

REVOKING AND CANCELLING APAs

31. The Department may revoke or cancel an APA when warranted (e.g., if taxpayers misrepresented or omitted information during the APA process, or did not comply with the terms and conditions of the APA).

32. The facts and circumstances giving rise to the possible cancellation or revocation would require in-depth examination, evaluation, and consultation with the taxpayer and the competent authority of the other countries. The conclusions reached would determine the appropriate action to be taken.

33. When an APA is canceled, the cancellation will be effective at the beginning of the year in which the basis for the cancellation occurred.

34. When an APA is revoked, the revocation will be retroactive to the first day of the first taxation year for which the APA was effective.

REVISING AND RENEWING APAs

35. The Department can revise an APA, with the consent of the taxpayer and the competent authority of the other countries involved, when there is a change in any critical assumption, tax law, or treaty provision, or if justified by changed circumstances.

36. The Department may renew APAs upon request by the taxpayer. The Department will conduct a review and evaluation of the renewal application, taking into account whatever revisions to the initial APA are necessary and appropriate, in light of changed facts and circumstances.

37. When appropriate, and with the taxpayer's concurrence, the Department will try to obtain agreement on renewing the APA with the competent authority of the relevant foreign tax administrations.

USE AND DISCLOSURE OF INFORMATION

38. The information the Department receives or generates during the APA process relates directly to the potential tax liability of the taxpayer under the Act. All information the Department acquires or produces during the APA process is considered to be provided, as in the case of a normal tax audit, for the purposes of administering the Act. The APA and such related information, including commercially sensitive and proprietary data, is subject to the confidentiality provisions of section 241 of the Act and the confidentiality provision contained in Canada's tax treaties.

39. The Department will address taxpayers' individual concerns or requests about the limitations on using and disclosing information provided in the course of pursuing an APA in more detail during the prefiling meetings.

Appendix D:
Sections 770 to 773 of the U.K. Income and Corporation Taxes Act of 1988

TRANSACTIONS BETWEEN ASSOCIATED PERSONS

770.—(1) Subject to the provisions of this section and section 771, where any property is sold and—

    (a) the buyer is a body of persons over whom the seller has control or the seller is a body of persons over whom the buyer has control or both the buyer and the seller are bodies of persons over whom the same person or persons has or have control; and

    (b) the property is sold at a price ("the actual price") which is either—

        (i) less than the price which it might have been expected to fetch if the parties to the transaction had been independent persons dealing at arm's length ("the arm's length price"), or

        (ii) greater than the arm's length price, then, in computing for tax purposes the income, profits or losses of the seller where the actual price was less than the arm's length price, and of the buyer where the actual price was greater than the arm's length price, the like consequences shall ensue as would have ensued if the property had been sold for the arm's length price.

(2) Subsection (1) above shall not apply—

    (a) in any case where—

        (i) the actual price is less than the arm's length price, and

        (ii) the buyer is resident in the United Kingdom and is carrying on a trade there, and

        (iii) the price of the property falls to be taken into account as a deduction in computing the profits or gains or losses of that trade for tax purposes; or

    (b) in any case where—

        (i) the actual price is greater than the arm's length price, and

        (ii) the seller is resident in the United Kingdom and is carrying on a trade there, and

    (iii) the price of the property falls to be taken into account as a trading receipt
      in computing the profits or gains or losses of that trade for tax purposes; or
  (c) in relation to any transaction in relation to which section 493(1) or (3) applies;
or
  (d) in relation to any other sale, unless the Board so direct.
(3) Where a direction is given under subsection (2)(d) above all such adjustments shall
be made, whether by assessment, repayment of tax or otherwise, as are necessary to give
effect to the direction.

771.—(1) For the purposes of this section a company is a petroleum company if—
  (a) its activities include any relevant activities; or
  (b) it is associated with a company whose activities include any relevant activities
    and its own activities include the ownership, operation or management of ships
    or pipelines (as defined in section 65 of the Pipelines Act 1962) used for trans-
    porting or conveying petroleum or petroleum products.
(2) ''Relevant activites'' means any of the following—
  (a) the acquisition or disposal of petroleum or of rights to acquire or dispose of
    petroleum;
  (b) the importation into or exportation from the United Kingdom of petroleum prod-
    ucts or the acquisition or disposal of rights to such importation or exportation;
  (c) the acquisition otherwise than for importation into the United Kingdom of petro-
    leum products outside the United Kingdom or the disposal outside the United
    Kingdom of petroleum products not exported from the United Kingdom by the
    company making the disposal;
  (d) the refining or processing of crude petroleum; and
  (e) the extraction of petroleum, either under rights authorising it or under contractual
    or other arrangements with persons by whom such rights are exercisable.
(3) Section 770(2) shall have effect with the omission of paragraphs (a) and (b) in any
case where—
  (a) either party to the transaction is a petroleum company or both are petroleum
    companies; and
  (b) the activities of either or both are or include activities—
    (i) the profits from which are or would be chargeable to overseas tax for which
     credit could be given under section 790 or in pursuance of arrangements
     having effect by virtue of section 788; or
    (ii) which are exploration or exploitation activities within the meaning of section
     830; and
  (c) the transaction is part of such activities or is connected with them.
(4) Where both the buyer and the seller are resident in the United Kingdom and the
Board, in pursuance of this section, direct that section 770(1) is to apply to the computation of the income, profits or losses of the one, the direction may extend the application of that subsection to the computation of the income, profits or losses of the other,
and where it does so adjustments shall be made under section 770(3) accordingly.
(5) Where any property is sold and either the buyer or the seller is a petroleum company
or both are petroleum companies, then if—
  (a) the sale is part of a transaction or series of transactions (whether or not between
    the same persons) and its terms are affected by those of the remainder of the
    transaction or transactions; or

(b) what is sold is petroleum extracted under rights exercisable by a company other than the buyer, and not less than 20 per cent of that company's ordinary share capital was at the time of the sale owned directly or indirectly by one or more of the following, that is to say, the buyer and any companies associated with the buyer;

section 770 shall apply in relation to the sale as if in subsection (1) of that section paragraph (a) were omitted.

(6) Where a petroleum company was a party to a sale of property, then, in determining for the purposes of section 770 what price the property might have been expected to fetch had the parties to the transaction been independent persons dealing at arm's length and what consequences would have ensued in computing the income, profits or losses of the seller or the buyer for tax purposes if the property had been sold for that price, it shall be assumed—

(a) that the terms of the transaction would have been such as might have been expected to secure both to the buyer and to the seller a reasonable profit from transactions of the same kind carried out on similar terms over a reasonable period; and

(b) that the seller would not have been compelled by law or by executive action of any government to demand a price fixed by law or such action or a price not less than one so fixed; and

(c) that, if the transaction was part of a transaction or series of transactions (whether or not between the same persons), its terms would not have been affected by those of the remainder of the transaction or transactions; and

(d) in a case where the whole of the property sold is not delivered by the seller within 12 months after the date of the sale—

   (i) that such part of the property as is delivered within that time would have fetched a price equal to that which it might have been expected to fetch if sold under a contract for the sale of that part and of no other property, being a contract made at the date of the sale; and

   (ii) that such part of the property not so delivered as is delivered in any calendar month would have fetched a price equal to that which it might have been expected to fetch if sold under a contract for the sale of that part and of no other property, being a contract made at the material time in that month; and no regard shall be had to the terms of similar transactions which were capable of being varied.

   In this subsection "calendar month" means a month of the calendar year and "material time," in relation to a calendar month, means noon on the middle day of the month which, in the case of a month containing an even number of days, shall be taken to be the last day of the first half of the month.

(7) In this section—

"petroleum" includes any mineral oil or relative hydrocarbon and, except in the expression "crude petroleum," includes natural gas; "petroleum products" means products derived from petroleum and wholly or substantially of a hydrocarbon nature.

(8) For the purposes of this section—

(a) two companies are associated with one another if one is under the control of the other or both are under the control of the same person or persons, and "control" has the meaning given by section 840;

(b) any question whether ordinary share capital is owned by a company directly or indirectly shall be determined as for the purposes of section 838;

(c) rights are exercisable by a company if they are exercisable by that company alone or jointly with another company or companies.

772.—(1) The Board may, by notice given to any body corporate, require it to give to the Board, within such time (not being less than 30 days) as may be specified in the notice, such particulars (which may include details of relevant documents) as may be so specified of any related transaction which appears to the Board—

(a) to be, or to be connected with, a transaction with respect to which the Board might give a direction under section 770; or

(b) to be relevant for determining whether such a direction could or should be given in any case; or

(c) to be relevant for determining for the purposes of that section what price any property sold would have fetched had the sale been one between independent persons dealing at arm's length.

(2) For the purposes of a notice under subsection (1) above, a transaction is a related transaction if, but only if, it is one to which the body corporate to which the notice is given, or a body corporate associated with that body, was a party; and for the purposes of this subsection, two bodies corporate are associated with one another if one is under the control of the other or both are under the control of the same person or persons.

(3) Where, in the case of a transaction with respect to which it appears to the Board that a direction under section 770 might be given—

(a) one of the parties is a body corporate resident outside the United Kingdom and a 51 percent subsidiary of a body corporate (''the parent body'') resident in the United Kingdom; and

(b) the other party is, or is a 51 percent subsidiary of, the parent body, the Board may, by notice given to the parent body, require it to make available for inspection any books, accounts or other documents or records whatsoever of the parent body or, subject to subsection (4) below, of any body of persons over which it has control which relate to that transaction, to any other transaction (of whatever nature) in the same assets, or to transactions (of whatever nature) in assets similar to those to which the first-mentioned transaction related.

(4) If, in a case in which under subsection (3) above the parent body is by notice required to make available for inspection any books, accounts, documents or records of a body of persons resident outside the United Kingdom over which the parent body has control, it appears to the Board, on the application of the parent body, that the circumstances are such that the requirement ought not to have effect, the Board shall direct that the parent body need not comply with the requirement.

(5) If, on an application under subsection (4) above, the Board refuse to give a direction under that subsection, the parent body may, by notice given to the Board within 30 days after the refusal, appeal to the Special Commissioners who, if satisfied that the requirement in question ought in the circumstances not to have effect, may determine accordingly.

(6) Where it appears to the Board that a body of persons may be a party to a transaction or transactions with respect to which a direction under section 770 might be given, then, for the purpose of assisting the Board to determine whether such a direction should be given, an inspector specifically authorised in that behalf by the Board may, at any reasonable time, on production if so required of his authority—

(a) enter any premises used in connection with the relevant trade carried on by that body of persons (that is to say, the trade in the course of which the transaction or transactions were effected),

(b) inspect there any books, accounts or other documents or records whatsoever relating to that trade which he considers it necessary for him to inspect for that purpose, and

(c) require any such books, accounts or other documents or records to be produced to him there for inspection.

(7) An inspector's authority for entering any premises under subjection (6) above shall state the name of the inspector and the name of the body of persons carrying on the trade in connection with which the premises are used.

(8) If and so far as the question in dispute on an appeal to the General Commissioners or, in Northern Ireland, to a county court against an assessment to tax arises from a direction of the Board under section 770 the question shall be referred to and determined by the Special Commissioners.

773.—(1) Nothing in sections 770 and 771 shall be construed as affecting the operation of any of the provisions of the 1968 Act or of Chapter I of Part III of the Finance Act 1971.

(2) In sections 770 and 772—

"body of persons" includes a partnership, and "control" has the meaning given by section 840;

and, for the purposes of this section, a sale shall be deemed to take place at the time of completion or when possession is given, whichever is the earlier.

(3) In determining for the purposes of sections 770 and 771 whether any person (alone or with others) has control over a body of persons—

(a) here shall be attributed to him any rights or powers of a nominee for him, that is to say, any rights or powers which another possesses on his behalf or may be required to exercise on his direction or behalf;

(b) there may also be attributed to him any rights or powers of a person with whom he is connected (within the meaning of section 839 but omitting subsections (5) to (7) and the exception in subsection (4)), including any rights or powers of a nominee for such a person, that is to say, any rights or powers which another possesses on behalf of such a person or may be required to exercise on his direction or behalf.

(4) Sections 770, 771, except subsection (5)(b), and 772 and this section shall, with the necessary adaptations, have effect in relation to lettings and hirings of property, grants and transfers of rights, interests or licences and the giving of business facilities of whatever kind as they have effect in relation to sales, and the references in those sections to sales, sellers, buyers and prices shall be deemed to be extended accordingly.

Appendix E:
Circular of the State Taxation Administration of the People's Republic of China on Tax Management Measures Concerning Business-Associated Enterprises, No. 237 (1992), October 29, 1992

ARTICLE 1

The following measures are formulated in accordance with the provisions of Article 13 of the Income Tax Law of the People's Republic of China for Foreign Investment Enterprises and Foreign Enterprises (hereinafter referred to as the Tax Law) and articles 52 to 58, Chapter 4, of the Rules for the Implementation thereof (hereinafter referred to as the Rules).

ARTICLE 2

Definition of associated enterprises: ''Having direct or indirect relationship of ownership or control in the areas of funds, operations, purchase and marketing''; ''being directly or indirectly owned or controlled by the same third party''; and ''having other connections in the area of interests'' mentioned in Article 52 of the Rules encompass mainly foreign investment enterprises or foreign enterprises (hereinafter referred to collectively as ''enterprises'') that have one of the following relations with other companies, enterprises or economic organizations other than companies and enterprises (hereinafter referred to collectively as ''other enterprises''):

1. holding, directly or indirectly, a minimum total of 25 percent of the shares of one or the other;
2. being owned, directly or indirectly, by the same third party, or at least 25 percent of the shares being controlled by the same third party;

3. loan funds from or to other enterprises making up at least 50 percent of the owned funds of enterprises, or 10 percent of the total loan funds of enterprises being guaranteed by other enterprises;

4. more than half of the senior managerial personnel such as board directors or directors, or one of the standing board directors of enterprises being assigned by other enterprises;

5. production and business operations of enterprises being normally conducted only when other enterprises providing them with royalties (including industrial property rights, proprietary technology, etc.);

6. raw materials, spare parts and fittings (including price and transaction terms, etc.) bought for production and business operations of enterprises being controlled or supplied by other enterprises;

7. marketing of products produced or commodities (including prices and transaction terms) being controlled by other enterprises;

8. having, in the area of interests, other connections including family and kin relations, that have actual control over production/business operations and transactions of enterprises.

ARTICLE 3

Enterprises must, when conducting business with their associated enterprises within a tax year, file their annual income tax returns with the local tax authorities together with the "Annual Tax Returns Concerning Business between Foreign Investment Enterprises/ Foreign Enterprises and Their Associated Enterprises."

ARTICLE 4

The local tax authorities shall, when conducting audits and investigations concerning business between enterprises and their associated enterprises, have the right to request that enterprises provide information as to prices, expense standards, etc.

ARTICLE 5

A written notice shall be issued when the local tax authorities require that enterprises provide information on prices, expense standards, etc., in respect to the business conducted with their associated enterprises, and enterprises shall report and submit the information within 60 days after receipt of the notice from the tax authorities.

ARTICLE 6

Where enterprises fail to file their tax returns within the prescribed time in accordance with the requirements, or refuse to provide information on transaction prices, expense standards, etc., the local tax authorities shall impose penalties in accordance with the provisions of Article 39 of the Tax Collection Management Law of the People's Republic of China.

ARTICLE 7

With respect to the business between enterprises and their associated enterprises, where prices or expenses are not charged or paid at the prevailing price levels of business between independent enterprises, and the amount of taxable income is thereby reduced, the local tax authorities have the right to make judgments and adjustments and to levy taxes accordingly. The adjustment methods shall be in accordance with the provisions of Articles 53 to 57 of the Rules.

ARTICLE 8

A notice of the adjusted amount and nature of the adjustments shall be served in those cases in which the local tax authorities make adjustments to the transfer pricing of enterprises.

ARTICLE 9

Adjustments to the transfer pricing of enterprises generally shall be restricted to the taxable income of the tax year under audit and investigation. Audits, investigations and adjustments generally shall be conducted within 3 years from the following year of the tax year. Where adjustment cases involve income of the previous years, adjustment can track back to a maximum of 10 years.

ARTICLE 10

Where enterprises do not make corresponding accounting adjustments to the taxable income derived from adjusting the transfer pricing of enterprises, the amount, received by their associated enterprises that exceeds what non-associated enterprises should receive, shall be deemed dividend distribution that does not enjoy the preferences of income tax exemption provided for in Article 19 of the Tax Law. Where income gained by the associated enterprises is derived from interest or royalties, the withholding income tax already withheld shall not be adjusted.

ARTICLE 11

In case of an objection to the transfer pricing adjustments, enterprises must first pay the amount of taxes within the prescribed time in accordance with the requirements of the local tax authorities, and then file an application for reconsideration or bring in a lawsuit in accordance with the provisions or Article 26 of the Tax Law, and provide, at the same time, information of prices, expense standards, etc. Where information is not provided or information provided is not sufficient, the local tax authorities shall refuse to reconsider the applications.

ARTICLE 12

Where adjustments to the transfer pricing of enterprises involve the implementation of some tax agreement clauses, adjustments shall be done in accordance with the provisions of the tax agreements.

ARTICLE 13

These measures shall go into effect on January 1, 1993.

Index

Aburdene, Patricia, 2, 4, 216
Adhikari, Ajay, 21
Advance Pricing Agreement or Arrangement (APA), 27, 93–105, 112, 128–29, 135, 208, 211, 227–28, 233–34; the Australian APA program, 194; the Canadian APA program, 147–49; Japan's Pre-Confirmation System, 208; the 1995 OECD guidelines, 128–29; the U.S. APA program, 93–105
Akamatsu, Akiya, 207
American Management Association, 18
Anderson, David, 146
Anderson, Philip, 192–94
Apple Computer, Inc., 109–10, 113, 208, 228
Apple Japan Inc., 208, 228
Arm's-length prices, 65–66
Arm's-length standard (principle), 72, 120–22, 131–32
Armstrong, Neal, 147
Aronson, Jonathan D., 16, 17
Asaki Breweries, 18
Asian Pacific Economic Council (APEC), 14
Association of Southeast Asian Nations (ASEAN), 14
Atkinson, Mark, 178–79

Australia, 10, 27, 187, 191–94
Australian Taxation Office (ATO), 93, 192–94, 227

Bach, Christopher L., 137
Baik, Sunghak Andrew, 207–8, 210, 227
Barber, Hoytl, 54
Barrier, Michael, 19
The Basic Arm's-Length Return Method (BALRM), 68
Baxter, George C., 138
Behling, Robert, 19
Bergguist, Philip J., 110
The best method rule, 71–72
Big Six accounting firms, 18
Bilateral trade: between Canada and the United States, 140–45; between Mexico and the United States, 151–54; between the United States and the Asian Pacific countries, 187–89
Bird, Richard M., 145
Bisat, Talal A., 31
BlanLuet, Gauthier, 172
Boeing, 17–18
Boidman, Nathan, 157, 176, 179
Bonturi, Marcos, 36, 38
Borkowski, Susan C., 103

About the Author

ROGER Y. W. TANG is a professor of accountancy at the Haworth College of Business Administration, Western Michigan University, where he also holds the Upjohn Chair of Business Administration. He has taught at the University of Nebraska, McGill University, the University of Calgary, and Hong Kong Baptist University, and is a member of the American Accounting Association, Academy of International Business, Institute of Management Accountants, and Institute of Certified Internal Auditors. Dr. Tang has published widely in the important journals serving his field and is author of three earlier books, including *Transfer Pricing in the 1990s: Tax and Management Perspectives* (Quorum, 1993).

ISBN 1-56720-039-7

EAN

9 781567 200393

HARDCOVER BAR CODE